2006

Caroline
Hope you have
a wonderful trip w/
lots of bfb to see
Mark

p. 66+
176-177

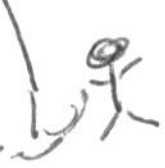

Galápagos
Diary

CONSERVATION IN THE GALÁPAGOS

The Charles Darwin Foundation, Inc.

The CDF, Inc. is affiliated with the Charles Darwin Foundation for the Galápagos Isles in program and mandate. The institution grew out of a project housed in the Smithsonian Institution for over 20 years, and was launched as an independent entity in late 1992 with the blessing and cooperation of the Smithsonian Institution.

CDF, Inc. is responsible for raising funds to support projects in Galápagos related to the conservation mandate of the Charles Darwin Foundation, and is the logistical base in the U.S. for projects and programs in Galápagos. The CDF, Inc. also conducts seminars, briefings, and other public education and advocacy efforts to inform the general public about conservation issues and current work being undertaken in Galápagos. Finally the CDF, Inc. is the headquarters for the international membership of over 10,000 'Friends of Galápagos', donors and institutions which support Galapagos conservation, and for the Darwin Scientific Foundation, an endowment fund from which the income is used for research, education and conservation of natural resources in Galapagos.

Address: 100 N. Washington St, Suite 232,Falls Church, VA 22046, USA
Tel: (703) 538-6833; fax: (703) 538-6835; e-mail: darwin@galapagos.org
Website: www.galapagos.org

The Charles Darwin Foundation for the Galápagos Isles

In 1959, the 100th anniversary of the publication of Darwin's seminal work, *The Origin of Species*, the Charles Darwin Foundation for the Galápagos Isles (CDF) was formed under the auspices of UNESCO, IUCN, and the Ecuadorian Government. The Foundation, under formal accord with the Government of Ecuador, was charged with advising the government on conservation of the Islands' biota and environment and establishing and operating an international research centre in the archipelago.

The government and the CDF have established a special relationship, recognized worldwide for its effectiveness and pioneering approach. It reflects a unique combination of advantages: a governmental agency with legal authority to manage the Islands' biota and natural resources and an international, independent NGO which conducts applied research and education programs to inform decisions and facilitate conservation and management, as well as obtain and channel international financial and technical support for both management and research/education.

The budget of the CDF is approximately $3 million per annum. Funds are raised annually from diverse public and private sources including the Frankfurt Zoo, research tables, project funds from the European Community, USAID, and UNDP among other, interest income from endowment., and individual donations.

Contact: Fernando Espinoza F., Secretary General, Av. 6 de Diciembre 4757 y Pasaje California, Quito, Ecuador.
E-mail: fcdarwi2.q.fcdarwin.org.ec

The Charles Darwin Research Station

The Charles Darwin Research Station (CDRS) is the operative arm of the Charles Darwin Foundation. Located in Puerto Ayora, on the island of Santa Cruz, the CDRS was established in 1960. Until 1968, the CDRS not only conducted research in the Islands and advised the government on conservation, but also conducted the first conservation management programs, due to the absence of a responsible government agency. Since 1969, the Galápagos National Park Service (GNPS) part of the Ministry of Agriculture, has been in charge of managing the Islands' natural resources and conserving its delicate biodiversity.

Current conservation priorities include enhancing the captive breeding program in Puerto Villamil, gathering baseline marine data (population dynamics, inventory, etc.) to inform the design and implementation of the newly established Galápagos Marine Resources Reserve (the second largest marine reserve in the world), feral animal control programs, eradication of introduced plants and establishment of seed banks, broad environmental education projects, and basic Station infrastructure needs (electrical and water systems and buildings).

Contact: Dr Robert Bensted-Smith, Director, Charles Darwin Research Station, Puerto Ayora, Isla Santa Cruz, Galápagos, Ecuador.
E-mail: director@fcdarwin.org.ec

Friends of Galápagos - Amigos de Galápagos

Friends receive regular information about conservation efforts in Galápagos.
Los Amigos reciben regularmente información sobre los esfuerzos por la conservación en Galápagos.

Charles Darwin Foundation (see details above)

• Become a Friend of Galápagos for 25 US$

Galápagos Conservation Trust

5 Derby Street, London, W1Y 7HD, UK. E-mail: gct@gct.org
Tel: +44 0207 629 5049
• Become a Friend of Galápagos for £25

Freunde der Galápagos Inseln (CH)

c/o Zoo Zurich, Zurichbergstr. 221, CH-8044 Zurich, Switzerland.
E-mail: galapagos@zoo.ch
Tel: +41 1 254 2670
• Become a Friend of Galápagos for Sfr 30 (single), Sfr 50 (couple)

Zooloogische Gesellschaft Frankfurt

Hilfe fur die bedhohte Tierwelt, Alfred-Brehm-Platz 16, D-60316 Frankfurt, Germany.
• Spenden mit dem Hinweis 'Galápagos' an: Frankfurter Sparkasse BLZ 500 502 01, Kontonummer: 80002. Spenden von mindestens 40._DM ermöglichen den Bezug der englischen Galápagos News mit einem deutschen Info_Blatt für ein Jahr.

Stichting Vrienden van de Galápagos Eilanden

c/o Adrian De Waard, 6, Charlotte de Bourboniaan, 2341 VD Oegstgeest, The Netherlands.
Tel: +31 0343 517132
• Become a Friend of Galápagos for NLG 50

The Galápagos Darwin Trust

Banque Internationale a Luxembourg, 2, Boulevard Royal, L-2953 Luxembourg.
• Donations marked 'For the Galápagos' may be made to Account No. 1-100/9071

Galápagos Diary

A COMPLETE GUIDE TO THE ARCHIPELAGO'S BIRDLIFE

HERMANN HEINZEL & BARNABY HALL
(concept • text • drawings)   (photos)

UNIVERSITY OF CALIFORNIA PRESS
Berkeley • Los Angeles

University of California Press
Berkeley and Los Angeles, California

Published by arrangement with
Christopher Helm (Publishers) Ltd.,
a subsidiary of A & C Black (Publishers) Ltd.

Library of Congress Cataloging-in-Publication Data

Heinzel, Hermann.
  Galapagos diary / Hermann Heinzel and Barnaby Hall.
      p. cm.
  ISBN 0-520-22794-8 (cloth : alk. paper) — ISBN 0-520-22836-7 (pbk. : alk. paper)
    1. Birds—Galapagos Islands. 2. Natural history—Galapagos Islands. I. Title.

  QL694.G2 H45 2000
  598'.09866'5—dc21

                                                                    00-034383

Designed by D & N Publishing, Berkshire, England

Printed in Singapore by Imago

          9   8   7   6   5   4   3   2   1

ACKNOWLEDGEMENTS

Our thanks first of all to Jenny Hall, Barnaby's mother, who encouraged us to make the trip to the Galápagos. Rod Hall arranged the entire trip by telephone and fax. Without their encouragement and organization, our trip would not have happened. Tony Castro, our local guide, has a deep knowledge and understanding of the Galápagos, which helped us find all the birds we wanted to see. At the same time, he made sure that we kept within all the regulations necessary to protect these islands. Tony was the best guide we could have had. Our thanks also to our very professional crew: Captain Marlon Zavala and his brother Roland; the cook, Aurelio Garcia; and Peter Tenorio, the seaman. Special thanks also to Maggie Sweetnam in London who typed the entire manuscript while simultaneously converting the 'Continental' English. Robert Kirk, our editor, was the easiest and kindest person to work with in spite of the inevitable delays in delivering the text.

Hermann Heinzel and **Barnaby Hall**

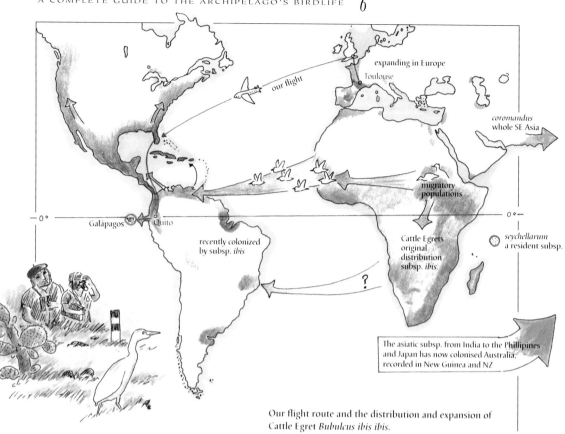

expanding in Europe

Toulouse

our flight

coromandus whole SE Asia

migratory populations

0°

Galápagos Quito

recently colonized by subsp. *ibis*

Cattle Egrets original distribution subsp. *ibis*

seychellarum a resident subsp.

0°

?

The asiatic subsp. from India to the Phillipines and Japan has now colonised Australia, recorded in New Guinea and NZ

Our flight route and the distribution and expansion of Cattle Egret *Bubulcus ibis ibis*.

I could not believe Barnaby when, in 1994, after visiting the Galápagos with his mother and brother, he told me he had seen **Cattle Egrets**. Although a keen birdwatcher, Barnaby was then still a young boy. I thought he had misidentified Great Egret, an uncommon but regular breeding bird on the larger islands. They generally feed along the coast, around lagoons, or in the intertidal zone. On my first visit to the archipelago, some 25 years ago, I had seen them, always single birds, in the grassland in the higher areas of St Cruz. It was here, in farmland amongst grazing cattle, that Barnaby told me he had seen numerous Cattle Egrets. He also told me that he had seen groups of 5–6 walking around amongst sleeping sealions on the rocky coast of Plaza. Great Egrets are found along the coast, but don't like rocky areas, and a small flock walking between sealions sounded highly unlikely.

Cattle Egrets are extraordinary opportunists. Their stronghold is in Africa and some parts of Asia, wherever large ungulates graze, and they are never found far from them. In the nineteenth century they found their way to the Americas, and have thrived alongside herds of introduced cattle. At first they were only found in farmland along the northern coast of Venezuela, but they very quickly colonized southern areas of the USA. From there, they moved northwards along the east coast and around the Gulf into Mexico. At the same time other birds moved into Central America from the south, moving northwards into Canada and west along the coast of Ecuador, where they have now filled all available habitat. Other groups, possibly also from Africa, have found their way to different parts of South America. Well, it was possible that they had found their way to the Galápagos, a much shorter journey than crossing the Atlantic Ocean from Africa to the Americas. I was well aware that in Europe they had already crossed the Pyrenees from Spain into southern France, and are still expanding their range northwards. The more golden-coloured Asiatic subspecies, *Bubulcus ibis coromandus*, expanded its range from India eastwards to Japan and the Philippines, and is now colonizing China and Australia. Having taken all this into consideration, I decided it quite possible that Cattle Egrets had pushed westwards to the Galápagos (even though there is no mention of this species in Michael Harris's 1984 field guide), and that they may be found in small flocks and not as the odd 'accidental'.

A few days later, Barnaby telephoned me to tell me his photos had arrived from London and I could come and look through them with him. As we looked, I couldn't find one with a Cattle Egret. He told me he hadn't taken any pictures of this bird as he could easily photograph it nearby, around Toulouse in France! There was one photo of an egret, but we decided it was a **Great Egret**. The long yellow bill and slender neck of Great make it very different from the shorter-billed, more stockily-built Cattle Egret. Although Barnaby was still sure that he had seen Cattle Egrets, I had sown some seeds of doubt: perhaps he had misidentified them. Eventually his mother half-jokingly suggested we both went there next year to find out for ourselves.

The idea took root, and we decided to make a trip to the Galápagos during the next long school holidays – but not just to solve the Cattle Egret mystery! To answer this particular riddle we could have written to Tony Castro, Barnaby's guide on his trip in 1994 and now a good family friend. We wanted to see all the other endemic and breeding birds; for Barnaby to take as many photos as possible, and for me to fill sketch book after sketch book.

Barnaby's father took over the logistics of the trip: flights, accommodation etc. We wanted to visit a dozen islands including small ones such as Plaza, Rábida, Daphne and Bartolomé. The two northern islands, Wolf and Darwin, although very interesting, were too far flung and would require too much time. To organize the itinerary we contacted Tony Castro, who would be our guide and who lived in Ayora on St Cruz. He arranged everything for us. Our plan was to use a small boat to give us flexibility in our island-hopping. We would be able to stay longer in the places where we wanted to, and we could move more freely between the islands. For some islands, such as Daphne, we would need a special permit, only given to small parties; perfect for us because we would be three in all (the crew would stay on the boat). It's quite easy to visit the islands these days, and you don't really need any special equipment. Even using one of the larger tourist boats it's possible to watch and photograph many species. There is of course an inherent problem in making the islands so accessible. Every year more and more people want to visit, thus endangering the very thing they have come to see. All in all, I think the Ecuadorian authorities manage tourism very well. Only small areas on each island can be visited so damage is limited. Large areas are left untouched, and the revenue from tourism goes to pay for the conservation of the fragile habitats. The major problems come with people who want to settle permanently in the archipelago. With more visitors, the service industry has to expand, which means more resident workers. Another major problem surrounds farming, where the demand for more food necessarily puts pressure on the islands' natural habitats. Introduced mammals, insects and plants also pose a threat. Large mammals such as donkeys, goats and cows can be very destructive, but their numbers can be controlled on the smaller islands. More problems actually come with rats, cats and dogs, which are difficult or, in some cases, nearly impossible to eradicate. Pigs destroy vegetation and dig up and consume both turtle and tortoise eggs and their young. Twenty-five years ago I had seen the danger posed by introduced plants on St Cruz and San Cristóbal, and I wanted to see what changes had occurred since then.

If we are prepared to abide by the rules laid down by the conservation authorities, and help in whatever way we can, there is every chance that we can save the Galápagos for future generations. And this could be the model for other areas where destruction has gone even further. At the moment there are only two bird species in serious danger in the Galápagos: Dark-rumped Petrel and, even more critically, Mangrove Finch. I very much hope that we can do enough to save these fascinating birds.

After a rather quick flight from Miami, with good views of Caribbean islands and the Andes just before landing, we arrived safely in Quito. I can't remember how long it took as I have no feeling of time when travelling. But neither Barnaby nor I liked the long and unnecessary wait to get through customs. We wanted to see birds outside the airport, but when we finally got through night had fallen. Our taxi drove hurriedly along the poor streets of Quito. The hotel was a surprise, however, built in a mixture of the Spanish-Colonial style, whatever that is, and had a very homely atmosphere. After a good meal, we were both ready for bed.

Next morning, before 6 o'clock, I was wakened by a loud, hurried but melodious birdsong. Looking out the window, it was still dark but I could see a Zenaida Dove on a roof, and a Rufous-collared Sparrow, delivering his pretty slow whistling song, 'tee-teeoo-teo tee tee' with a little trill at the end, a song I know well. With better light I saw more birds approaching along the ground in the manner of Rock Buntings, their European cousins. Now there were doves everywhere, smaller than European Collared Doves and shorter-tailed than American Mourning Doves. Some showed beautiful pink breasts in the rising sun. They were Eared Doves. All at once a large bird passed by and settled on a telephone wire, and at first I thought it was a kind of sparrowhawk. It seemed like an oversized European Blackbird with reddish legs and an orange bill. It was the singer. A second bird appeared with a paler throat, possibly a female. They were too big for Glossy-black Thrushes and too brownish. I made sketches of all of them, because it was still too dark for Barnaby's camera, and left details of their identification until later.

Returning to the airport, there were many Eared Doves searching for food on the street and two small parakeets high up in a tree. They flew past, screaming loudly, and too quickly for identification since we also had to watch our luggage. We saw two beautiful tanagers in a large *Araucaria* pine, one with a yellow belly and blue head, the other drab, very noisy and easy to identify as Blue-and-yellow Tanager, *Thraupis bonariensis*.

We left Quito for Guayaquil where we changed planes. Beside the runway, Barnaby spotted a large iguana bobbing its head. It looked as though it was sending us greetings for its cousins in the Galápagos. A large 'albus' egret stalked in the grass next to the runway and then six Cattle Egrets flew in the same direction as us. (I don't think they were on their way to the Galápagos!)

Between Ecuador and the Galápagos there is only water — the wide Pacific. How did the landbirds get there? There is no direct ocean current and most landbirds had their nearest 'families' in the Carribean and not in South America. The last to arrive in the Galápagos, the ani, was possibly brought by man, or was it an illegal traveller on a ship? Could one of the birds we saw in Quito reach the islands? Surely not the thrush, bunting or tanager. These are mountain birds; but the bunting also lives in Peru, along the coast. Why is there no parakeet in the Galápagos? On the other side of the Pacific there are many members of the parrot family that have found their way to outlying islands from Asia; and South America is parrot-rich. Well, Cattle Egret has reached the islands, as Barnaby saw the previous year when he visited with his mother and brother. The larger 'albus' egret has been a Galápagos bird for a long time. These puzzling thoughts occupied me on the flight to Baltra.

Landing on Baltra is rather disappointing. It's a dull dry island, desert-like, and the wildlife there was possibly adversely affected during World War II when it was a US army base. Now, as a tourist or islander, we profit from the military occupation because there is a runway and airport left over from this unfortunate time. It is operated by the Ecuadorian airforce and open to civil aircraft. The fauna and flora is particularly sensitive, and exploring the island outside the airport and tourist harbour is forbidden. It is hoped that the present airport has no long term detrimental effect on the environment. We met Tony Castro our guide. Barnaby knew him from the year before and I had met his father over 25 years ago when he was perhaps the best Galápagos guide.

On my first visit I had come by boat, also from Guayaquil, but to Puerto Baquerizo Moreno, the administrative capital of the archipelago, on San Cristóbal. It was then a rather long and uncomfortable journey across the Pacific, and you only saw a few birds once you left the Ecuadorian coast. I saw only a few albatrosses and some petrels on the 950+ km journey, mostly too far from the boat for proper identification. There were some flocks of Sabine's gulls, visitors from the high north, which came close to our boat. I suppose this way of travelling to the islands is still possible. Ships come from the mainland irregularly, bringing food, fresh water and other necessities for the ever-growing population and burgeoning tourist industry. Perhaps these ships still carry some passengers. Flying is of course quicker and more comfortable, but it also allows more people to come to the islands. There are now three airports, one on Baltra, the second on San Cristóbal, which is less busy and the third, located near Puerto Vilamil, on Isabela, has now been open for a few years.

not a real crest
← just pointed

spot

black stripes
grey
a whitish spot
reddish rufous collar

sitting on a wall singing
it's still poor light

shape like
a European
Reed-Bunting

bill not
so heavy

black spots

rufous

flesh coloured legs

orange
eye ring

a juvenile
all striped breast

pointing
upwards

strong
reddish
orange

greyish
blank

two wing bars
Zonotrichia capensis

Rufous collared
sparrow

like all American
sparrows
it is a
bunting

paler

long
strong

pale belly

long

broad tail

A very large thrush, dull grey in colour
Long orange legs, reddish bill in some more
yellowish. One had a paler throat.

A bird came flying over a wall
like a kind of sparrow hawk
it was a thrush. Later they were
all over the roofs, one singing
rather hurried in tempo but melodious
unlike our Blackbird 'Keart Keart'

identified at home : **Great Thrush**
Turdus fuscates

grey

earth brown
spots (black)

pinkish

back no black
more olive green

bright blue

a sweet
'chuck'

conspicuous
in flight

sitting a bit miserably
on a wall it is still clearly
smaller than a Collared Dove
shorter tailed than Mourning Dove
Zenaida auriculata
Eared Dove

olive back
some blue

rounded wings

rump
yellowish

◁ **Blue-and-yellow Tanager**
Thraupis bonariensis
both very noisy in a large Araucaria tree
just outside the airport entrance

female with
much blue on
her head
more than on birds
I had seen in
Argentina
was this a young male?

both looked
finch like
(larger than a
Greenfinch)

earth
brown

shiny

greyish

pinkish

not very shy

some
white

about a dozen or more doves
on the street just outside the airport

9 July 95
Quito/Ecuador

short

rather
long legs

The first sketch inside the airport
waiting for our luggage, second
bird outside the building slightly
larger, more thick-set, both are
Small Ground-finches (females?)
    9 July Baltra

long

Waiting to cross   long neck
the channel, many noddies
flying past. They had
rather long necks

Barnaby's first photos were of
ground-finches digging in the soil
just outside our bungalow. He could
approach them to within about 2 m,
before they flew into a nearby bush,
but then came back immediately he
left. All the time we were there, two
species were present, Small and
Medium.

While waiting for our bus to take us to the nearby Itabaca Channel we watched some Small Ground-finches, all in female plumage, searching in the dust just outside the airport. They took no notice of us. High in the air some large birds were circling and sailing around like overgrown Black Kites – frigatebirds – they were too far away to determine the species and our binoculars were still packed away.

During the two-minute channel crossing to St Cruz, some Galápagos Doves flew in front of us. Brown pelicans, Blue-footed Boobies and Audubon's Shearwaters were fishing in the channel, while rather long-necked noddies flew past. Once on St Cruz, waiting for another bus, we had time to watch more ground-finches, mostly Small but also many Mediums, of different sizes and with different bill shapes. Some were really beautiful all-black males, others had only black heads, and the females also varied, some greyer, some paler, others had broad fawn wingbars. At first I thought there were 3–4 different species and I could not tell if some were Small or Medium Ground-finches. In a bush near-by was an old finch nest, a round bulky construction with a side entrance. There were two Small Tree-finches moving around in another bush amongst the leaves, both females and paler than the ground-finches, with short bills, giving them a doll-like appearance.

The road to Ayora, on the other side of St Cruz, was a simple grav-el track straight across the highlands during our visit (now largely paved), first through a dry vegetation zone with pale grey Santo Palo trees and other bushes, now barren. There were the same bulky finch nests in some bushes we had seen at the bus stop. Before reaching Ayora, the road passes through 3–4 different vegetation zones. After bright sunshine near the coast, we had light rain in the 'terra alta'. Many birds flew over the road or sat in the roadside bushes but we drove past too quickly to identify them. I don't know why the driver was in such a hurry; fast driving is a real danger for all wildlife.

Arriving in Ayora after an absence of 25 years what changes I found! It is now home to around 12,000 people. The bus terminal is in front of the busy little harbour, next to an albatross monument, possibly the only one of its kind in the world. Ground-finches were again every-where, under and on the monument, in the street, on the quay, in the harbour – mostly Smalls, some Mediums. We booked into our hotel, a collection of bungalows next to a lagoon, a wonderful place for bird-watching. There were finches all around, and Yellow Warblers, but also waterbirds and seabirds, an ideal place to stay. Barnaby got out his camera and I my sketch book, and we started working at the front of our hotel.

From within a small shrubby tree, right in front of our hotel, we heard a bird singing as though talking to itself, babbling away with some melodious phrases; it reminded me of an Orphean Warbler, many of which I've heard singing in southern France. Barnaby tried to take a 'shot', which was not easy between all the branches. The bird was smaller than a European Song Thrush, longer-tailed with a pale unspotted breast and a dark cheek patch, a Galápagos Mockingbird. I saw the bright yellow mouth when the bill opened. Next morning at 5.30 it was singing again in the same tree, this time much louder and even more melodious.

There were mostly grey females around the hotel, and some, possibly young males, with darker heads. Only one in a dozen were all-black adult males with white undertail-coverts, which in some seem to be pinkish brown, but I think this was only through staining by the reddish dust in which they were digging in search of seeds.

It's already getting dark and difficult to take a photo. Ground-finches are still feeding and even more are arriving. There are only Small Ground-finches, all in female plumage, and no black males amongst them. Do Small Ground-finches have better eyes or do they just have more difficulty finding food when Mediums are present?

Next to the hotel in a lagoon was a young **Lava Heron**, well camouflaged between wet lava blocks and fallen golden brown mangrove leaves, stalking around as though in slow motion, spearing small prey in a flash, quicker than the eye could follow.

We spent the whole afternoon just around our hotel, and most of the time I watched ground-finches. They were attracted to two small areas just in front of our door. There was a permanent toing and froing, and 20–30 birds were present most of the time. It was a flock, but each bird seemed to act independently, unlike other seed-eaters in countries where many predators are present. They spent most of the time digging in the soil, often only the back of a bird could be seen. Most were Small Ground-finches, but many Mediums were also present. Large Ground-finches with their heavy bills, short tails and broad wings were flying past high in the air but did not join the feeding flock. Most of the birds present were in female or female-like plumage. I counted ten grey-coloured to one all-black male. The colour of their plumage is of no help in identification.

In both species there are strongly streaked individuals, others have very few streaks, some have dark heads, nearly black with pale bills, others pale heads with black bills, some show broad orange-brown wing-bars, strong breast stripes and brown undertail-coverts. One had a longish pointed bill, this was possibly a Sharp-billed Finch. I made some sketches of this bird. The Mediums were most puzzling, some are just slightly larger than Smalls but have larger bills; others are nearly the same size as Large Ground-finches but have smaller bills and their plumage, as mentioned above, is of no help in identification. Behind our bungalow on a wall was a dripping water pipe. This was attractive to all birds, Large, Medium and Small Ground-finches; some female Small Treefinches and also multi-coloured Yellow Warblers came to drink. In the nearby bushes there were also many finches, perched on branches. They often look different and more thick-set than when on the ground. All four species were feeding in an exotic flowering bush, biting off the pinkish flowers and chewing the stems.

The nearby lagoon was also a good spot for birds. At low tide, Moorhens came walking out of the dense vegetation and joined a young Lava Heron in more open space. The Moorhens are the same species that can be seen in a London park or in the United States (where they are called Common Gallinules). Two were still in their brownish juvenile plumage with greenish bill and frontal disc. Two adults seemed larger than European Moorhens, with brighter orange-red bills and frontal discs, but this impression was possibly caused by the light in the dark green mangrove. They were a bit timid, but not really shy. Not so the Lava Heron, which we could nearly touch. Lava Heron is an old endemic species which evolved in the Galápagos far away from predators, while the Moorhen is a more recent arrival, and although this could still have been some thousand years ago, there is in the Moorhen a genetic memory of predators. Later in the evening an adult, slate-coloured Lava Heron arrived and chased the young bird away.

After a simple but good dinner, Tony came with our captain and we fixed the route for our tour of the islands. We wanted to visit all the islands open to visitors, except the two outlying northern islands, Darwin and Wolf. We wanted to see as many bird species as possible, to photograph and sketch them. Our goal was to see all of the Galápagos breeding birds. It was not the right time for the regular visitors. They appear in the Galápagos during the northern winter months, but some, mostly younger birds, stay all year round in small numbers, so it was possible that we would see some of them. At this point, on our first day, we had already seen 22 different Galápagos species including some Cattle Egrets which came flying over our hotel as if to greet us.

A **Lava Heron** sitting motionless in dense vegetation in a mangrove beside the road to the Darwin Station, difficult to see (and photograph), waiting above the incoming tide for prey, suddenly stabbing at something very small. I thought it would fall from its perch. It swallowed the prey and waited again.

A beautiful brightly coloured **Brown Pelican** in full breeding plumage on a boat, as if it were the captain.

Next morning, 10 July, at 5.30 the mockingbird was already singing in the same tree as yesterday. Its singing was louder this time and more musical than the previous afternoon. Another Mocker, possibly its mate, was hopping on the ground under the tree. Normally Galápagos Mockers, with their peculiar social system, stay in family groups all the year round but these were just two together. Small Ground-finches came from all directions, mostly alone, sometimes two or three together, to feed in the same area as yesterday. They were the first finches to arrive and the last to leave yesterday evening. The different coloured 'Sharp-billed' with its orange-brown eyestripe and throat was also there. A Large-billed Flycatcher was singing his tuneful song from a rooftop.

At 8.00 am we left on foot to visit the Charles Darwin Research Station near Ayora, which is in the dry vegetation zone. On the road we saw a number of large Darwin's finches mostly in small groups of 4–5, pecking seeds from the dust. They must have good eyesight because I could find no seeds myself. Again, like yesterday, they were in different plumages resembling Small/Medium Ground-finches, but possibly all a bit darker. Grey females, grey males with black heads and many jet black males with white undertail-coverts and all different bill colours from pale brown to all black. They looked strong but fluffy in their feathers when hopping around, their upright tails often spread.

There were numerous dome-shaped bulky finch nests in the roadside bushes. I think it was impossible to tell which species had built them. This one was occupied by a Small Ground-finch. It was coming out of the entrance hole, but on our way back, three hours later, there was a Large Ground-finch beside the nest.

all black exept rump

others had only black heads

When searching for food on the ground, the finches resemble large-billed quail or even hens, especially when cocking their short tails. They not only look like hens, they also behave like them, scratching the ground with their feet, pecking at seeds and scratching again. Often they dig little holes and only their backs can be seen. But they don't take dust baths like Old World sparrows.

sometimes they even look like a thick-set, thick-billed Fantail Pigeon with drooping wings and open, spread tail.

The Charles Darwin Research Station was established in 1960 to further scientific work and conservation in the Galápagos. In 1965 a breeding programme was started with the endangered subspecies of giant tortoise; initially with the form from Pinzón, then with those from other islands. The need for this work was obvious; for instance only 14 tortoises remained alive on Española. All were brought to the Darwin Station on Santa Cruz. Eggs were collected from other islands before rats or dogs could steal them, and these were artificially incubated. To date, more than 1,000 tortoises have been reared and the first taken back to their islands where they can breed when sexually mature at around 25 years. At the same time, a programme was established to eliminate introduced animals such as dogs, pigs and rats, as well as goats and donkeys; not an easy operation.

A similar breeding programme was started later for land iguanas where, on Santa Cruz for instance, only 60 were left in 1976. Luckily for Baltra land iguana, a scientist took some to Seymour before they became extinct on their home island, and they have survived. In 1978, the first of the programme's newly bred iguanas were taken to their original homes where they have now started to breed again.

A young giant tortoise born at the Darwin Station. They stay here for their first few years until big enough to survive on their home island. There they would be easy prey to the introduced rats and feral dogs when still small.

Giant tortoises have been famous since the discovery of the islands to which they give their name. Galápagos means saddle in Spanish after the tortoise carapaces found on some islands. Together with the Aldabra tortoise from the Seychelles, they are the largest of their kind now living. On Santa Cruz, with their dome-shaped carapaces, they can weigh up to 250 kg. The saddle-backs from Española are much smaller. When looking at their faces, one has the impression of an unreal prehistoric animal.

Cactus-finches resemble ground-finches with longer, slightly curved pointed bills. The females are more heavily streaked and with rather dark heads.

In the open pens, where the larger young tortoises live, there are large concrete pans with fresh water that are particularly attractive to many Darwin's finches and other birds. We saw at least four finch species at any one time: numerous Large Ground-finches with their enormous bills, Medium and Small Ground-finches, males in full black breeding plumage, many more than we had seen yesterday in the flocks near our hotel in Ayora. New species for us were the more elegant cactus-finches. They were all bathing, casually sitting in the water, splashing water slowly around them, not like our European sparrows which are always hurried. There were also some Yellow Warblers, Mockers and Large-billed Flycatchers but we did not see any tree-finches. Possibly they don't like it down here in the dry vegetation zone. It was not easy for Barnaby to take photographs in the shade of the bushes where the finches preferred to bathe. Flashbulbs are not allowed.

In the afternoon we went in a dinghy along the steep lava cliffs in Ayora harbour where we saw some Blue-footed Boobies on their nests. We landed next to the Angermayers' house, surrounded by marine iguanas. The Angermayers are early settlers of German origin who still live there. From there we walked along the 'Playa de los Alemanes'.

There was a **Brown Pelican** colony in the mangrove bushes of the lagoon near the 'Playa de los Alemanes'. Often both parents sat on the rather untidy nest platforms made of sticks and twigs. None was actually breeding. Their striking white and chestnut heads and necks are very showy. Some had a golden/yellow tinge to the head and a silvery shine on the wings. The young birds are rather drab, brownish and dull white. Most of them were just sitting there and there was no noise in the colony: pelicans are silent birds. It's peculiar to see these large seabirds sitting in a bush, but that's where they breed.

We also saw other seabirds besides Brown Pelicans. Large Magnificent Frigatebirds flew overhead, an adult male with just a little red on its chin and a female that seemed to be larger with a white breast but dark throat. All the others were younger birds with white heads, their colours indicating that they were between immature and adult. All were Magnificent Frigatebirds. In the male I could see the greyish legs which are pinkish in the similar but more pelagic Great Frigatebird. A Lava Gull, still in brownish immature plumage came to see if we had some food. We had seen both the frigate-birds and the gull before, along the cliffs and in the harbour. Lava Herons, always found singly, were sitting in the lower parts of the mangroves. One showed its silvery slate back and yellow feet in direct fast flight low over the water. Some Cattle Egrets flew past. They did not settle down, but with their short compact bodies and pale bill, were easy to identify. They are not rare now. Barnaby had seen a few the previous year. Tony told us we would see many more up in the highlands. Twenty five years ago I found none.

An adult **Lava Heron**, not yet in bright full breeding plumage.

In the Galápagos there is always something special. All over the world, gulls, when adult, are normally white birds with grey or even black backs and wings. Here in the Galápagos, one gull is all dark and remains this way year round. This is **Lava Gull**, a good name for this grey and black species, which is the colour of wet lava. A similar gull from the western coast of South America is all dark but only as a non-breeding bird. When breeding, Grey Gull, *Larus modestus*, has a silvery pale head. The even paler Heermann's Gull, *Larus heermanii*, from the Californian coast, is all dark only in first-winter plumage, like a brown-black crow with a yellow bill.

It is not only colour which separates the Galápagos gull: unlike others it is a solitary bird, mostly seen alone or in pairs, only occassionally 3–4 together. It is not a colonial nester like other gulls, the nest being placed alongside saline lagoons or on a sandy coast and well away from other breeding birds. Their movements are also slower, not so nervous as other gulls, and their voice is seldom heard (not noisy like most gulls). Their call is similar to that of a European gull but also reminds me of a heron.

We walked along a mudflat with some open shallow water and a very flat dry landscape behind it, with palm-like cactus trees and candelabras, in warm bright sunshine and with a clear deep blue sky.

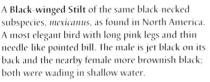

A **Black-winged Stilt** of the same black-necked subspecies, *mexicanus*, as found in North America. A most elegant bird with long pink legs and thin needle like pointed bill. The male is jet black on its back and the nearby female more brownish black; both were wading in shallow water.

There were two single **Whimbrels** on the mudflat. When standing still they blended exactly with their surroundings. We spotted them only when they moved around. They were of the subspecies *hudsonicus*, more buffish brown, not so grey as European Whimbrel. This was our first northern vagrant, a bird breeding in Alaska and Arctic Canada, not in the Galápagos like the stilt.

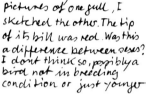

pictures of one gull, I sketched the other. The tip of its bill was red. Was this a difference between sexes? I don't think so, possibly a bird not in breeding condition or just younger

Two **Lava Gulls** were on the sandy 'Playa de los Alemanes', walking along the tideline. From a distance they looked dark ash grey, but when close the hood is distinctively dark slate black and typically with white around the eyes. When I threw a piece of banana towards one, it came slowly, picked the morsel up and swallowed it. Their movements are rather slow, as though they have all the time in the world. The other gull found something on dry ground, took it to the water and washed it before swallowing. The whole scene was peaceful, even a bit melancholy.

After the beach, we passed a saltpan empty of birds. Far away a Blue Heron and Great Egret were both sitting close together in a bush, half asleep. We could note well the difference in size but it was too far away for Barnaby's camera. It was an unreal dry landscape, salt crusts without vegetation. Tony wanted to show us a 'Barranco' just behind the saltpans: a deep gorge with an underground connection to the sea. The water in the barranco was of the same deep blue as the sky above; a fantastic sight, and well worth visiting. There were no birds and the absolute silence was broken just once by a Mocker's song. In the silence its song seemed even more melodious.

On our return, the herons were still in the same bush we had passed an hour ago on our way to the barranco. Now there were some Small Ground-finches in the low vegetation near the saltpans and a Yellow Warbler in grey plumage, lacking any yellow, and singing its high-pitched warbling song. On the mudflat the Whimbrels now had the company of another northern vagrant, a Semipalmated Plover, in non-breeding plumage, running over the mud like a wound-up children's toy. It looked like a smallish, short-billed European Ringed Plover. When it flew off there were no white markings in its wings and it looked more like a Little Ringed Plover.

Back on the 'Angermayers'' landing, we had to wait for our dinghy. There were two **Lava Gulls** just a few metres from us on a lava block. We could study them easily and they seemed to be as interested in us as we were in them. Their dark hoods showed up well against the slate-coloured back. Both had some red at the tips of their bills, unlike the pair we had seen earlier on the beach. I noticed they have rather long legs for a gull. A younger Lava was flying past, its back and head the same dark colour and with a small pale rump patch. A **Yellow Warbler**, an all-yellow male with a rusty reddish front patch, looked even brighter on the black lava. It looked into every little crack and hole and 'warbled' between glances, just like the grey bird we had seen on the saltpan.

Below our feet on lava blocks, like little mice, the ever present Small Ground-finches. Their colour matched the lava well. At first I thought they were searching for flies or other insects because it was low tide, but on closer inspection, I noticed rice had been scattered there.

Perhaps the Angermayers from the nearby house had left it for them since they also fed the marine iguanas around their house. The **Yellow Warbler** also joined in. Normally it's an insect-eater but I watched very closely and saw it take rice several times. Possibly small seeds are part of the normal diet as in so many seed-eating birds, or was this just an adaptation to unnatural circumstances?

There was not one black male among more than 20 finches, all were in female plumage. Do males retire earlier to bed? A I noticed yesterday next to our hotel only females were present late in the evening.

grey green

pale stripe

On the return crossing to Ayora harbour, there were many frigatebirds in the air. Again, all in different plumages: two adults, some immatures at different stages, but mostly juveniles with white heads. Two attacked an incoming Blue-footed Booby but with no success. It landed safely next to its two hungry chicks waiting on the cliff ledge. **Brown Pelicans**, all in adult plumage, were swimming around tourists' boats, waiting for food to be thrown to them. We counted 11 Lava Gulls, always singles, flying in different directions. Most were in the all-dark, black-ish/brown juvenile plumage with the paler rump. Dark slate grey adults with black heads also showed this paler rump. Others were in a plumage between juvenile and adult: dark on head and breast, paler on lower belly, pale rump and a terminal broad black band on the grey tail. Only one younger bird came close to our dinghy and followed for a short while.

When we landed there was a **Lava Heron** in the shallow water, not afraid of us in the dinghy nor the people standing around. It came out of the water and inspected a lava block for some possible prey. Another walked on the pier between some tourists. This was an adult in slate-grey plumage with a beautiful silky silvery sheen to its slightly elongated back feathers. On its crown a short crest, not long and egret-like as in many other herons, and its legs were bright orange. When the younger bird walked onto the pier, the adult raised its crest and chased the intruder away. They don't seem to like company or competition for food.

Back on 'our lagoon' next to the hotel it was low tide. **The Common Gallinules**, or Moorhens, as they are called in Britain, were there again, two adults and three full-grown young birds. I had more time to watch them. They are not really as different from the American/European as I had first thought. The frontal disc looks really bright red and the red joints on the legs show up very well. In Europe, they don't let you observe them so closely. Here they are not so confident as the Lava Herons but not so shy as they are at home in France. Later, two more adults came and all seven fed peacefully next to each other, jerking their tails and showing their black-centred white bottoms. One walked into the dark mangrove and there I could easily see how this white undertail serves as a flashing signal.

A **Lava Heron** in immature plumage. It looked like a cross between a Striated and a Lava Heron. This could be possible since both species occur in the Galápagos. The Striated, a possible newcomer, is rarer and only found in a few places. The taxonomic relationship of these two species is not clear yet; it could be that they are just different colour forms of one species.

Mockingbird
9 July 95

black bill

Dark-billed
Cuckoo
11 July Ayora
in the same tree as the
Mockingbird two days before

white
edges
on tail

11 July, about 7 o'clock in the morning, I thought I saw the Mocker we had seen on our first and second day in the same tree but the bird looked different, sitting upright, very still, not singing. It had a long dark tail and short, stout curved black bill. I sketched it from the doorstep, but when I approached, it flew off with rapid wingbeats. Then I saw it was a cuckoo.

Later we drove up to the terra alta farmland region where our vehicle ran out of petrol. I had time to walk up the road between high exotic trees. Guava trees laden with fruit were everywhere. Tree-finches, I thought Medium, were eating the papayas, but no, this could not be. They are not found on St Cruz, so they must have been Small Tree-finches. I heard the low chuckling call of cuckoos and twice saw one flying over the road. They are shy birds and I could not approach them. Like all American *Coccyzus* cuckoos, those in the Galápagos are not parasitic breeders (unlike European Cuckoo); they make their own nests. As always, Small Ground-finches were present between the exotic trees. Once I saw them in a farm amongst chickens and pigs, and above them tree-finches. Now I was sure these were Small Tree-finches. I heard a Mocker singing and some Yellow Warblers calling, otherwise it was rather poor for birdwatching.

Remainders of the original
woodland behind a fence
The rest was cut and the area
is now grazed by cattle

Some poor clumps of ferns and
other endemic plants between
introduced grass. I thought the
land rather poor for breeding
good quality cattle

Warbler Finch
like a little Wren
or a kinglet

In some areas the terra alta has been completely altered by man. Large areas are now cattle grassland where there are no birds. I wonder if this clearance was necessary. Even worse was the introduction of the quinine tree during the last world war. A remedy for malaria is made from the bark, but there is no malaria in the Galápagos. Now the plant is established, it colonizes large areas very quickly. The fight against it is very difficult, almost impossible. The chinchona looks beautiful when in flower and has handsome large leaves, but no wildlife is found in them. The only birds we saw there were Warbler Finches, a new species for us. These birds were not shy but always on the move, quicker than European Chiffchaff or wrens; too quick for the camera but okay for my sketch book. Tony wanted to show us Barn Owls in a cave off a very large lava flow, but we failed to spot them. There were many pellets lying on the cave floor, fantastic material for scientists. One Galápagos mammal, a kind of hamster, is known only from such a pellet in which its skull was found. I believe this was on Isabela.

There is now another cuckoo living in the Galápagos, **Smooth-billed Ani**. It is not known if the anis came by themselves or were introduced by man. Anis are sedentary birds, not migrants, and do not fly very well, although in South America they sometimes 'wander'. It is said they take ticks from cattle, so someone might have brought them to the islands illegally for that purpose. The first birds were seen in 1960 and were identified as Groove-billed Anis, *Crotophaga sulcirostris*. They were first seen on Santa Cruz in 1980 but this time the species was Smooth-billed, *Crotophaga ani*. They now breed there in large numbers and have found their way to other islands, even though they are poor flyers. They are often seen in flocks of 10–50, mostly near cows, sitting upright in bushes or tall grass, like black witches. As newcomers they are shy but not secretive like Dark-billed.

Plans have been made to eradicate them but this has now become very difficult. This might be possible on Santa Fé and Pinzón, where they also breed, but on a large island like St Cruz it is hopeless. Now they are there, they will probably stay, and if they did come by themselves, which is unlikely, they would have the right to be there since all birds were once newcomers.

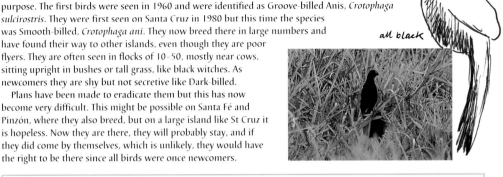

all black

While standing with Tony next to our van and talking about the quality of cattle on the islands, a **Cattle Egret** came and settled on the car as if willing to join in the discussion.

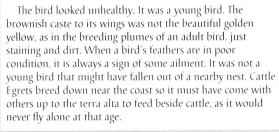

The bird looked unhealthy. It was a young bird. The brownish caste to its wings was not the beautiful golden yellow, as in the breeding plumes of an adult bird, just staining and dirt. When a bird's feathers are in poor condition, it is always a sign of some ailment. It was not a young bird that might have fallen out of a nearby nest. Cattle Egrets breed down near the coast so it must have come with others up to the terra alta to feed beside cattle, as it would never fly alone at that age.

Examining the bird in the hand (only allowed in this case so Tony could try to establish the nature of its ailment) it was as skinny as a razor blade. I hoped it was not suffering from a disease the egrets had brought with them when they settled in the Galápagos about 25 years ago. This could be fatal to other birds like Lava Heron (even tourists can bring disease).

On farmland, along a road with large trees, we watched some finches. A large clump of moss fell from an exotic tree. Up there, under a large branch, was a Woodpecker Finch, working like a little bulldozer, with its bill pulling the moss from the bark. It was amazing how powerful this finch was at its work. Hanging under a branch, often on one leg, pulling away pieces as large and even larger than my palm. Under the tree, Small and Medium Ground-finches were waiting for the falling moss and searched in it for insects. They were not at all afraid when the large clump sailed down. They seemed used to it. Later the Woodpecker Finch took a bath in a small puddle with other finches. It did this rather quickly, as if it did not like to be on the ground too long.

Along a cattle trail, under a fence, there was a rich flora of endemic and exotic plants. Many birds of different species, all three ground-finches, many black males, a Woodpecker Finch, tree- and Warbler Finches were searching for food, especially in the moss and lichen.

Small Tree-finches moving as quick as mercury, all in female plumage, searching in nearby bushes. The even smaller, similarly-coloured Warbler Finch with its thin insect-eater's bill was also there. Often when the bill is not clearly seen, it is difficult to separate the two species. Both are so agile and quick, always on the move. I would have liked to have seen a male Small Tree-finch in breeding plumage with its all-black head.

Like a red flash, a male **Vermillion Flycatcher** always came back to the same stake or wire after catching a flying insect.

Females are not easy to spot in their duller more delicate plumage, greyish brown and yellowish with no trace of red, resembling the larger Galápagos Flycatcher.

The bright Vermillion males are really an exception among the rather drab Galápagos landbirds. Vermillions are widespread from the arid southwestern United States down across Central America to northern Chile and central Argentina. In the Galápagos there are two subspecies: on most islands *Pyrocephalus rubius nanus*, more pinkish than most continental subspecies, and on St Cristóbal the even smaller and paler subspecies *dubius*.

Barnaby with his camera. He did not have highly sophisticated equipment like many tourists. Sometimes it was difficult for him to get close to the birds since there are strict limits on access. Here in the farmland there are no such limitations. The birds were shier, keeping their distance. They had already learned to be wary.

But even here on farmland there are no real problems with distance. When you stay still the birds will come to you. All you need is patience, and even with a 'snap-shot' camera you can take good pictures of most birds if all you want is 'souvenir' photos of Galápagos species. A hide is not necessary since on most islands there is little human disturbance and the birds are quite tame. Often it's you who has to move away from the birds to avoid getting too close! Sometimes it feels as though you are in a zoo.

A male **Yellow Warbler**, of subspecies *aureola* from the Galápagos and Cocos islands, with its rusty crown patch. North American subspecies have all-yellow heads, rust-red in some Central American subspecies.

A dumpy **Small Ground-finch** in female plumage and with a very pale bill. Bill colour changes during the season but not shape, which is always proportionally smaller, the bill only slightly curved on the upper edge and more pointed than in often similar-sized Medium Ground-finches.

A female Small Ground-finch with a dark upper mandible was in our bathroom when we came back from the terra alta. We had to catch her to release her from the room. Touching the birds is normally forbidden.

Male Vermillion Flycatchers usually like to perch in the open, along fences or on dead branches in the lower parts of bushes or trees. From here they drop to the ground, catch their insect prey and flutter quickly back to perch again. Females behave in a similar manner but they are more secretive, perching less in the open. Both sexes catch insects in flight. Males are very territorial and make spectacular aerial display flights raising the crest, fluffing breast feathers, flying upwards with furious wing-flapping, gaining height slowly, up to 10 m, sometimes even higher. The body is held vertically, wings raised, showing as much red as possible, finally dropping down to perch or rising just before touching the ground again and repeating this display several times. All this is accompanied by a rapid peeping musical 'tee-tui-tui tinka-tui-tweet-tuiteet' call, interspersed with bill-snapping, like the sound of castanets. It is not only adult males that show this display. We saw a young male, brownish on back and whitish on breast with a pink caste to the belly, displaying in the same way. Many males in the Galápagos breed in a plumage which resembles that of a female from the Continent. Galápagos females have yellowish bellies and no trace of pink.

Another colourful highlight is Yellow Warbler in full adult male breeding plumage. Bright yellow all over with only a little green on wings and back, a beautiful rusty orange on the crown and with breast streaks of the same colour. There is nearly always one of these brightly coloured males around somewhere but most are in other stages of plumage, from grey-green with pale whitish undersides to those without any trace of yellow. All colours and combinations to full yellow are possible. The grey birds are not always females, and some females can be very yellow. Sexing is not easy, sometimes even impossible outside the breeding season, except for brightly coloured males. I heard greys singing like males.

Warblers are virtually everywhere. They are the only species of their kind on the islands so they can occupy all habitats. We saw them down on the lava rocks on the seashore at low tide, in gardens and on the streets of Ayora, even at the airport, in the cactus around a saltpan in the dry zone and everywhere in the terra alta in dense natural or sparse farmland vegetation. We often heard their song, a rapid series of high-pitched sweet notes finishing with a short warble, even though it was July and after their breeding period, which is in the rainy season from December to April. We often saw several birds together in a loose flock and we could hear their bills snapping as they caught insects. This noisy bill-snapping is a typical habit of Yellow Warbler and not heard in Warbler Finches.

Up here, finches were everywhere. All three ground-finches were present, mostly Small, some Mediums, fewer Large but many Small Tree-finches yet always less common than Small Ground-finches.

Most were in their pale yellowish female plumage. Only one had some dark feathers on its face and was without the pale ring (like spectacles) around the eyes, so typical in female plumage. They are a bit larger and more strongly built than Warbler Finches, but just as agile, hanging upside-down under a branch or even on large leaves in a very acrobatic manner, often on one leg only. Towards the evening, just before leaving, we saw a beautiful male in breeding plumage with black head, breast and back. He was in the company of some Large Tree-finches in grey-brown female plumage with yellow underparts. In two days we had seen eight, out of the 13 Darwin's finches, not counting the possible Sharp-billed Finch from Ayora. Santa Cruz, like Santiago and Isabela, has ten finch species; no other islands have as many.

On 11 July at 9.30 in the evening we went on board our boat, the *Española*, and left Ayora harbour for the Plazas, arriving next morning at 4 am after a calm passage in the canal between the twin islets. The sun rose as we arrived. On one side was Plaza Norte, with steep lava cliffs and many Swallow-tailed Gulls and some noddies flying around or sitting on the cliffs. On the other side, was Plaza Sur, with a flat beach where dozens of sealions were lying between the lava blocks, some bulls in the water controlling their harems on land. Plaza Sur is just over 1 km long and is about 13 ha in size. On one side the land slopes down to the sea; on the other it rises to a steep cliff 25 m high. Plaza Norte is smaller and not open to visitors. Both lie close to the coast of St Cruz. There is a small jetty for dry landing on Plaza Sur, but before we could land we had to clap our hands to gently chase away a sleeping sealion in our path.

Northern Plaza

Landing with seal

southern Plaza

seal

A solitary **Ruddy Turnstone** on the Plaza lava beach must have been here since last year. Normally they arrive from their breeding haunts in August, often in large numbers; they return in March. A few remain all year round in the Galápagos but they don't breed here.

prickly pear fruit and pads are the perfect food for land iguanas and that's where they get their liquid on a dry island without open fresh water

Land Iguana
Conolophus subcristatus

After a delicious meal, *(above)* it seems to be very happy and looks as though it is smiling. Their mouths must be incredibly tough. They can eat the prickly pear figs or pads without removing the spines, but I watched one while it rolled the fig over a stone with its feet to scrape off the spines. They also eat other juicy green plants, some insects and even carrion.

Just after landing, having passed the sealion on the landing jetty, beneath some large prickly pear cactuses, you will nearly always see another territory holder, an old brightly coloured male **land iguana**. Large and beautiful with its yellowish head and forelegs, and a row of spines on its back, it really looks like a small dinosaur. They can grow to more than one metre in length and old males reach nearly 15 kg in weight. There are some 300 adults on this tiny island. Most of the year they stay on the western side in the cactus forest. During the breeding season in January, the females move into the more open parts on the eastern side where they find sandier areas to dig their nest burrows and lay their eggs. Here they eat mostly from the juicy *Sesuvium* leaves, and later in the season when the bright yellow portulac flowers are out, they live mainly on this delicacy. There are no introduced mammals on Plaza, the reason for such a healthy iguana population.

Under the same large prickly pear cactuses a **Lava Heron**, in its typical hunched posture, slowly stalked around taking flies from fallen cactus fruit. It was entirely slate grey but with a green gloss to its elongated back feathers and a small pale whitish stripe down its throat and neck.

Its legs and bill were dull grey. The legs of breeding birds are bright orange-yellow, contrasting with the slate grey plumage, and the bill is shiny black, as we had seen the day before in Ayora. So this bird here must be a non-breeding individual. There is no fixed breeding season as there is with northern herons. Lava Heron can breed all year round but mostly does so from September to March. This bird was not at all shy, even less so than the birds we had seen on Santa Cruz. It came and caught a fly on my shoe. I stood on the tourist trail and made sketches and could have touched it, but this is not allowed with any wild creature in the Galápagos.

There is an easy walk on Plaza, a trail of about 950 m (also a shorter one of only 500 m), moving gently from the dry landing place up to the steep cliffs (25–30 m high) on the southern side. On the right there is a dense cactus forest covering about one third of this island, where most land iguanas were located when we visited. On the left side of the trail, which is more open, there are some single or small groups of short cactus trees, mostly under 3–4 m. The whole of this part of the island is covered by a carpet of *Sesuvium*, a perennial herb with fleshy leaves.

Now, in July, it was a golden to deep red. In the wetter season, when the plants are green, they are eaten by iguanas. The fleshy leaves are salty. Perhaps in this way the ancestors of marine iguanas, which were once green land iguanas, acquired the taste for salty sea plants. Yellow Warblers were hopping around everywhere on the lava blocks and in the low vegetation. One very bright yellow male, with reddish cap and flank stripes searched lower down on the shoreline between the sunbathing sealions for flies and possibly other edible matter in the dung (always a malodorous waste product).

The mostly white wings with black tips, grey shoulders and back make a very conspicuous pattern in flight. Then the closed tail is deeply forked (see *inset above*), but squarish when wide open. The flight is very elegant, a bit tern-like.

Swallow-tailed Gulls reign high up, all along the ridge, on both Plazas. There are large colonies on the steep lava cliffs where they breed among other seabirds. For me they are the most elegant and beautiful seabirds in the Galápagos, and the most photogenic gulls in the world. In shape and colour they are pure elegance. Not shy at all, they let you watch their private life very closely, and the couples are very tender with each other. Their large dark eyes are impressive, much larger than in any other gull, enabling them to search at night, generally far out on the open sea, for their preferred food, small fish and squid. They are the only nocturnal gulls in the world. Night fishing avoids competition with other seabirds and they also escape pirating by frigatebirds.

The adults have a conspicuous white patch at the base of the black bill, on their blackish hood, and there is a pale ivory tip to the bill. This helps the single chick to recognise its parents when they return in the dark with food. During the day the adults stay around the breeding colony and do not follow ships as do Lava Gulls. After breeding, which can be in any month of the year, the Swallow-tails stay out at sea for about 4–5 months, far away from their colony.

At the edge of the Swallow-tailed cliff, watching some birds below. This is over 25 m above the sea, and one should not go too close to the edge since the lava is not very solid, often slippery and can break off. It's better to keep away and observe from a safe distance.

F rom the cliff on Plaza we watched a **Cattle Egret** below us, near the northern shore. It had adopted sealions, under some cactus trees, as if they were buffaloes under *Acacia* trees in its African homeland. Ground-finches were feeding between rocks and *Sesuvium* plants nearby, when the Cattle Egret stalked slowly towards them and with a very quick dart caught a black male. The victim fluttered its wings. The egret danced around while the wings covered its eyes then swallowed the poor little bird whole. This took place about 80 m from us. I could see it very clearly with my binoculars but it was too far away for Barnaby to get a really good shot. I wondered if Cattle Egret pose a new danger for small endemic birds or has Lava Heron a similar hunting technique? Other finches nearby were unaware and just kept feeding near the scene of this drama.

A t the highest point, just at the end of the tourist trail, there is an important Galápagos sealion bachelor colony, out of reach of territorial bull sealions. I wondered why they chose this place and how they were able to climb over the steep lava cliffs some 30 m high. The sealions, of all ages and mostly large, were just lying around, idle and peaceful, possibly dreaming of the time when they themselves would have a harem on the lower northern shores. How peaceful it looked, but there was an evil smell in the air; the lava was 'polished' with sealion excrement.

The young Swallow-tail is long-legged like all gull chicks but otherwise looks more like a young tern. The brown on the head is natural but the normally white belly is stained here in the sealion colony. Swallow-tails always lay just one egg and do this every nine or ten months, beginning when about 40 months old. They can live 20–30 years.

Sealions off duty can be very lazy, especially in the 'bachelor' colony, but this one has taken it too far. Only his bones remain and a young Swallow-tail thinks this a good place for a siesta. I hope it will not stay as long in the same place as the sealion. Its parents will wake it when they come home tonight with food.

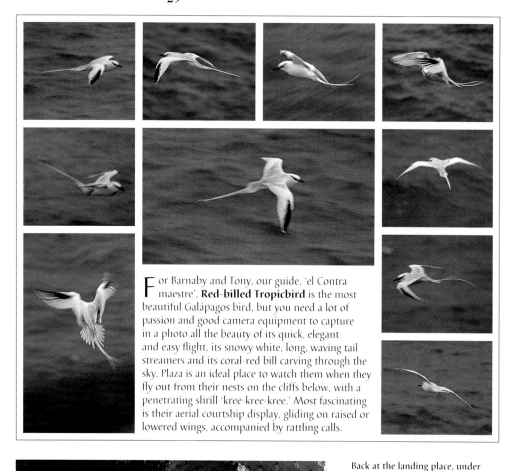

For Barnaby and Tony, our guide, 'el Contra
maestre', **Red-billed Tropicbird** is the most
beautiful Galápagos bird, but you need a lot of
passion and good camera equipment to capture
in a photo all the beauty of its quick, elegant
and easy flight, its snowy white, long, waving tail
streamers and its coral-red bill carving through the
sky. Plaza is an ideal place to watch them when they
fly out from their nests on the cliffs below, with a
penetrating shrill 'kree-kree-kree.' Most fascinating
is their aerial courtship display, gliding on raised or
lowered wings, accompanied by rattling calls.

Back at the landing place, under
the cactus trees, the same Lava
Heron was still just sitting there on
a lava rock, like an island warden
watching the passing tourists.

It was as though he was keeping
an eye on us and making sure we
kept inside the tourist trail, which
is marked by the typical short
black and white posts. A beautiful
all-black cactus-finch was singing in
the *Opuntia* above him, in front of
a nest deep in the shade of the spiny
prickly pear, too dark for a photo.

a typical trail post

The Lava Heron was not the only one on watch. The same dark-coloured **land iguana** was still there. I do not know if this was just a very dark-coloured female or if it was one of the hybrids between land and marine iguana found on Plaza. It is possible since they both belong to the same family and are more closely related than appears, and may even have the same ancestor.

We saw a Wandering Tattler on the rocky shore, a greyish wader from North America, a visitor we had not seen before. There was also a Turnstone but not the drab one we had seen on landing. This one was in bright breeding plumage. Two snowy white and jet black yellow-billed Masked Boobies and many Common Noddies were flying in the straits between the two Plazas. We had also seen Masked Boobies on the cliffs above the 'bachelor' sealion colony. I do not know if they were just resting or breeding there. Blue-footed Boobies and Brown Pelicans were fishing close to the shore. It is incredible to see them dive between the lava blocks so close to the shore. The water could not have been deep. On the other side, on Plaza Norte, there seemed to be more Swallow-tailed Gulls, most sitting on the edge of the cliffs, with only a few flying around.

We had lunch on board, watching the peaceful picture around us and hearing the barking of the patrolling sealions in the water in front of their harems on land. Slowly we sailed north, away from the Plazas towards Seymour, our next island.

We saw only a few birds en route to the next island. **Blue-footed Boobies**, mostly singles, were around all the time. One followed our ship for a while, sailing above us with angled wings. A single all-brown **Common Noddy**, long-tailed and without a pale cap, passed in a straight line, moving faster than our boat. A small group of five Audubon's Shearwaters flapped and glided over the low waves. I relaxed on deck to enjoy the calm sea in bright equatorial sunshine.

We sailed slowly along the coast of Santa Cruz, and as soon as we passed Rocas Gordon seabirds became more numerous. We saw Blue-footed Boobies all the time, and while passing Punta Carrión near the Canal de Itabaca, many shearwaters were swimming or gliding and fluttering low over the water. Sometimes large flocks were in the company of noddies and, near the Baltra coast, with Brown Pelicans. Along the Baltra coast there were many **frigatebirds** in the air. We saw them in all their different plumages. I could identify Magnificent Frigatebirds but some males could have been Greaters. Called Greater Frigatebird in English, their scientific name is *Fregata minor*, and *minor* means small. They are not so common in the Galápagos, concentrated in only a few colonies, but their Spanish name is Fragata Común. As you can see, names can be misleading!

We passed the small Isla Mosquera, which is more of a sandbank than a real island. Numerous Brown Pelicans and some Great Blue Herons stood on the flat beach, mostly asleep. Beyond we could already see Seymour, also flat, an uplifted lava plateau a bit like Baltra, with low cliffs around the coast. The island is known for its submarine fossils, its endemic Palo Santo, *Bursera malacophylla*, found there and on Baltra and small Daphne. The prickly pear cactuses are only bushy on this island and not tree-like as on Plaza. There were many Swallow-tailed Gulls on the cliffs, some still breeding, possibly sitting on an egg or small chick, while other unguarded chicks were already walking around. Again, as on Plaza, they reminded me of tern chicks, and were also similar to young kittiwakes, but much longer-legged. They need long legs to walk over the rough lava blocks, which they did easily and often quite rapidly.

Next to the gulls there were nesting noddies. They prefer to build their nests in the shade of boulders, where often all you can see is the white cap of the adults. Like the gulls, many had a single chick, which was entirely chocolate-brown; but unlike the gulls they preferred not to wander around in the sun.

On Seymour we saw a young **Swallow-tailed Gull** in flight, clearly showing its forked tail with black terminal band. In flight, you can also see the white belly of this juvenile, which is unique in young gulls. It's possible that this is what made me think of their tern-like appearance.

With the chocolate-brown head, mantle and wings, **young Blue-footed Boobies** look quite different from the adults, more like tropical Brown Boobies, which don't occur in the Galápagos. When younger and still partly downy (*below and right*), they resemble a Masked Booby with a dark bill. They sleep in the funniest places, often on the tourist trail.

Seymour is to frigatebirds what the Plazas are to Swallow-tailed Gulls. Certainly there are many Swallow-tails breeding on the low cliffs, but most impressive is the large frigatebird colony. First the trail passes between the typical Blue-footed nests, just a scrape in the ground within a white circle painted by the droppings of the chicks. Arriving in a more vegetated area, mostly of yellow cordia and salt bushes, there were frigatebirds, with their flimsy nests, in the bushes. At first the whole colony looked chaotic. Some males were still courting, other adults or females sat on their nests, possibly breeding, others fed chicks of different ages, many fully feathered, full-grown young perched in the bushes and some adults were just sitting around. We saw many dried and mummified corpses of young birds under the bushes. Life must be very tough in such a colony.

The majority were Magnificent Frigatebirds, particularly in the middle of the colony, most Greater frigatebirds had their nests around the edge. I don't know if this is the rule. Often in a colony of breeding birds, the most numerous species holds the safer area in the centre. Magnificent are also slightly larger and have longer bills than Greaters. Possibly this gives them supremacy.

Blue-footed Boobies were also breeding on the ground in open spaces. It must be very difficult for them to get there with food for their chicks but we did not see frigatebirds harassing the boobies; perhaps they don't pirate inside the colony. Masked Boobies were also present. One was even sitting on a frigatebird nest, guarding the still small chick of the owner, a peculiar habit for a cliff-nester, and on the nest of its enemy!

Female Great Frigatebird has a pinkish eye ring, female Magnificent's is blue. In both males the eye ring is also blue. Both females and male Great Frigatebird have pinkish feet, while male Magnificent has grey feet. You seldom see them, but legs can be a good field mark. The chin colour in both females is different, as shown in the drawing opposite, but look at the photo and you won't see this. It's a better field mark when they are in flight. Males in flight are often almost impossible to identify; a task for specialists.

Breeding is a long affair in the frigatebird world. After endless courting by the male, waiting until a female has made her choice, the building of the nest begins. Frigatebirds build flattish platforms of twigs and sticks, all gathered by the male while the female builds. The nest can be quite substantial but it is generally a flimsy construction, depending upon the material the male can supply. There is a permanent chasing and stealing of everything brought in by any bird. Once the nest is ready, both birds will often sit together for another ten days before the female is ready to lay her single egg. Both parents incubate in turn for seven weeks, then for up to 170 days the chicks are fed by the parents (that's nearly half a year, a long time for a bird). Often the male will leave the family before the young are independent and start courting again in order to breed with another female.

Incubating; often sitting in the baking sun for 10-14 days before the partner returns from feeding out at sea to take its turn. This means that until the egg hatches, they feed only 4-5 times. During this period the male's red pouch shrinks away to a small area of pink skin, frequently invisible.

Greater Frigatebirds need even more time for the young to become independent. They incubate for 55 days and the chick stays on the nest for five months. Once fledged, it must be fed for another 10–12 months before going its own way. The parents can't bring food regularly and many young starve, often when they are almost independent. Many pairs fail to get that far. Over two thirds of the eggs laid are lost during the incubation period. Many eggs are lost when the adults take off from the nest. Their legs are so short, they cannot jump off like other large birds. Often the ground under the bushes is littered with broken eggs, a feast for mockingbirds, finches and the introduced rats which possibly also steal eggs and chicks from the nests. Not many reach the stage of a fledgling, and even fewer mature into the superb flying machines that adult frigatebirds become, never settling on the water, spending most of their lives in the air.

With the whole head white, this is a juvenile Magnificent Frigatebird. Greaters at this age have a rust-red head and breast. Only a few will reach this age; sitting on the nest and waiting, often for days, for a parent to bring food.

Worldwide there are five different frigatebird species, and in each
the males are similar: shiny black all
over, except for Christmas Frigatebird from the Indian Ocean, where
the male has a white belly patch,
which is otherwise a female feature.

Male courtship is similar and there
is nothing like it in the entire bird
world, really something special. The
whole display is built up around the
enormous male pouch which is scarlet and inflated. Outside the courting
period this pouch is invisible, shriv-
elled-up pinkish skin. While courting, the male inflates this pouch into
an enormous balloon (this takes
20–30 minutes). They can inflate or
deflate the pouch at will and can even
fly with it inflated, which looks very
peculiar. When a female of their own
species flies over the bushes on which
the waiting males are sitting, they get
excited and open their wings (which
span over 280 cm). The head is
thrown backwards, the bill points in
the air. The undersurface of the
wings, which have a silvery flash, are
shown to the females, the head waves
sideways and they make a rattling
noise with the bill and wings. It's a
real 'concert' and spectacle when
several males court together.

There are two different species in
the Galápagos, and the courting
males can spot the right females 100 m

up in the air. Males look exactly alike when on the wing but females of all five species have a distinctive pattern of black and white underneath as does the juvenile. The males do not court when the wrong species flies overhead. How the females recognize the 'right' males I do not know. Magnificent have a purple sheen to the head and back, while in Great Frigatebirds it is blue-green. Great also have a brown band across the upperwing, but when the females arrive, the males show their silvery underwings, the same pattern in both species. Perhaps the females see the shiny iridescent purple or blue-green males in a different way from humans, and from a greater distance too. The female descends, attracted by the display, and lands opposite the male she has selected. The male 'freezes' and utters a rattle like the noise of a fisherman's reel. They never fight or snap at each other with their long powerful hooked bills even when close together. If they did, this could be disastrous for the inflated red pouch. Once a female has accepted a male, pair-forming and nest-building follow quickly thereafter. Unsuccessful males will sit waiting in the bushes with inflated pouches until the 'right' female passes overhead and the whole ceremony starts again. This could go on for weeks.

When an adult frigatebird comes back from sea with food for its young, others waiting nearby also try to steal some, but frigatebirds just feed their own young. The young are fed by regurgitation, inserting the head deep into the parent's gullet, flapping wings in excitment, all while sitting balanced on a thin branch.

Waiting, waiting for days and days, apathetically sitting on a small branch in a bush, often in bright baking sunshine, waiting until one of the parents returns with food. This young Magnificent could already fly but could not catch or steal food for itself. They have to learn this skill from their parents; it's not inborn as in other seabirds, like boobies, which plunge dive and look after themselves much earlier in life.

Waiting in company is possibly easier than waiting alone, but when the other gets food, hunger must be even greater. Not many juveniles reach the stage of these two here. Most starve earlier and many will still die after the long apprenticeship, at the point when adults stop feeding the young and they have not learnt enough to survive.

The male in front, with the green sheen to its head, must be a Great Frigatebird, but he has no visible wingbar. He turned his single egg with his bill, then shuffled his body a little and kept on incubating, possibly for another ten days. The two breeding females behind could be Magnificent, but I am not sure. Identification of the young with their white heads is easy, they are Magnificent Frigatebirds. Great Frigatebirds have rust-red heads at this age.

While walking slowly through the frigatebird colony I asked myself why such a state of affairs exists with so many eggs being lost before they hatch, so many chicks falling out of their nests and so many starving to death. Only a few will reach the age where they can fly out to sea, independent of their parents. Once they reach that stage they can live for a long time, spending most of their life on the wing, but they don't like to roam too far from these islands. Frigatebirds, or Man O' War birds as they are often called by sailors, have always been a signal that land is close. Only occasionally will they fly far out to sea, but they are the only seabirds which regularly cross the land between the Caribbean and the Pacific Ocean.

After finishing the flimsy nest, the female, often in company with her male, will sit for over a week before she lays her egg. Thereafter the male takes over and incubates for the first ten days. Both partners have three turns during the incubation period.

Some Blue-footed Boobies were still courting. Here the smaller male, with open wings, is in front of the larger female. This size difference is the rule with boobies. The female's pupil appears to be larger than the male's.

Blue-footed Boobies are very common and literally everywhere. Their large, bright blue feet differ in colour individually.

After our visit to Seymour we went along the rocky coast with our dinghy to look for Galápagos fur seal. The first one we saw was in the water, a rather large-headed male, patrolling the shore where his females were lying in the shade of some rocks on the rugged beach (unlike sealions that like to lie in the baking sun). They looked rather short with broad heads and long-haired dense coats, which made them look a bit like bears. Their ears seemed to be longer than those of sealions, and they had larger round eyes and relatively larger front flippers. When on land they are always between rocks and boulders so they need longer flippers to climb, at which they are much better than the beach-loving sealions. The whole scene was quiet and peaceful. Only once did we hear the bull's hoarse and guttural voice, quite different from a sealion's barking.

This Yellow Warbler looks like a Northern Wheatear on the sandy beach.

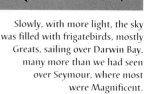

Slowly, with more light, the sky was filled with frigatebirds, mostly Greats, sailing over Darwin Bay, many more than we had seen over Seymour, where most were Magnificent.

Our first **Galápagos Dove**, colourful and quail-like, was even tamer than feral London pigeons. We saw them everywhere on Genovesa.

Just behind the landing beach there is a Swallow-tailed Gull colony. Youngsters of all ages walked around, shier than the adult birds. Stay strictly to the trail as the camouflaged eggs simply lie on the ground. We saw two beside the trail.

We had had a fantastic night at sea. After a short sleep I went on deck. The moon reflected a beautiful silvery light over the calm sea. I watched colourful lightning far away on the horizon, a spectacle I had never seen before, an explosion of red, orange, blue and green. Swallow-tailed Gulls, like silent white ghosts, passed our ship over the black water. They took no notice of our boat, flying in a straight line in one direction, possibly to waters rich in squid and small fish, their preferred food. Once, higher in the night sky, I saw a larger, darker bird. Against the moonlight its silhouette was like a booby but not so heavy as that of long-tailed Blue-footed; it must have been a Red-footed Booby, a bird we had not yet seen.

Towards Tower, or Genovesa as it is now called, gulls became more common, all now flying in the same direction we were sailing, towards the island. When we arrived at Bahía Darwin it was still dark, much darker than before on the open sea. We dropped anchor not far from another, larger ship in the middle of the calm bay.

When the sun rose we saw more and more birds around us, hundreds of them. Most were Swallow-tailed Gulls and only one Lava Gull, which we first heard calling, and then it settled on the dinghy behind our boat. Some shearwaters were flying into the still dark cliffs of the sunken crater which forms Bahía Darwin. Trees were growing on the ridge of the low cliffs. I think they were Palo Santos. Their silhouettes looked like uncombed hair. The bay is nearly circular, a sunken crater open to the sea only on the southern side where the cliffs have broken off and disappeared into the water. A fantastic place in this early morning light.

The higher the sun rose the more birds appeared, now mostly Great Frigatebirds and some young and female Magnificents, possibly also males, but in this light identification was not possible. The most numerous birds were Red-footed Boobies, most coming from the sea, hurried, and sometimes harassed by a frigatebird, but we saw no successful attack. In contrast, we saw many Masked-Boobies but only a few Blue-footed, and no Brown Pelicans. Perhaps for the latter two the waters around Genovesa are too deep; both like fishing along shallow shores. Tropicbirds were numerous, a wonderful picture as these elegant white birds with their long tail streamers flew along the dark cliffs.

To the north, at the head of the bay, there is a small beach seemingly of white sand, but it was bony white coral washed up by the sea. There are only a few coral banks in the Galápagos, most waters are too deep and also too cold for them. Coral needs a constant temperature, above 21 °C.

A large female finch cleaning her feathers. Without seeing the bill, identification is impossible.

Is it a Large Ground-finch or is it Large Cactus-finch, the bird we wanted to see on Genovesa?

Genovesa has some interesting, easily observed finch specialities. A bird which I first thought was just a Small Ground-finch was a Sharp-billed Ground-finch. On other islands this variable species is a highland bird, but not here on Genovesa. They were everywhere, replacing Small Ground-finch which is absent on this island. They are very similar to Small Ground-finch, possibly a bit rounder and with a straighter and more pointed bill. The females were rather dark and all were heavily streaked. Only DNA examination could separate Small and Sharp-billed Ground-finches.

The other specialty is Genovesa Cactus-finch, which we found in large numbers in the prickly pear cactuses all along the visitors' trail. They are larger and more heavily built than the cactus-finches we saw the previous day on Plaza, and they looked 'calmer'. On Genovesa, the bill is longer and heavier than in birds on Plaza. They are now regarded as a subspecies of Large Cactus-finch. The females are like Sharp-beakeds, very dark and heavily streaked. Large Ground-finch is also common and they have very large bills on this island, even larger than in birds on St Cruz. These three, and the more common Warbler Finch, are the only Darwin's finches on Genovesa.

Warbler Finch, normally a bird of more moist vegetated habitats, is very common on dry desert-like Genovesa. Very dull, some had small, pale pearly spots on the head and very faint pale streaks on the dark back. The bill is long, thin and pointed, thinner and sharper than that of Yellow Warbler.

At last she turned her head and showed the large and heavy bill – a female Large Ground-finch. Large Cactus-finch, a bird we wanted to see, has a more elongated, narrower bill here on Genovesa, and the female is also much darker.

These Sharp-beakeds, hopping around everywhere like Small Ground-finches, with their cocked tails sometimes looked to me like dark, fat wrens. The longer, pointed bill is characteristic, and it seemed to me that they also have slightly longer legs than those of Small Ground-finch, but it is difficult to tell when they are not side by side.

sharp pointed bill

This Sharp-beaked, rather greyish on the back, behaved like a tree-finch (not present on Genovesa), turning around in a chala bush, searching for insects, looking on the undersides of leaves and probing small yellow flowers with its pointed bill.

Tower Mockingbird, or now more aptly named **Genovesa Mockingbird**, is similar to birds from St Cruz, but possibly a bit smaller. The few we saw had longer, more curved bills. The pale neck band is large and conspicuous. None had dark breast spots; there was only a rusty patch and the flank stripes seemed to be very faint. They ran along the beach, often at great speed, spreading their wings to keep balance. We did not see any flying. I was under the impression they had not only a longer bill but also longer legs. One sat on a low lava block with open fluffy feathers, singing a rather simple song, similar to but not so melodious as I had heard from the birds on St Cruz. This could possibly be individual variation.

A tender pair of Swallow-tails on their nest on the lava cliffs. Others were breeding lower down near the shore on the coral beach.

A Swallow-tail chick, still small, climbing over the lava boulders with its long legs, under a prickly pear cactus, an unusual sight for a highly pelagic seabird.

Genovesa is a flat and dry desert-like island. Palo Santo trees and prickly pear cactuses dominate vegetation at higher levels. When we visited Genovesa, the Palo Santos were leafless and their whitish or silvery grey trunks made the trees look dead. *Waltheria ovata*, chalas, *Croton scouleri*, muyuyo and *Cordia lutea*, with large yellow flowers, are common bushes and shrubs. On the coast, which is mostly surrounded by deep waters, are some **red mangroves** and salt bushes as in the photo above in Darwin Bay (left, on the coral beach with the typically low cliffs behind).

The island is quite small, only 14 km³, and rather flat, the highest point is 76 m. The low, often rough and steep cliffs make ideal nest sites for many birds, and there are bushes and trees inland for Red-footed Boobies. Surrounded by food-rich deep waters, and with Short-eared Owl the only predator, this is a seabird paradise.

Lying so far northeast, 100 km away from the main Galápagos islands, there are no endemic land mammals. On the coast there are sealions and a small fur seal colony. Giant tortoises, snakes, lizards and land iguanas are all missing. There are marine iguanas, a small all-black form. We did not see many of them but there was one fairly high up, far away from water on the southern side, climbing in sharp lava like a land iguana on the other islands. Why it did this, I can't say; or is this the first step in returning to land in the absence of land iguana?

Far out at sea, surrounded by fish and squid-rich deep waters, Genovesa is really a paradise for seabirds, perfectly situated for the more pelagic species. Blue-footed Boobies, the most common seabird around the other Galápagos islands, are rare here. The **Masked Booby**, (*above*) brilliant white with black wings and a yellow bill, has a flourishing colony on Genovesa, possibly the largest in the Galápagos, but **Red-footed Booby**, (*below*) the most pelagic fisher of all, really owns this island. The world's largest colony is found here and about 140,000 pairs breed.

Masked are ground-nesters on cliffs, Red-footed nest in shrubs and trees. Frigatebirds are also common, mostly pelagic Great but also some Magnificent. Audubon's Shearwaters, Red-billed Tropicbirds and Swallow-tailed Gulls nest in large numbers on the steeper cliffs but Lava gull is rare; there are no large flat beaches which, as scavengers, they need. Two storm-petrels are also common: Wedge-rumped in very large numbers, and the less numerous Band-rumped. These two and young Red-footed Boobies are the main prey of the diurnal Short-eared Owl. In the lagoon at Darwin Bay, there are many Yellow-crowned and some Lava Herons but they are also often seen on the cliffs. Landbirds are few on Genovesa. Galápagos Doves and Yellow Warblers are common; less so the mockingbird. There are only four finch species but these are rather special. Apart from Darwin, far to the north, this is the only island where two large-billed finches live together: Large Ground-finch and Large Cactus-finch, which has a medium-sized bill. Medium and Small Ground-finches are absent, the latter replaced by Sharp-beaked Ground-finch. Warbler Finch is omnipresent, even along the beach. Pintails occur when rain is plentiful. Barn Owl, Galápagos Hawk and the two flycatchers are absent.

This rock, white with droppings, is a favourite spot for boobies to sunbathe. Their droppings, the guano, is sold along the Peruvian and Namibian coast as a highly valued agricultural fertilizer. Several attempts to develop this business in the Galápagos failed. It is only possible on a very small scale, mostly for local use. Heavy rains in the wet season wash the guano into the sea where it fertilizes the water.

Masked is the largest booby on the islands and, as with all other boobies, the female is slightly larger and more heavily built (as seen in this photo). Not only bigger than the male, she also has a deeper, raucous trumpeting voice, while the adult male produces a piping whistle. They are not rare, breeding on most Galápagos islands, but never in dense colonies like the other two boobies. Colonies are widely spread over an island and single pairs often breed at the edge of other boobies' colonies. They prefer open bare terrain, with a steep slope, and nest mostly on cliffs but will also use flat sandy ground or clearings amidst dense bushes and trees, where Red-footed boobies also build their nests. Young and immature look very much like same-aged Blue-footed Boobies and have even been mistaken for Brown Boobies, *Sula leucogaster*, a non-Galápagos bird (*see* p. 181).

No other large seabird is such a brilliant white as Masked Booby. The black wing feathers and the black, naked skin mask make this white even more striking. There is no real difference in colour between sexes, but the larger females have a formidable bill, which can be yellow, pinkish or even orange/pink, but more often greenish. These three colours, brilliant white, jet black and yellow, with piercing orange eyes, gives this booby a dazzling look, the aristocrat of the family on this island.

bright

male

often more greenish

strong bill   female

Their large feet, webbed between all four toes, typical for boobies, are drab grey or grey willow-green. We saw none with yellow legs as so often quoted in literature. When courting, they often use their brightly coloured bills and long necks in sky-pointing, whereas Red or Blue-footed Boobies show their brightly coloured feet.

In other parts of the world Masked Boobies have black tails but not so in the Galápagos where the subspecies is *granti*. The tail is slate grey, often very pale (*see* p. 181).

We had already seen this on Seymour, a Masked Booby on a frigatebird nest (*see* page 139). On Seymour, the booby fed the chick, here on Genovesa the ground-nesting booby was just sitting on the tree nest and the frigatebird chick looked very unhappy, but we saw no aggression by the booby towards the chick. Why does a rock/ground nester settle on a tree nest? What was it doing there? The photo above and the three on the right are not of the same bird; one picture was taken on Seymour and two taken here on Genovesa so it is a regular habit unique to Masked Booby.

This is what a happy, fat downy frigatebird chick looks like, with its father (*left*), and alone (*right*), waiting for food in bright sunshine.

Of the three Galápagos boobies, **Red-footed** is the smallest. In fact the male, at only 950 g, is the smallest booby in the world, and the female weighs only about 1000 g. Compared with the 2300–3600 g of a Northern Gannet, they really are bantam-weights. On Genovesa, about 140,000 pairs nest, spread over the whole island. Red-footed are not seen so often as the coastal-fishing Blue-footed Booby which nests on all islands. Red-footed Boobies are more numerous but their colonies are restricted to Genovesa, San Cristóbal and Marchena and the two outlying islands, Wolf and Darwin, with a smaller colony on Gardner Islet. They can only breed where the strong eagle-like Galápagos Hawk is absent. The small Red-footeds would be easy prey for the hawk.

There are two colour phases in the Galápagos, a rare white form, which looks a bit like Masked Booby, and the more common brown phase, which makes up about 95% of the population. There are also intermediate birds and the browns can be of different shades. When adult and in breeding condition, they have delicate bill and face colours of pink and blue, different in each individual. The bare face skin is bright blue and the eyes are large, which indicates that they are mostly nocturnal fishers, a reason why Red-footed are not often seen around the islands. They are also more pelagic than Blue-footed Boobies, fishing far out at sea, away from the islands.

Red-footed's nest in colonies, but these are never so dense as those of Blue-footed. Nests are seldom less than two metres apart, and there is little or no fighting, unlike in Northern Gannet colonies. Tree-nesting birds have a defined territory and avoid trouble if they stay out of reach. The young stay in the nest, and if one falls out it is not allowed to climb back in but is treated as an intruder and chased away. Good children stay at home when small!

The endemic Galápagos subspecies *S. s. websteri*, has a dark, nearly black tail in all colour phases, while the other populations of this tropical species around the world have white tails when adult. Masked Booby, on the contrary, is black-tailed elsewhere and paler-tailed in the Galápagos. Another peculiar feature of these islands.

◄ An intermediate colour phase with pale head and dark wings. Some have even paler heads with a golden tinge. Here the bright bill/face colours and pattern (with large eyes) are clearly shown. This is the standard pattern, some have more pinkish bills, possibly younger birds. One had a more violet bill and another a greenish bill, and some have purple faces, but all adults have red legs.

Red-footed are unique in the family. While all other boobies and gannets breed on the ground and do not make nests, Red-footed build flimsy plat-forms with twigs and sticks in bushes and trees. Their feet are extremely flexible, adapted to perch on very thin branches, which no other booby can do. Sometimes they will even settle on large ships, especially sailing boats.

Generally, they lay only one egg which both parents incubate in turns for about 45 days. Then the chick has to be fed for another 130 days on the nest and, after fledging, for another three months before they can fish for themselves. This is a very long period for such a small booby, much longer than for the larger Blue-footed. Not many chicks fledge. The ground under the bushes and trees in a colony is often littered with bro-ken eggs and dried corpses of chicks of all ages, mummified by the hot Galápagos sun. Many fall out of the nest and cannot climb up again to the platform. Even more are lost through starvation when parents are strug-gling to find sufficient fish at sea. The chicks grow very slowly when food is scarce and quickly lose weight, but with plenty of food they can put weight on very quickly to build up reserves for difficult periods.

Both brown and white morph youngsters are chocolate ►
brown with dark, grey/black bills, faces and legs. With
age they gradually acquire their definitive adult plumage.

These two **Red-footed Boobies** were lucky, reaching an age when they could wander around their nest in the colony. There will still be three months when they depend upon their parents, before the dangerous adventure starts in looking after themselves far out at·sea. In both photos the typical juvenile plumage, with black bill and face, is clearly illustrated as well as the long tail and long narrow wings (a wingspan of nearly 1 metre when fully adult).

You can watch the small, compact **Lava Heron** virtually everywhere on Genovesa. Slate grey with bright yellow eyes when adult, all-brown with black stripes when young. Legs are grey in non-breeding birds, yellow to bright orange and even red in breeding plumage, and the bill is then shiny black.

The large **Great Blue Heron** is rare on Genovesa. We saw only one, sitting like a statue in the mangrove, an adult in full breeding plumage, showing the beauty of this species. A truly photogenic bird.

The Great Blue Heron is rare, Lava Heron common, but **Yellow-crowned Night Heron** is abundant on Genovesa. When you pass one, sitting motionless in a sheltered spot, squat-looking, apparently asleep, it will sometimes momentarily look at you with its bright red eyes.

It quickly closes its eyes again to finish its dreams. The crown is not straw yellow as in North American birds. The name 'rusty-crowned' would better suit the Galápagos bird of the endemic subspecies *pauper*.

It will often fall into a deep sleep. They really are night herons, only becoming active at dusk like owls, and in flight the rounded wings and 'hunched' look enforce this similarity; while young birds with their large yellow eyes and light, brown-spotted plumage resemble owls even more.

◀ These four photos, each of a different individual, look very similar and show a plump, hunched grey bird with a short thick bill. However, once active, though a little bulky, they are surprisingly elegant, large-eyed herons.

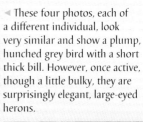

▲ At least one is doing something, sitting in the shade, holding its wings upside-down in the bright sunshine. After a quarter of an hour it was still in the same position, possibly asleep.

G enovesa, like Plaza, has a good population of **Red-billed Tropicbirds**. Their aerial display is always fascinating. They glide along the dark lava cliffs with stiff wings raised or bent downwards, and with strong flapping turn high into the blue sky, the long streamers trailing behind and often looking like a waving flag. They are quarrelsome, noisy birds with a shrill, loud rattling voice. Their nests, often only a small hole in a narrow ledge, are on the crater's steep cliffs, where they sit with just their head in the shade and the long tail streamers hanging outside. I wondered if all were sitting on eggs or small chicks, possibly some were just resting there, sometimes a pair together. There were no chicks visible or young birds flying around. Had the breeding season just started?

T here were some small, brown, quail-like birds bustling and digging under the black cliffs on the white beach. Once closer we could see they were Galápagos Doves, turning over the bleached coral pebbles with their long curved bills. They were beautiful little doves, delicately patterned and coloured, with a bright blue rim to the eyes.

It was incredible to see the size of pebbles they could turn over and even throw aside with their bills. I would have liked to take some pebbles with me to weigh them at home; this is not possible without a licence. Next time I will take scales with me. I had kept and bred these doves in an aviary at home and now I understand why they always threw the seeds out of their dishes when I fed them. It is an inherited habit from the home islands; birds forage by digging, and never use their legs (as chickens do).

Sometimes their posture reminds me of an Old World sandgrouse.

Identifying a storm-petrel is not easy. These are **Wedge-rumped**, *O. tethys*, the most likely species to be seen in daytime over the colony. Band-rumped, *O. castro*, which also breed here, visit the nesting sites at night, and are larger with less white on the rump. Both nest side by side, even between the round (white-marked) Masked Booby nests.

On the southern side of the sunken crater is another place small groups can visit. The landing point lies below the Prince Philip Steps, named in honour of H.R.H. The Duke of Edinburgh after his visit to the island on 4 November 1964. It is a dry landing, on lava, and sometimes a bit difficult to negotiate. After a steep but easy climb, you arrive on a rather flat plateau, covered with sparse bushes and trees where many Red-footed Boobies and Great Frigatebirds breed. In the more open spaces there are Masked Boobies with their typically white-ringed nests; some Blue-footed breed here too. Galápagos Doves search for food under the bushes, but they are not so numerous as on the other side of the crater.

The further you walk the more open the plateau becomes and more Masked Boobies breed on the flat ground. Later it becomes really desert-like with only a few low bushes, and on the real lava plateau, the beautiful **lava cactus** is about the only decoration in the bare reddish landscape. Storm-petrels breed here; small, swallow-sized seabirds (*see* p. 168). You must keep strictly to the visitors' trail. The storm-petrels have their nests under the thin crisp layers of lava, in crevices and holes, and you can easily break into them. About 200,000 pairs of Wedge-rumped breed on Genovesa and most of them are here. Thousands and thousands were around us in the sky. Band-rumped Storm-petrels, active at night, also breed here, but less abundantly.

We looked especially for Short-eared Owl, found a moulted feather and remains of the many storm-petrels the owl had plucked, but failed to see the owl itself.

A female **Great Frigatebird**, common on Genovesa, with typical red eye-ring and faintly coppery neck.

A **Galápagos Dove** digging on the beach, searching for food under sparse shrubs where Red-footed Boobies breed.

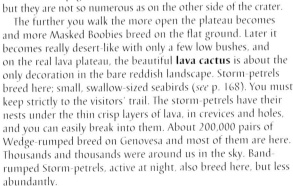

We left Genovesa late in the evening. Numerous Swallow-tailed Gulls were flying out to open waters. The sea became very rough and I had a very unpleasant night. The trip seemed endless until we arrived at 2.15 am at Playa Espumilla on Santiago.

The open bay on Playa Espumilla was calm and flat, a relief after the rough night at sea. We anchored and had to wait till sun rise to disembark. Before us was a long white sandy beach with only a few seals and a lagoon with high trees behind. It appeared completely changed since my last visit a long time ago. Tony told us that in 1983 El Niño had changed the whole coast in this part of Santiago and it was only now recovering slowly. After a good breakfast we landed on a beach decorated with hundreds of red crabs. We had to walk slowly along the beach towards the lagoon since this is a favourite breeding place of green sea turtles and you can easily tread on a fresh nest.

Behind the lagoon was a saltpan, almost completely dry. Weeks ago there must have been rich birdlife here because we saw so many footprints in the dry mud; mostly flamingos, a bird which we had not seen until now, herons, with their long prints, and many waders of different sizes as well as gulls. We found the dried corpse of a Franklin's Gull, *Larus pipixcan*, a common visitor from North America between October and May. There were some Yellow Warblers hopping over the dry mud in search of insects; otherwise it was calm and silent.

The landscape reminded me of Africa, a mixture of bushland and savanna in the dry season: low grass, leafless trees and some grey/green bushes.

We saw only one snake during the whole visit. A slender constrictor (*Dromicus*) about 1 m long, coming out between lava boulders and disappearing quickly again, harmless to us but possibly venomous to often large prey.

We wanted to walk further into the bush behind the saltpan. Our captain, who is also a park warden, wanted to shoot a goat for food. We stalked slowly through the often dense vegetation where ground-finches, Small, Mediums and a few Large, were searching under the shrubs, and some Small Tree-finches were in the bushes. Most amazing of all was the number of Galápagos Doves. They burst out of the bushes as we passed. They were not so tame as on Genovesa; perhaps there is some shooting here. They appeared to profit from the presence of goats, which had trodden down the vegetation under many bushes where the doves were now digging for seeds. Behind us was the Cerro Cowan, over 900 m high.

With our field glasses we saw some flocks of goat on the slopes. They are not the only feral animals responsible for the visible destruction on this island. Pigs and burros are also present and in the dust we saw rat tracks. Goats have already been eradicated on some smaller islands – St Fé, Rábida – and some larger ones too – Española, Marchena and Pinta. I hope Santiago will soon join this list; eradication is in progress. To exterminate them all will be a long and difficult task and not easy on this island, particularly with its rough terrain. Pigs are even more difficult to control. Only two islands, Fernandina and Genovesa, are entirely free from introduced animals and plants.

While stalking through the dense vegetation a small flock of about a dozen **Smooth-billed Anis** followed us, warning the goats with their 'aa-ak, aa-ak' calls; an introduced bird helping the introduced mammal! The anis were very shy, keeping at a distance, high in the trees, not so confident as the Galápagos Flycatchers which were also following us. I wonder if the abundant doves had already learnt that these warning calls mean danger?

Goats were everywhere. We could smell them, we heard them running away, their horns clicking against dry branches, and we saw degraded vegetation, and their droppings in the dust under each bush. They behaved like wild animals and it was difficult for Barnaby to take a good photo. At last, on a ridge, some stood still looking at us, and our captain had the opportunity to take two proper shots. One young 'chivo' for our cook and an old male for the hawks that were following us.

Galápagos Hawks descended straight away and did not wait for us to cut open the goat for them. They looked more like small powerful eagles rather than plump *Buteo* hawks.

They did not stop eating till the crop was full and round like a balloon

It was a real feast for them. More than a dozen hawks came. The large females were first and started tearing open one side of the goat while we were still cutting the other.

The smaller males, still with powerful talons, were waiting nearby, some only 2-3 m away; others were higher in the surrounding trees.

Amongst more than a dozen adults, mostly smaller males, there was only one young hawk, keeping its distance from the others, sitting on the ground and waiting its turn. It was paler, especially the head, with a dark, buff-mottled underside and some paler mottling in the wings. Here you also see the typical longish bill of this species, this possibly allows them to eat crabs out of their shells, or young sea turtles. The claws of this young hawk were already strong.

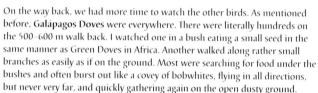

On the way back, we had more time to watch the other birds. As mentioned before, **Galápagos Doves** were everywhere. There were literally hundreds on the 500-600 m walk back. I watched one in a bush eating a small seed in the same manner as Green Doves in Africa. Another walked along rather small branches as easily as if on the ground. Most were searching for food under the bushes and often burst out like a covey of bobwhites, flying in all directions, but never very far, and quickly gathering again on the open dusty ground.

Back on the saltpan a **Yellow-crowned Night Heron**, not asleep as they all were on Genovesa, walking slowly (when space allowed). It caught a lizard which then tried to escape.

We crossed the saltpan again and I tried to identify some of the footprints. The flamingos were easy, also the stilts. Ducks had been there too. The different small wader prints were a puzzle: at least four different-sized species, which had now returned to North America, had left their prints, preserved in the dry mud until the next rain, which could be as long as one or two years away. Back on board we had a delicious meal. While we were on land, Peter had been out fishing and Aurelio had already prepared the fish. A fresher meal would not be possible. I don't know what kind of fish it was, but it was very good.

We sailed slowly along the coast, with fantastic views all around. On one side Isabela and the volcanic Wolf far away on the horizon, on the other side a black lava bank close to the Santiago coast, and behind, the hill of Santiago, covered with green bushes and large silvery Palo Santo trees. We passed along some 'tuff' cliffs and a broad lava flow from 1897, now 100 years old and still without vegetation. We anchored at Puerto Egas. Here, in the 1920s, Norwegians exploited saltpans in a crater filled with salt water, and later in the 1960s Hector Egas, an Ecuadorian, worked a salt mine. The enterprise failed to make money and the area is now a flamingo sanctuary.

On Puerto Egas I wanted to first visit the black lava flow, which was full of red crabs and further on many seabirds and some waders, but our crew wanted to play soccer with the crew of another boat against some young American tourists. They needed Tony, our guide, and Barnaby for the Ecuadorian team. At the end of the game all the players had a thick cover of fine, floury lava dust. They had played on a slightly sloping field in a layer of lava dust about 10 cm thick. Result: Ecuador vs USA, 3:3. Everyone was happy, even Barnaby who had a deep wound on his leg; under the dust there was sharp lava. I hoped that by now the lava flow was sterile.

We could now visit the lava flow. On the seaward side near the open water were a dozen oystercatchers in groups of 2–3. They looked very much like European Oystercatchers but in flight there was half as much white visible on the rear end. There were also some other waders, one Grey Plover, six tattlers, two Sanderlings, about 15 Semipalmated Plovers, one Western Sandpiper, one Whimbrel, but no turnstones. This must be a good place for waders in the northern winter, from October till May, when large numbers visit the Galápagos. Most fascinating on this lava flow were the red lava crabs. There were hundreds, even thousands, running in all directions. I watched a territorial fight between two males with their large pincers held high in the air. The black juveniles seemed to keep in groups away from the red adults, mostly on the more sheltered sides of the lava blocks.

The **Sally lightfoot** or **red lava crab**, *Grapsus grapsus*, is abundant not only here on Puerto Egas. Adults are bright red above and blue below but black when young. Don't touch them; they can give a nasty pinch and are always alert and not easily approached. Keep still and they take no notice of you and will even walk over your feet.

We saw **sealions** on every landing. Here in Puerto Egas they are common but not always seen. They like to lie in shelters as this 'moulting' bull is doing here. You can get very close, but be careful. They are generally harmless, but if you get too close they can become annoyed and snap at you. Sealions have teeth like lions! So be careful and respect them, especially harem-holding bulls which are often aggressive and might regard you as an intruding rival. They can move very fast even though they look leaden.

Before giving birth, the female moves out of the harem to the edge of the colony. Here the pup is born and the mother will stay with it throughout the first week. The pups weigh about 5 kg at birth but will double their weight in a few weeks. The female is on heat again within 2–3 weeks of the pup's birth. The fertilized egg is delayed for 2–3 months and then develops in about nine months, so the cycle is around one year. When the pups are one month old, they are gathered together in a nursery, and when the mothers are out fishing an older female is always on guard. The bull also patrols out in the water so no youngsters are allowed to go into the sea. The danger from sharks is too great.

The endemic Galápagos Oystercatcher, *H. p. galapagensis*, has a heavy bill, and the border on the breast between black and white is irregular; otherwise, it is similar to American Oystercatcher.

Galápagos and Californian sealions are the same species. The endemic Galápagos subspecies, *wollebacki*, differs mainly in size, being smaller and more elegant. Despite this, a male can weigh about 300 kg; females are only 50–80 kg. The bulls are dark, nearly black, and typically have a high forehead, while the female is brown and longer-faced. They are very playful and in many ways remind me of human beings. The other member of the family, the fur seal, is seen less often but is nearly as numerous as the ever-present sealion. Fur seals prefer rough, rocky shores and coasts with plenty of shade. They are smaller, shorter and have bear-like faces. Less tolerant of heat, they keep to shade in the daytime and prefer colder water. They fish at night. As on Genovesa, Santiago is a good place to watch them. The social behaviour and breeding cycle are similar in both species.

Whilst watching some waders far out on a black lava flow, a large flock, or more accurately, an enormous crowd of seabirds arrived, mostly boobies and pelicans. Plunging into the water, fluttering around, swimming, diving, it was impossible to follow a single bird in this whirl. Coming closer and closer to the shore, following a shoal of fish, there were Blue-footed Boobies, Brown Pelicans, some noddies and shearwaters. A frigatebird high above the spectacle did not join the crowd over the water but followed them. Even near the shore, between the black lava blocks, the boobies and pelicans kept on diving, sometimes 'paddling' over lava blocks and rocks then jumping into the water again. It was as if the water around them was boiling. Some sealions also jumped into the water to feed or were simply afraid of all those wings around them. It must have been as huge a feast for their stomachs as it was for our eyes. When the shoal turned back to the open sea, the whole crowd followed.

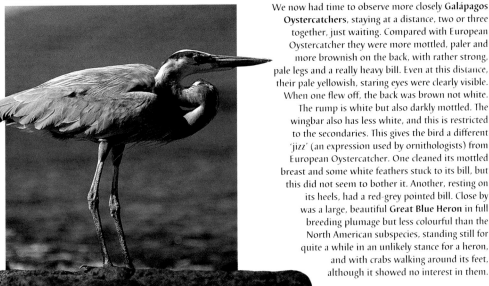

We now had time to observe more closely **Galápagos Oystercatchers**, staying at a distance, two or three together, just waiting. Compared with European Oystercatcher they were more mottled, paler and more brownish on the back, with rather strong, pale legs and a really heavy bill. Even at this distance, their pale yellowish, staring eyes were clearly visible. When one flew off, the back was brown not white. The rump is white but also darkly mottled. The wingbar also has less white, and this is restricted to the secondaries. This gives the bird a different 'jizz' (an expression used by ornithologists) from European Oystercatcher. One cleaned its mottled breast and some white feathers stuck to its bill, but this did not seem to bother it. Another, resting on its heels, had a red-grey pointed bill. Close by was a large, beautiful **Great Blue Heron** in full breeding plumage but less colourful than the North American subspecies, standing still for quite a while in an unlikely stance for a heron, and with crabs walking around its feet, although it showed no interest in them.

Next to the lava flow at Puerto Egas, as if it had not recovered after it was burnt 100 years ago, there is a dry and dusty desert-like bushland. Possibly after rain, when the grass is green and there are new leaves on the bushes, this landscape has some charm; now it was just melancholy with a few bushes, lava gravel, dry grass and dust blown up by the wind. **Galápagos Doves** can survive even in this habitat. One was searching around in the dry vegetation to find food. It looked perfectly healthy, did not bother about us and just got on with its busy search.

I wonder if they nest here. Galápagos Doves are optimists, they adapt to every kind of habitat from sea level up to the terra alta, both dry and wet. After rain, and this could be more than a year away, food would be plentiful even in this barren land, and they could start breeding. About three weeks after courtship they build their nest, a rather simple construction, often just placed on the ground in the shade under a sheet of lava. Sometimes they use an old mockingbird nest or build their own in an *Opuntia* tree, using grass and twigs to construct a simple platform. The normal clutch has two eggs, never more, and these are incubated by both parents, for about two weeks. The chicks fledge after a further 14 days, rather quick for a bird of this size.

The only other landbirds were four **Small Ground-finches**, all of which were in female plumage, searching for food under a bush. We had seen Yellow Warblers on the naked lava flow but not here in this dry habitat. Perhaps there are few insects here, but Tony showed us a scorpion which preys on insects and spiders so there must have been some. It was a **yellow scorpion**, *Hodruides lunatus*, one of two endemic Galápagos species. Normally during the day they are hidden under a rock or in vegetation, only coming out at night to hunt. The sting of both species is painful but not dangerous. The poison seems to have no effect on lava lizards which prey on the scorpions. Be careful though, it's best not to turn over rocks to find a scorpion: it could be painful and is also forbidden. We passed this desert bush and walked along another 'branch' of the lava flow. It resembled a lunar landscape, but with water, at least in some years.

Brown pelicans were patrolling for prey along the edge of the lava flow. One flew very low, its feet trailing in the water, so low it had to turn to dive into the sea. It is incredible what little depth of water is needed for such a large bird to dive successfully. Blue-footed Boobies often dive from great heights into very shallow water. To brake, they have longer tails than the other two Galápagos boobies. I have often wondered how they manage to avoid smashing themselves on the sharp lava rocks.

A **Galápagos Hawk** sitting on the lava flow near the shore. It looked much more like a large buzzard, not so eagle-like as the birds we had just seen on Espumilla. The rounded head gave it a more 'friendly' expression. I think it was a male. Its claws looked powerful. I do not know what it was doing there, there were no crabs to catch, but a bit farther away there was a sealion with a new born pup. Perhaps the hawk was after the placenta which must have been lying somewhere between the rocks. They are powerful hunters but also scavenge.

Brown Pelican occurs on all the islands. Except on Genovesa, I do not think we were ever without one wherever we anchored. Often several, mostly young birds, swam around our boat or sat on the dinghy, waiting for some scraps to be thrown overboard by Aurelio our cook. Locally they are called Pelícano Cafe, after the coffee colour, particularly on the neck, which is often bright reddish, coffee-brown. Some call them Alcatras, an old Spanish name for pelican, a word of Arabian origin: al-gattas. This means sea-eagle, but some say white sea-raven. Al-gattas is also the origin of the English albatross. So the pelican is in the company of the sea-eagle, white sea-raven and albatross. Often pelicans like sitting high up on a lava ridge.

Brown Pelican is the smallest member of a family of eight species. Being small can be a source of pride. Napoleon was not very tall and he became emperor of France. Barnaby took this photo on the tough, rugged Santiago cliffs. The birds remind me of Napoleon, standing there, fierce and proud like a statue; don't you agree? It's just like a monument. There should be a real one somewhere in the Galápagos like the albatross monument in the harbour at Ayora. Perhaps the pelicans are jealous of this and play 'monument' each day themselves!

Another bird in the Galápagos with a peculiar name is Great Frigatebird. Next to Magnificent Frigatebird it is the largest of a family of five species. When Linnaeus gave all the known birds a Latin name in 1758, he thought then the only frigatebird was just an all-black, small pelican and gave it the name *Pelecanus aquila*. In 1789, Gmelin described another frigatebird as *Pelecanus minor*. That was what we now know as Great Frigatebird, yet *minor* means small. At that time this was correct when comparing their size and weight. A Dalmatian Pelican, the only known pelican at that time, has a wingspan of 300 cm and weighs 7–14 kg. Brown Pelican has a wingspan of around 200 cm and weighs only 3–3.5 kg. Great Frigatebird only weighs about 1.5 kg but has a wingpsan over 220 cm. Frigatebirds really are flying machines, always on the wing. Their short legs are only good for set-

An immature Yellow-crowned Night Heron, like a guardian at the entrance to hidden treasure, standing motionless, watching us. Large black frigatebirds on their long pointed wings patrol outside, silent shadows in the air. A scene from *A Thousand and One Nights.*

tling on branches or rocky outcrops, and they cannot really walk well with them, just shuffling over the ground. Sailing around is their metier, masters of the air, on their long and pointed wings, longer than in any other bird of equivalent body weight. With the forked tail, they always remind me of a European Red Kite, but overgrown and black. Their pirating of other seabirds is well known, robbing food for their own chicks, but they catch most of their food themselves. They often fly far out at sea, staying away for a week or more, all the time on the wing.

Contrary to common belief, they can swim but don't like to do so and avoid contact with water as much as possible. Only once did I see two frigatebirds bathing, in brackish water, dipping their bodies into the water while holding their wings stiffly above. Their favourite food is flying fish but with the long hooked bill they can also catch other fish from just under the surface. They never plunge dive like Brown Pelican, which does so masterfully, the only pelican that can dive from any height above the surface. Male frigatebirds courting over the colony with the red pouch inflated like a balloon are an unreal sight. Often the pouch is only half full and shrivelled, as in the photo above, hanging under the bill like a red plastic bag. Almost mystic birds from another world, I could watch them for hours in their acrobatic yet powerful flight.

While watching the frigatebirds high in the air from our ship in the evening light, I saw a young **Yellow-crowned Night Heron** down in the lava cliffs outside a deep black cave, standing there like a warden at the entrance to a cave of treasure; the black lava around it in a golden glitter. It was not asleep like most of the night herons we had seen, but looked at us. Below it, an adult walked over the sharp lava with its long legs and toes making wide steps, as if climbing a staircase very quickly. At last, after all the sleeping Yellow-crowned, one which was active!

It is only 15 miles from Puerto Egas, Santiago, to Caleta Shipton on Isabela, where we anchored for the night. No other boat was in sight. The sea was calm and hundreds of Audubon's Shearwaters flew past our boat, all travelling in the same direction, towards Isla Cowley, which could be seen at a distance off the Isabela coast. Whole flocks of shearwaters settled on the water, swimming with heads under the surface, some diving. Suddenly the whole flock fluttered over the water, paddling their feet, and flew off in the same direction. Noddies and Blue-footed Boobies also flew towards Cowley but not in direct flight like the shearwaters. Sealions barked loudly around our boat, a sound from the Galápagos you never forget. Behind us was the 1097-m high Volcán Alcedo which we would climb tomorrow. We had an early night and planned to get up at 5.00 am next morning. Thes ad braying of a donkey caried far out from the dense bush. I wondered if we would see one next day.

We were up very early next morning planning to depart at 6.00 o'clock, but were delayed half an hour. The walk is very easy: first the trail leads over a rough lava flow without vegetation; later there are some Palo Santo trees, shrub-like in shape, but taller, with dense bushes around them. The trail leads along a narrow barranco, only 3–4 m deep. There, in a small cave we saw a bird we had not yet seen before, the nocturnal **Barn Owl**, pressed into the shadows. It looked like a Euro/American Barn Owl, but somehow different in colour. Smaller, it looked even violet on its back, and proportioned differently. Behind the owl we could just see a downy white chick. The adult flew some 6–7 m further away into even deeper shade. Above the barranco, a Vermillion Flycatcher in a bush took no notice of the predator. The owl was not harassed as is so often seen in Europe. We watched it for quite a while and, as we walked on, it remained in the same place.

A bird of light and
sunshine Vermillion
Flycatcher. Red male
above and yellow
female below

We saw **Vermillion Flycatchers**, the jewel of Galápagos landbirds, all the time on our walk to the Alcedo, mostly the more conspicuous red males but also many yellow females and the slightly larger, but not so brightly yellow, Large-billed Flycatcher. Both species are territorial but seem to live together here.

Cactus-finches and also ground-finches always like when possible to build their round nest with its side entrance hole between two cactus pads. The nests vary in size, often nearly as big as a small football, made of twigs and grasses, rather rough outside and lined with hair and feathers inside. All lay similar brown-speckled pale eggs.

All the way along, often in great concentrations, we saw finches. Mostly ground-finches, Small, Medium and Large in that order of abundance, but also cactus-finches and some Vegetarian Finches. Small Tree-finches were common, less so Large Tree-finch. Near the ridge of the Alcedo, on the steeper part of the trail, we saw some Woodpecker Finches, and Warbler Finches were more numerous here than lower down.

The 10-km trail from Caleta Shipton to the ridge of the Volcán Alcedo is an easy walk. Passing through the dry zone there are bushes, often dense, and towards the steeper part more and more trees. There is always somewhere shady where you can stop for a rest. And it's just at those places where birdwatching is best. There were no Galápagos Doves nor anis along the trail, birds which had been so common on Santiago. Here, several times we could watch Dark-billed Cuckoos, which were not so shy as on St Cruz. We could see the two flycatchers nearly all the time. Large-billed Flycatchers (or Galápagos Flycatcher) were extremely tame; one even took an insect from my hand, and when we were drinking water, came very close. The more common Vermillion Flycatcher seems to be a bird of higher altitudes, but we saw our first 3 km from the coast.

A new bird to us was Galápagos Martin, and we saw the first, an all-black male, near the ridge of the volcano. There were Mockers everywhere, but not tame. Yellow Warbler was the first landbird we saw when we landed on the rocky shore, and from then on they were ever-present on the way to the volcano. Finches were plentiful. There are nine species on Isabel, and on the walk we saw eight of them. Mangrove Finch lives on the other side of the island, is very rare and localized, and only found in large dense mangroves. Also new to us was the large Vegetarian Finch, sitting upright in a tree, parrot-like with its large curved bill. Other finches, often 4–5 species together, were in large concentrations of 50 or more, just in or under one tree. All along the trail we saw their round ball-like nests in bushes or *Opuntia* cactus.

Everywhere we found goat droppings and could often hear goats calling or running away through the dense vegetation. We did see some. They mostly behaved like wild animals, but sometimes they were more domesticated and not so secretive as on Santiago. Donkeys are wilder. We saw only two at a distance, watching us, but their droppings, often next to those of tortoise, showed us they must be common here. The first giant tortoise was a young individual. Tony thought it must be around eight years old. Later, higher up, we saw many more and everywhere their large fibrous droppings. Some large old tortoises were just ahead of us on the trail; when we came closer they hissed and withdrew their long necks. In the bushes we could see the tracks they had 'bulldozed' and we heard some pushing through the vegetation. There were no donkey droppings up on the steeper parts but this is probably not the reason there are more tortoises. At night it is damper here; donkeys do not like this but tortoises enjoy it. A fantastic walk (for which you need a special permit), not arduous and with only the last section being really dry and dusty and a bit tiring in the hot sun.

A male Large Ground-finch. It was interesting to see here on this side of Isabela more full-black males of all species and also black-headed tree-finches than we had seen on St Cruz or the other islands we had visited.

After a 5-hour walk with many stops for birdwatching, we arrived at the Alcedo ridge. Once at the top, we had a fantastic view in and over the crater. The crater is about 7–8 km long and more than 6 km wide. The floor is covered with greyish green bushes and open spaces with ponds. The southern slope has an active fumarole with a tall column of steam. The eastern slope is covered in a white blanket of pumice. Galápagos Martins were flying in and out of the crater. They were males, bluish black in colour and we only saw one sooty-coloured female. Perhaps they were breeding somewhere down in the 200-m high caldera where the males disappeared under the wild overhanging lava rocks. We watched them for quite a while but taking photos was very difficult. They are so quick in flight. A Woodpecker Finch searched for insects on dead wood and lava boulders just a few metres from us.

The stockily built, broad-winged Galápagos Martin reminded me of an American Purple or European Crag Martin flying around the calderas on stiff wings, with rapid short wingbeats and long glides.

♂ and ♀ playing

Frigate bird

all dark head (rounded)

lighter panel

all dark

barred underwing flight feathers

barred tail

moulting flight feathers

new tail feathers growing

In the distance, three **Galápagos Hawks**, two smaller males and a large female, played together. One male stayed apart from the female and showed his 'plunge-dive' display on folded wings, diving again and again. The other two passed something from claw to claw several times. Was it prey? We could not see clearly. Sometimes one flew upside-down holding its feet outstretched. Another smaller male came close towards us, circling overhead and we could see very clearly the underside pattern and buzzard-like shape in flight, not at all like an eagle as it so often resembles when perched.

On our return to the coast we saw more giant tortoises. Since we had to be back on our boat before nightfall we had little time left for bird-watching. With a permit one can stay longer on the Alcedo and can even go into the crater, but the nights can be wet and cold and you have to carry all food, water and camping materials as well as warm clothes. That morning we had marked the place where we had seen the **Barn Owl**. It was still there, now sitting in the small hole with the chick behind. The owl held a large rat in its claws (had it hunted in daytime?), with its long tail it looked like a black rat, a less aggressive species than the shorter-tailed brown rat.

Before going on board we swam in the sea; it was really cold but good after our long walk from the Alcedo. We made it back in two hours compared with the outward five. Many shearwaters swam around our ship, and pelicans and Blue-footed Boobies sat on the cliffs. There were hundreds of shearwaters around us. We were really tired, had a quick meal of 'cabra', or 'chivo' as they call goat on the Galápagos, and were soon in our cabins for an early night.

Landing

During the night we sailed northwards along the Isabela coast. At Punta Albemarle and again at Punta Flores we turned and it was already light when we passed Cabo Berkeley. We arrived at Punta Vincente Roca, just below the Volcano Ecuador, where we dropped anchor. It was still early morning. From the sea it looked a rather dull place (not many visitors stop here). On the right were steep, worn reddish brown lava cliffs with green patches. There were only a few Swallow-tailed Gulls gliding around. Noddies flew in and out of a large cave near the waterline; possibly they breed there. Some young birds, already on the wing, were sitting outside, mostly very close to the water.

Above all this the air was full of **Blue-footed Boobies** going out to or coming in from the open sea, hundreds of them, showing us their masterly flying skills. Some Magnificent Frigatebirds were above them but did not attack the boobies. We wanted to visit the booby colony above us, on the left side, sloping towards the Punta Vincente. From the boat we could already see many birds high up on the slope and heard others which were on flat ground out of sight. The high whistles of the males and the duck-like hoarse calls of the females vibrated in the air.

We walked up to the summit beyond, keeping outside the colonies, and gained a fantastic view over the breeding birds. Many were sitting on eggs; others had young of different ages, often two or three in one nest. There must have been thousands of birds. Some were still courting. The scene was similar to a Northern Gannet colony but with more space between each nest, and calmer, more relaxed – more Latin American! Two Galápagos Hawks flew high over the colonies, keeping at a distance as though inspecting the goings-on below. There must be lots of flies on the guano around the nests; a pair of martins swooped down to the breeding birds, went up to the ridge again and played in the wind. Yellow Warblers, as always, were everywhere, but only a few ground-finches (they looked like Mediums). We saw nests in the bushes and *Opuntia* cactuses at the colony edges, and it appeared some were occupied by finches which were flying in and out. A restful place, yet full of life.

On the edge of a Blue-footed Booby colony, showing the typical spacing of nests. In some places they can be close to each other but never so packed as in a Northern Gannet colony. Perhaps they are more quarrelsome, or there is just more space available, or the fishing waters around the Isabela coast cannot support a larger population.

When the chicks are still small they stay inside the white ring around the nest, the centre of their territory. Later, the youngsters walk around but never wander too far. When still small, one parent will stay with the chicks while the other is out at sea searching for food. The parents protect young against predators such as frigatebirds, and for the smallest chicks provide cover from the hot sun. I wonder if they would also defend their young against feral cats: I found a cat skeleton under a cactus bush. In most nests we saw two chicks, and there were only a few corpses lying around, unlike the scene in the Red-footed Booby colonies on Genovesa.

On the steeper slopes, nests are more widely spaced, and here many more pairs were still incubating or sitting on smaller chicks than on more level ground where the nests are closer together. Some pairs, mostly on the edge of the colony, were still courting, as was this pair below. I could not understand this since Blue-footed Booby has no fixed season and breeds all year round. A pair could raise a brood every seven or nine months. Perhaps breeding peaks during the year at the best nesting places in the flat part of the colony.

Blue-footed Boobies are really comical birds with their large, bright blue webbed feet. When a pair is seen together on the ground, the sexes can easily be separated. Females are larger and more strongly built. They weigh about 30% more than males. Males have a piping, whistling voice, females a hoarse raucous duck-like call. The most reliable way to separate sexes is by pupil size (*see below*).

the bill of the male often looks longer and is always more slender, spear-like

the female has a stronger heavier bill

male

female

for fishing in shallow coastal waters Blue-footed have rather long tails compared with other boobies

variable in both sexes paler or darker

The pupil in the male looks smaller and thus for appears to 'stare' at you

these neck feathers have a rather typically spiky look in both sexes

the female's pupil is similar to the male's but there is an extra dark pigmented ring around it, so she seems to have larger more friendly eyes

male

female

The legs in both are bright blue, but greenish or even purplish legs are not uncommon, the males have a tendency to brighter colours (not a rule)

webbed between all three

Males not only have a smaller, lighter build which is most noticeable in the neck, but they often also cock the tail more so it is touching the head

These are typical Blue-footed nests encircled with white guano rings, as though painted on the ground. Both parents incubate in turn and later feed the youngsters (normally two). The early feeding is mainly done by the male who takes smaller prey in the shallow waters near the colony. About midway through raising the young, the male gives up and thereafter the female feeds alone, leaving her now well-feathered larger chicks alone, often for a long time, while she is fishing in deeper waters farther away. Males are then often seen sitting on rocks and in the rougher parts around the colony.

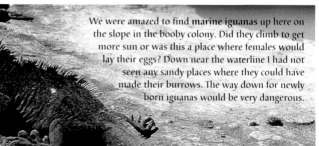

We were amazed to find **marine iguanas** up here on the slope in the booby colony. Did they climb to get more sun or was this a place where females would lay their eggs? Down near the waterline I had not seen any sandy places where they could have made their burrows. The way down for newly born iguanas would be very dangerous.

Marine iguanas need their large spider-like toes to cling to the rocks to prevent being washed away while feeding, at the tideline or even under the sea's surface. Algae is their sole food.

The long, strongly flattened tail is a powerful swimming aid. Land iguanas have more rounded tails.

As with so many other places, I would have liked to stay longer at Punta Vincente Roca. When we arrived this morning it did not look like a very interesting place. Once we were up on the slope near the booby colony it changed completely. We made some very interesting observations but time was too short to understand more about the social structure of such a large colony. At the edge of the sloping colony we also saw two pairs of Masked Boobies. Perhaps it was not the right time of the year for them. Unlike Blue-footed, Masked have an annual breeding cycle which changes from island to island.

They don't nest in such large colonies as other boobies or gannets. The nests are more widely spaced, which has led to different social behaviour from Northern Gannet. On this side of Isabela they are rare, preferring warmer waters for fishing.

Mockingbirds, which we had not seen as we climbed, were now in the lower areas near the bushes, searching for food between the boobies. We only saw what looked like Medium Ground-finches. Down on the beach noddies were now more numerous than this morning and pelicans were sitting on the rocks. Lava Herons searched near the tideline between the lava boulders. They seem territorial even when young, chasing each other when approached too closely. Magnificent Frigatebirds were also more numerous and some chased boobies as they came in from the sea. I wondered how they knew which booby was carrying food and which not.

Our first **Flightless Cormorant** coming out of the water, like an oily submarine, next to our dinghy.

Looking back to Punta Vincente Roca we could see that half of the old 600-m high Volcano Ecuador has been eroded by the sea. The water into which we sailed, between Isabela and Fernandina, must be rich in fish. There were many Dark-rumped Petrels and Audubon's Shearwaters, Band-rumped Storm-petrels, Blue-footed Boobies and Swallow-tailed Gulls, all fishing, but none in large flocks. Only the noddies were plentiful: a single flock stretched from Isabela right over to Fernandina.

Fernandina, dominated by the 1450-m high active Volcano La Cumbre, is the most westerly island in the Galápagos. Beyond this are more than 5500 km of open sea to the islands of French Polynesia. Fernandina is mostly barren rough lava but with many fresh flows. The only place one can visit is the most northeasterly point of this round island, Punta Espinosa, with its interesting lagoons, mangroves, black lava flows and few sandy beaches.

It is just over 25 km from Punta Vincente Roca on Isabela to Punta Espinosa on Fernandina. While we had breakfast in the early morning, before our visit to the Blue-footed Booby colonies, there were 30–40 Brown Pelicans fishing around our ship. Now, during our crossing, five hours later, there were none; no frigatebirds either. Blue-footed Boobies came from the nearby coast of Isabela, flew past our boat and out to the open sea. They were always single or in small groups of three to six, generally flying in line, one behind the other, low over the water or in 'packs' higher in the air. Only a few flew towards the coast but none of those flying was fishing. There must be more fish in the open waters.

Noddies hovered over the water, often in large flocks, catching food and sometimes in the company of diving Audubon's Shearwaters. Single Swallow-tailed Gulls took no notice of our boat, while a pair of Lava Gulls followed us all the way across. Near Punta Espinosa, which looks fantastic with its green mangroves and long black lava banks stretching far into the sea, I watched a Galápagos Hawk coming from nearby Isabela, six to seven km away, sailing over the lagoons before disappearing behind a cloud far inland over Fernandina.

The hawk made the crossing so easily, I wondered if it did this every day. If it crossed wider stretches of water with the same ease it could recolonize San Cristóbal and Floreana where it has been eradicated by humans.

Our first **Waved Albatross**, an exciting sight. Single birds far away from our boat, gliding over the sea. They are the largest birds in the Galápagos, long-winged, with a huge, long bill and short tail which gives them their typically short-reared shape. Even at that distance, we could see the golden gloss to their white heads.

We saw our first Galápagos Penguin, an adult bird, more than 2 km off the Fernandina coast. It was rather shy, keeping away from our boat, sometimes diving. It disappeared suddenly. We saw another close to the shore on a low lava bank, this one looked at us and was not shy. As we came closer to Punta Espinosa, penguins were on nearly all the lava banks or small islets, sometimes in small groups of three to five, with others jumping out of the water to join them.

From a distance the shiny black lava flows looked empty but close up they are full of life. All the Fernandina seabirds were present. We saw Blue-footed Boobies, Brown Pelicans, Flightless Cormorants, Galápagos Penguins, and some northern waders and noddies. Lava Gulls, mostly in pairs, were not easy to spot since their plumage blends with the black lava. Even so far out at sea, away from the green lagoon behind, some finches and bright, easily visible Yellow Warblers, were hopping around between sleeping sealions.

Fernandina marine iguanas are fairly small and all-black. There were hundreds, possibly thousands. Some banks were completely covered with them, all adults of nearly the same size. We never saw small young among them. Do they hide away from adults or from predators? When and what do they eat when still small? This was a great puzzle to all of us.

Marine iguanas, miniature Galápagos monsters, are fantastically well adapted to life in water. What an evolutionary step from an arboreal ancestor to life in salt water, where they dive for food, often deep under the surface. They spend most of their time out of the water and still love and need the sun, like their cousin the land iguana, which would never go into salt water.

▲
Flightless Cormorants standing on black lava rocks, silhouetted against the sky. They build their nests here, just above the tideline in a small colony of a few pairs. They never breed in large colonies like other members of the family.

A male coming home with a present for his mate. This could be seaweed, ▶ a branch, sea urchin, or even a dead fish or plastic bag. The female will add this to the ever-growing, bulky nest throughout the breeding period.

Going slowly along the coast of Punta Espinosa, Fernandina, we saw our first Flightless Cormorants on land, where they kept to the black lava flows. There were several small breeding colonies. In one I counted ten nests, which is a large colony for this bird. Their distribution in the archipelago is very restricted. They are found only in the colder waters of the Cromwell and Humboldt currents, rich with fish, in suitable areas around the Fernandina coast and on the western side of Isabela from Punta Morena northwards, with only a few breeding colonies on the eastern side, southwards as far as Punta Garcia. The whole population of this endemic species is no more than approximately 700–800 pairs. This seems to be a very low number, but they have never been numerous since suitable habitats are restricted.

Climbing on the rocks with its miniature wings held open to keep its balance.

They always remain along the coast, never wandering far away from their colonies, and seldom swim and fish further than 100 m from shore. I don't know if there is any contact between the Isabela and Fernandina colonies. The Canal Bolivar between the two islands is only 5 km wide at its narrowest point. We saw several ringed cormorants. Could this be a study to determine if they cross the channel?

There is probably little regular contact between populations on the two islands where cormorants breed, and little change in the make-up of the breeding colony on each island. The smallest females always choose the largest males within their colony. While he feeds the full-grown young alone, she will pair with another male to breed again. Females may never breed with the same male again.

There was only one other ship at anchor when we landed on Punta Espinosa; the only other visitors. Close to the dry landing place the rocks were covered with marine iguanas and we had to be careful not to tread on them. A small track led us to a pa-hoe-hoe lava field, which looks like a piece of landscape art. We passed some cormorant colonies where we could watch very closely. Barnaby took some good photos but this film did not develop.

Merging well with the black lava. Only the bright leg ring (for scientific research) shows up.

From a distance you can see the black lava 'painted' white with bird droppings, showing clearly some of the cormorants' favourite resting places or colonies. Such places are never far from open water. They do not like to walk long distances over the razor-sharp rocks. The silhouettes of cormorants often look like little men standing very straight.

E ven more like little men are **Galápagos Penguins**, which are nearly the same size as the cormorants but with much shorter necks. They are more widespread in the archipelago when not breeding. They only breed on Isabela and Fernandina, and Punta Espinosa is a good place to watch them. Like cormorants, but possibly more numerous, they also breed in small widely separated colonies, often of only a few pairs. They lay their two eggs in holes under lava, further away from the shore than cormorants. With their short strong feet they are better walkers. Rather shy at sea, they are very tame on land. Most are seen asleep; they are more active at night when you can often hear their donkey-like braying.

A young ringed **Flightless Cormorant**. They are very similar to the adults but browner. Their plumage looks neater, not so ragged as the adults', whose feathers are often worn. Young birds have dull brown eyes, the adults' are bright turquoise.

Punta Espinosa, the only place you can visit on Fernandina, is one of the best places to watch the two flightless Galápagos birds. Both breed here. The penguins hide their nests in holes under rocks and sometimes under dense vegetation. You only see them outside, sometimes in small groups of three to four together, often asleep. Cormorants build their nests in the open, often rather large constructions which they continue building during the entire incubation period. Every time the male comes back from sea he must bring a 'present' to his mate to add to the nest. When food is plentiful, the female will leave her mate to raise the chicks while she starts breeding with another attractive male. Here on Punta Espinosa you can watch their ceremonial family life (with its element of passion) very closely.

Many other species are also present. We saw 12 Wandering Tattlers resting next to penguins. Most interesting of all were Small Ground-finches, Yellow Warblers and a mockingbird far out on the northeastern corner of Espinosa in a cormorant colony, searching between the nests for food. This lava bank is far away from any vegetation. A Galápagos Dove was seen around the colony, I wondered what it was searching for. Lava Herons, always singles, are everywhere on the black rocks; generally you hear them before you see them. Barnaby thought their alarm call sounded like a harsh, sharp 'Keoup'; I thought it more like 'quark-quark'. We saw a pair of Lava Gulls that we would have overlooked had they not been standing beside a Whimbrel which, being brown, showed up well against the black rocks.

A Brown Pelican coming home from the sea. There was a breeding colony in the mangrove and on some nests there were adult birds not yet in full plumage next to chicks. I wonder if they breed before they acquire their complete breeding plumage like the bird pictured here.

A bird I hoped to find in the large mangrove at Punta Espinosa was the rare Mangrove Finch. Time was short and we did not see one. Possibly they are no longer found on Fernandina. There were many Small Tree-finches searching for food in the mangrove, often hanging upside-down on long branches, more like a tit than a finch. A pair of Vermillion Flycatchers, normally a highland bird, were down here in the mangrove. I saw the female first and thought it was a Large-billed Flycatcher but then the bright male appeared too. A Galápagos Hawk, on a dead tree, called and a second smaller one came and settled beside it. They stayed there for more than an hour, motionless, calling from time to time. A Great Blue Heron with a very short crest, not so long as in North American birds, stayed on its nest (much larger than the nearby pelican nests), beside two chicks with hedgehog-like heads.

Our boat, the *Española*, waiting for us in the Canal Bolivar near Punta Espinosa. In the background are the mountains of Isabela which show how close Fernandina is to that island. Even small landbirds could easily cross the narrow channel.

Sunset in tropical countries is very short, and often spectacular. After a short time the sea and sky were black with only a large circle of indigo blue around the orange sun and a deep red glow over the disappearing land.

Lago Darwin, on Isabela, a round crater lake, separated from the sea by a small ridge of land. The brackish water often looks turquoise with a green rim like a table cloth.

Typical dry vegetation (with Palo Santo trees and a variety of shrubs) around Lago Darwin.

The broad, easy, visitors' trail, which is like a botanical walk, leading to the cone viewpoint.

Young Brown Pelican on a favourite rest at the ridge (again a Napoleon?).

Tagus Cove on Isabela, formed by a broken tuff crater, was named after a British warship in 1814. Pirates and whalers once sheltered here. You can still see where many of them engraved the names of their ships and the year they visited in large letters on the cliffs on the right-hand side. This is now strictly forbidden.

Landing here is sometimes a bit difficult but the short climb up to Lago Darwin (some call it Lago Beagle) is easy, though perhaps not for everyone. The lake is filled with 'dead' salt water and it is said to be without life. We saw 13 White-cheeked Pintails and four stilts. I wondered what they were eating down there as we watched them for quite a while from the trail above the lake. Possibly they eat insects that fall into the water. There must have been a lot, as the stilts, especially, were very busy picking things from the surface. The trail is like a botanical garden with dry vegetation, dominated by Palo Santo trees, waltherias and chala shrubs, also some Galápagos cotton showed its bright purple-centred yellow flowers. There were too many shrubs and plants to name them all.

In many shrubs we saw abandoned finch nests. Present were all three ground-finches, Small, Medium and Large, and also Small and Large Tree-finch. A Large-billed Flycatcher followed us as we walked, a Mocker took no notice of us, and Yellow Warblers, as always, were everywhere. It was a short climb to the cone viewpoint, from where we had a fantastic view over the lava fields of Darwin Volcano, while a pair of Galápagos Martins sailed over our heads.

An all-black adult **Lava Heron**, this one sitting like a little statue, exposed and easy to see on the black lava. When they are asleep between lava blocks, it's often easy to miss them, even when they are near.

From Tagus Cove, with dolphins accompanying our ship, and at some distance from the Isabela coast, we sailed southwards for three hours to Bahía Urbina. The sea was very rough, and I did not feel well. There were not many birds at sea, only some storm-petrels. A rather large fish jumped over the deck, too large to be a flying fish. At Bahía Urbina the sea was still rough and we had to wait before disembarking. The coast looked wild, with rocks and boulders poking out of the water, and cormorants and pelicans sitting on them.

In 1954 a 6-km coastal strip, coral banks and all, was lifted, in some places over 5 m, and pushed over 1 km out into the sea. On this newly formed land you can still see the dead coral and other sea organisms. The former coastline, now further inland, forms a steep cliff, in some places with Palo Santo trees. Cormorants had their colonies on the coral banks. I counted 27 birds on one. Further away from the rough coast, where low salt bushes and different acacias now grow, there is a Brown Pelican colony, the largest we had seen until now. I counted over 50 nests. Great Blue Herons were standing motionless on low lava blocks near the water. I don't think they breed here. Lava Herons were common. I counted over a dozen, always singles, some in juvenile plumage. There were only a few Small Ground-finches and, oddly, we saw more Small Tree-finches. A pair was hopping over an old lava bank near the water, the female very pale, the male with black head and strong flank stripes. As always, Yellow Warblers were all around; some very bright males and pale grey females showing up well against the black rocks.

Punta Espinosa was a very good place for Flightless Cormorants, but here on Bahía Urbina it was even better. We could watch them very closely and Barnaby had no problems with his camera this time.

Why did only one cormorant in a family of 37 species worldwide become flightless? I believe there might be a simple answer: all other cormorants are either migratory or travel far from their often enormous breeding colonies to fish in richer waters, necessitating strong wings. The Galápagos species is sedentary, lives in small colonies along the western Isabela coast and around Fernandina, in waters rich with fish. Strong wings are not needed, fishing is even easier without wings, as penguins demonstrate.

Galápagos Cormorants are also the only purely tropical species living all year round next to piratic frigatebirds. When a flying seabird comes home from fishing, its pouch filled with food for the young, the powerful frigatebirds attack and do not give up until the victim drops its prey. Walking a short distance over the rocky shores to fish not only saves having to fly but is safer. Flightless Cormorants have developed even further, and only pass food to the chicks when it is half digested to a liquid pulp, so the frigatebirds cannot steal so easily as they do from pelicans and boobies. Once I saw a Small Ground-finch catching drops of liquid which fell down when a parent was feeding its nearly full grown chick. A fantastic adaptation for a seed-eater.

The bill is long and strong with a powerful hook at its tip. Watching these birds at close quarters, the bills appear stronger and larger than in any other cormorant. Noticeable too, the bill has no visible nose hole.

thick neck

hook

It looks rather peculiar for this cormorant to spread its tiny wings to dry, as all other flying cormorant species do. We do not know if wings are spread just to dry or if this also has a social function.

The pouch is not as well developed as it is in most pelicans and cormorants.

thick neck

pouch

The tail is long, stiff and wedge-shaped; each feather has a strong quill. When back on land after fishing, cleaning these feathers is often the first job; each feather passing through the bill. The tail always needs to be in perfect condition since it is used as a rudder when diving. On the surface birds swim mostly submerged, with only the snake-like neck held above water.

large webbed feet

Peculiar swelling which I have not noticed in any other cormorant.

A juvenile fishing from a mangrove branch. It is unbelievable how acrobatic the bird can be and how long it can stretch its neck when catching prey well below the perch, hanging upside-down and feeding like a parrot.

Green Heron – Striated Heron – Lava Heron: Are they three different species or subspecies of a widely distributed small heron? If so, they should all be lumped as one species, Mangrove Heron. Only Great White Egret and the Cattle Egret are as widely distributed in the warmer areas of the world. Both these egrets also breed in the Galápagos. Lava Heron, *Butorides (striatus) sundervalli*, is an old Galápagos endemic, found on all islands in intertidal zones and in mangroves. Striated Heron, *Butorides striatus*, has at present only been observed on St Cruz, Isabela, Fernandina, Pinzón and Pinta where there are large mangroves. Perhaps Striated is only a colour phase of the all-dark slate-coloured Lava Heron, or is it a more recent colonist (at least over a 100 years) and still only found in mangroves? The adult birds of both species are easily identified in the field when in typical plumage; but be careful, some Striated are rather dark and some Lava have streaks on the neck and often a rather greenish sheen on the back. This could be the result of interbreeding or, more likely, the first Galápagos colonist was a more greenish heron, like Striated now. As an adaptation to the lava habitat they have become slate black. The juvenile and immature plumages of many bird species often show ancestral colours, which moult into the definitive plumage – slate black in Lava Heron. On Genovesa, where Striated Herons don't occur, we saw some immatures in intermediate plumage, resembling hybrids. Striated may occasionally come and pair with Lava Herons, the island being in sight of Marchena, which is close to Pinta, where Striated breed.

Their way of life is very similar. Both start nesting, up to three times in a year, shortly after the first heavy rains. Unlike most other heron species they breed in solitary pairs not in colonies, and defend the often small territory very fiercely.

grey green

pale edges

striated

leg colour varies could also be grey or red

STRIATED HERON

slate grey

see also page 19

somehere slightly striated

leg colour also varies, greyish yellow or red

LAVA HERON

Young birds are not always so easy to recognise. Here, I would ▶ say the bird in this photograph is a young Striated Heron; Lavas are darker when still in this plumage, but be careful, 100% identification in this plumage is always difficult.

From a long way off we could see the large Brown Pelican colony in low salt bushes on the higher land in Bahía Urbina. Birds were flying in from and out to sea, mostly in adult plumage.

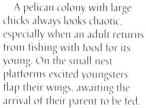

A pelican colony with large chicks always looks chaotic, especially when an adult returns from fishing with food for its young. On the small nest platforms excited youngsters flap their wings, awaiting the arrival of their parent to be fed.

A young bird exercising its wing to improve the power and strength of the muscles before its first flight.

Well-fed, nearly full-grown young pelicans waiting for the next serving.

Las Islas Mariela are two small islands covered with Palo Santo trees, guarding the entrance to the large, calm Bahía Elizabeth. I made a quick sketch of this wonderful scene because the light was too poor for Barnaby when we arrived at 5.30 in the morning.

An Audubon's Shearwater (easily identified). The Dark-rumped Petrel, has a white forehead and would never stay so close to a boat. It is a pelagic feeder, only approaching the shore at dawn or dusk.

We left the Bahía Urbina at night. The sea was quite rough, which is often the case in the Canal Bolívar between Fernandina and Isabela. I felt unwell and was relieved when we anchored early in the morning at Bahía Elizabeth in waters as calm and flat as a table top. The sun rose slowly over Isabela, and to our right in the Sierra Negra, the Santo Tomás volcano looked like a black wall surrounded only by some white clouds, turning pink with the sunrise.

Two cormorants and a few penguins were fishing around our boat. The cormorants, with their long sleek necks and upward-pointing bills looked more like sea snakes than birds as they swam with their bodies under the surface of the water, diving all the time, often for long periods. The penguins looked quite different with their short necks and stubby bills. They can dive for even longer than cormorants.

When Aurelio, our cook, cleaned some fish we had caught at night neither the cormorants nor the penguins were interested in the offal. By contrast, frigatebirds and pelicans arrived as soon as Aurelio came on deck with fish. They were not interested in the large bits, like fish heads, but they caught all the small pieces. The frigatebirds were masters at snapping up the smallest morsels, skimming the water with their bills. The pelicans also dived after small pieces. An Elliot's Storm-petrel stayed around our boat and got its share. I could easily identify it, which is not always possible with these tiny fluttering seabirds. Some Audubon's Shearwaters also fished near our boat, swimming on the surface and pecking at little pieces. They frequently held their heads under water, like dabbling ducks, and then dived, but only briefly. With the light constantly changing it formed a really tranquil early morning picture.

Nearby, on some rough lava, were resting Blue-footed Boobies and penguins. We could see how small the Galápagos Penguins are compared with the boobies. Blue-footed Boobies can be over 10% smaller than our Northern Gannets. The penguins were younger birds, still lacking the head and chest markings of the adult. Some had pale faces, but neverthless they were fully grown. Smaller, younger birds like to hide under rocks. With their upright stance, they looked more like gnomes than real birds.

B efore disembarking, we visited the large lagoon in our dinghy.
The water was as still as an inland lake, surrounded by luxurious
jungle-like vegetation with large and beautiful trees of different
species. Beyond this rich green mangrove, we could see the dry lava
fields where only silvery leafless Palo Santos and cactuses grew. A real
contrast, jungle and near-desert, just a few metres apart. There were
pelican colonies in the larger bushes in the lagoon, and Lava and
Striated Herons were fishing in the shade of the mangrove.

A bird we really wanted to find here was Mangrove Finch, but none
appeared. The habitat is ideal for this rare species. There were finches
in the trees, others flew over our heads from one side of the mangrove
to some larger trees farther away, but none looked like a Mangrove
Finch. This is the rarest Galápagos finch and is possibly near extinction.
It looks a little like a smaller version of Woodpecker Finch. I had seen
them 25 years ago but why not now? Why have they become so rare?
Their habitat is still the same and there is no more disturbance now
than 25 years ago. Perhaps we should have stayed another week or so
to find them. Twice I heard a song, something like Woodpecker Finch's
song, more a 'tur-tur-tur', repeated again and again: could it have been
a Mangrove Finch? To make things more difficult there was the loud
barking of sealions in the mangroves.

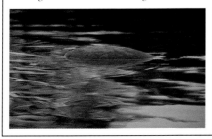

We identified three different
marine turtles swimming like
ghosts in the shallow water.
Most were green turtles, the
only species permanently
present in the Galápagos.
It was not easy to take a
picture of them, even when
they were close to the surface.

Two widely spaced colonies of Brown Pelicans were in Bahía Elizabeth lagoon. All the nests were in bushes just 3–5 m above the water; none was higher up in the trees. All nests had two half-grown, well-fed chicks so there must be rich fishing waters nearby. We saw only a few adults. The scene was much calmer than we had seen the day before.

From the land, the contrast of lava, dry and with only sparse vegetation on one side, and luxurious mangrove, green and full of life on the other, was even more marked than when seen from the dinghy.

There were open ponds surrounded by green bushes quite a distance from the lagoon. A sealion had found its way under the lava, swimming up to sunbathe. A strong smell around the pond told us that it came here regularly. Behind this little, private pool black lava sloped gently upwards to the distant Sierra Negra.

I walked up a narrow track behind the lagoon and was amazed to find some marine iguanas this far from open water. Did they come here to feed? First they had to cross the calm lagoon, creeping under the mangrove trees. Perhaps, like the sealion, they swam under the lava in the canal and then walked further on over the sharp black lava. It was at least 400–500 m from open water. Will some marine iguanas (unless they become easy prey to hawks) become land iguanas again?

I walked back down to the lagoon and searched for Mangrove Finch. There were many Small, and some Medium Ground-finches, and a few Small Tree-finches but not one Mangrove Finch. Only once, near a cormorant colony in an old dead tree, could a mysterious bird have been one; or was this wishful thinking?

A cormorant colony of five pairs was near the water, to the right of the large tree, on the sharp lava ridge of a small pool. Here the breeding bird clearly shows the long stiff wedge-shaped tail, and on the left, the standing bird, the short wings and peculiarly shaped legs.

Flightless Cormorants appear vaguely prehistoric. Above, a chick looks out from under its father. On the right the small male, after giving a present to its larger mate, is waiting with half-open wings so that she will let him sit on the eggs.

At Punta Moreno there were many cormorants on the large, black, flat lava flow, some drying their wings, and never far from the waterline.

Here in this rich lagoon was our last chance to see Mangrove Finch. The habitat is ideal, dense mangrove with large trees, but there were still none of these rare finches. I regretted not stopping on Punta Tortuga, higher up on the Isabela coast, where I had seen Mangrove Finches years ago. I don't know if Tortuga is still open to visitors. Perhaps the better way, instead of walking around to find this bird would be just to sit down in the mangrove and wait and let the birds come to you?

We had a very calm crossing from Bahía Elizabeth to Punta Moreno. While sitting on deck, eating a good fresh lobster, we watched about 30 Abatrosses sitting in a line like toy ducks. Even far off, at more than 500-600 m, their white, gold-tinged heads were very conspicuous. Their dark rear ends were rather high above the water. Two Lava Gulls followed our boat all the way. For a while they were joined by a small flock of six Elliot's Storm-petrels, scavenging behind the boat. Frigatebirds also appeared, looked at us but quickly lost interest until our cook cleaned some fish; they then followed the boat. Punta Moreno, with its large lava fields stretching down from the Sierra Negra on one side and the Cerro Azul volcano on the other, has a particular wild beauty. From a distance the lava field looked empty and desert-like, but a few pioneer lava cactus had begun to grow. In sheltered cracks *Scalesia affinis* tries to get a hold in this dry world. The most interesting part of Punta Moreno is the oasis-like mangrove surrounding a large pond filled with brackish water. Pelicans had some nests there, all with small chicks. Lava and Striated Herons were fishing in the lagoon. We saw many Yellow Warblers and some mockingbirds but, unusually, there were no finches, except for one all-black male Small Ground-finch. Perhaps the desert-like lava flow is a barrier for the finches. Down in the mangrove the vegetation is rich, varied and luxurious. I searched everywhere we were permitted to go but found no finches; this was the first place they were absent.

At first, **American Oystercatchers** appear to be similar to European Oystercatchers but their back and wings are more brownish, and they are not so gregarious. Here in the Galápagos they are found on all rocky shores. The local subspecies, *galapagensis*, has an irregularly bordered lower breast-band, a stronger bill and shorter legs than its North American cousin.

A Flightless Cormorant leaving the water looks 'oily' all over. They never walk far from the waterline, do not breed far from the shore and, when in the water fishing, are seldom found further than 100 m from the land. Like Galápagos Oystercatcher, they are not so gregarious as their Continental counterparts and are seldom found in groups of more than four or five pairs.

Like cormorants, Galápagos Penguins are not very gregarious. Here on Punta Moreno there is a colony of about five pairs. With short necks and chubby bills, the silhouette is quite different from long-necked cormorants. The back is normally seen when swimming; cormorants are mostly submerged.

We left Punta Moreno at 4.30 in the afternoon for Villamil, the harbour town on the southern side of Isabela. The sea was rather rough. According to the map, we had seen the most interesting places open to visitors on Fernandina and Isabela but I would have liked to see more places on Fernandina (for instance, the mangroves near Punta Mangle) but these are not open to visitors. I regretted not stopping at Punta Tortuga on Isabela. Now sailing southwards, Mangrove Finch would be unobservable because mangrove on Isabela's east coast, at Punta Davis (just opposite the Islas los Hermanos), where Mangrove Finches may live, is not open to visitors.

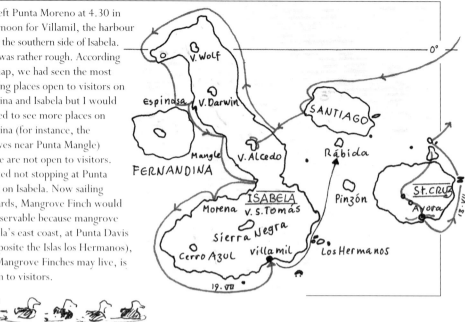

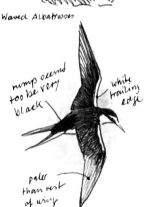

Waved Albatross

rump seemd too be very black

white trailing edge

paler than rest of wing

I noticed two Sooty Terns in a flock of Audubon's Shearwaters, flying just above them, dipping down to the water's surface, not diving. They looked very elegant with long wings (black above, white below) and with two long tail streamers, easy to identify. (Here, near Isabela, they were far from their breeding haunts on Wolf and Darwin.)

With the light still good, we saw albatrosses again, while we were quite far off the coast of Punta Moreno. It must have been near the same spot I had seen them that morning. This time we were closer but still too far away for Barnaby's camera. The sea was still quite rough but I did manage to sketch them. Otherwise, as we sailed southwards, there was not much birdlife. I was preparing to go below deck when a large flock of Audubon's Shearwaters passed by, accompanied by two Sooty Terns. Never leave the scene too early!

We sailed all night, far from the coast. Through the morning haze, I could see the Cerro Azul volcano. Large birds passed our boat like shadows; some were shearwaters, but larger than Audubon's, and it was difficult to identify them. We arrived in Bahía Villamil at 6.00 o'clock in the morning. This was a real South Pacific picture. A broad, white sandy beach with large palm trees, here and there houses under the palms, and in the early morning light, Santo Tomás volcano in the background. There were three tourist vessels among the fishing boats in the bay, their crews still asleep. We landed by dinghy to the right of the little town and walked along a small path through a lagoon containing numerous brackish ponds of varying size. Every pond had some Moorhens, a few ducks and flamingos; one had a Lava Gull searching for food. There were ground-finches everywhere, Small, Medium and Large, only a few Small Tree-finches but, as usual, many Yellow Warblers and some mockingbirds on the track and in the surrounding bushes.

The village was disappointing. The houses, once rather attractive, looked neglected, giving a sad impression so different from the more lively town of Ayora on St Cruz. This has now changed with the new airport at Villamil.

Many more people have come to live on the island, which has meant more houses and hotels have been built, and more tourists now start their tour of the archipelago on Isabela, visiting areas on the island in greater numbers than before. Here in Villamil was where we saw large numbers of black rats crossing the roads, more than we had seen elsewhere. They have certainly benefited from these changes, but the impact on the environment has yet to be fully assessed.

legs are pink with red knees

only half of the legs are seen

1/3 black, a bill like a nose

the flamingos bill with its lamellae, is a perfect tool to filter minuscule food, mostly algae and brine shrimp

long pink neck

back paler

flamingos swim well in deep water like pink swans

black wing tips not seen, only in flying birds

The Galápagos Flamingo, like Galápagos Penguin, Cormorant or Oystercatcher (*see* p. 85) is not a gregarious bird. They are seen mainly in small groups or often alone, unlike the same species in the Caribbean or the Camargue, where there are always thousands together when breeding.

Walking along the lagoon trail, with many square man-made ponds, we saw flamingos, always alone, except for one view of a pair. White-cheeked Pintails were always seen in twos. At first I thought they were pairs, but on careful observation I noticed they were all males. They were quite nervous and when we approached too close they flew to another pond. In flight, we could see clearly their bright green shiny speculum. Perhaps shooting has made them shy.

On the dark water the white cheeks and long pale tail show up very well.

There is a large lagoon just behind the village of Villamil which was more like a sandy, muddy saltpan, and nearly dry. At the edge two **Ruddy Turnstones** were there in full breeding plumage, possibly a pair, but sexing them in the field is not easy. Females are duller on the back and more streaked on the head. Some individuals are found all year round in the Galápagos and perhaps this species will breed one day.

Four **Semipalmated Plovers**, like turnstones, were visitors from northern North America, and ran over the saltpan like little mechanical toys. There were three males chasing each other as if guarding territory. The female was courted by a male but showed no interest. They could also breed here but the Galápagos are far to the south of their normal breeding range. They are most common here from August to May.

tail less pointed browner than male

cheeks mottled

less red

flank design rounder than males

overall males are brighter

♀

There were only female **White-cheeked Pintails** here, not shy or nervous like the males on the other side of the village. When I approached one female with a nearly full grown duckling she stayed only 2 m away in the water under a bush. I could possibly have moved even closer.

We were on our way to visit the tortoise reserve/breeding station and saw a female duck with four half-grown ducklings on one of the ponds we passed. Perhaps this was the reason the males were alone on the other lagoon: off duty while the females raised the brood. The males may have started moulting, causing them to become shier. As we walked along the dusty road, we often saw rats crossing. They had the long tails and big ears typical of black rats; not so aggressive as brown rats but still a great danger for endemic wildlife. On our return, we visited the village but there was not much to see. It was lunchtime and everyone seemed to be asleep. As we waited for our dinghy on the white beach, we watched a Lava Gull with only one foot that we had seen earlier that morning. A lone Whimbrel walked along the shore and four turnstones flew inland towards the saltpan.

We left Villamil at about 2.50 pm, sailing northwest towards Rábida, which we wanted to visit next. At first we stayed close to the Isabela coast, near the Islas Los Hermanos, four beautifully shaped islands that appeared very dry. From our boat we could see only a little vegetation on them. Opposite, on Isabela, the long stretch of mangrove near Punta Davis was of greater interest to me and I would have liked to have stopped and explored. This would have been our last chance to see the mysterious Mangrove Finch, but the area is not open to visitors. I hope they still live there in this mangrove, far away from the other populations on the eastern side of Isabela and the three areas of mangrove on Fernandina.

I remained alone on deck and watched seabirds. There were many Elliot's Storm-petrels, often three or four at a time following our boat. Numerous Blue-footed Boobies flew in small groups in different directions but were not fishing these waters. Distant albatrosses passed or settled on the sea. Swallow-tailed Gulls passed, not taking any notice of us. Three unidentified dolphins played around our boat. When we had passed Los Hermanos, a Lava Gull followed us, sometimes settling for a while on the dinghy. A large, dark storm-petrel with a fairly long tail flew behind us in a straight line, a fixed height from the water's surface and not dancing around like the Elliot's. I observed it very closely and made sketches. It had no white on its rump and could only have been Black Storm-petrel, which breeds on islands along the Californian coast and spends the nothern winter mostly along the Peruvian coast. There are only two records from the Galápagos.

Black Storm-petrel, entirely dark with two small wingbars but black underwings, is larger than the common Elliot's Storm-petrel. Previously there were only two recordings in the Galápagos so this sighting must be the third. They are common along the Ecuador coast (*see* p. 169).

It is not easy to take a good picture of these fast-flying tiny seabirds as they dance and walk over the surface with their long legs. Neither is identification easy. This one is an **Elliot's Storm-petrel**, with its square tail and white rump patch. The white belly patch is not easily seen. It's the only petrel that follows boats.

strong flight

back sooty black brown shine

long wings
black rump
fairly long notched tail
small wingbar
silvery shine

Here on Rábida we could see small downy chicks in nearly every nest. In the colony at Bahía Urbina on Isabela, which we had visited three days earlier, the chicks were nearly all full-grown and some could fly. Each colony may have its particular breeding cycle.

Some birds were still incubating or had just hatched chicks which we could not see. This all-brown bird had no white head feathers. Only the red around its eyes indicates that it is in breeding condition.

already breeding but head not white (mottled)

brown duller than 'full' adult

golden cast

mottled

not all adults have these white ornamental tufts

Rábida, the red island, where beach, rocks and everything beyond seemed red. Even the seals lying on the beach were stained red. The salt water in the lagoon was reddish and, even more peculiar, nearly all breeding **Brown Pelicans** in the mangrove colony had mostly reddish brown heads. I had thought these pelicans breed only when they have white, gold-tinged heads. Here they were breeding with brown heads. We had seen this previously in the colony at Bahía Urbina on Isabela, but here on Rábida nearly all breeders were in this brown-headed plumage.

We also sailed along the Rábida coast in our dinghy to watch some fur seals and again saw pelican nests. Here the chicks were larger but still in their down that looked like greyish fur, as if they had copied the fur seals below. Why were these chicks larger? Is the rocky coast a better breeding place or is it occupied by older, more experienced pelicans? If so, they should have had white heads. Most were brown-headed as in the mangrove colony.

The juvenile's bill is dark grey. When breeding, the upper mandible becomes paler with a yellow nail at the tip and a scarlet caste to the edge. I do not know how long the colour changes take.

Brown Pelicans can breed when approximately two years old, quite early for such a large bird. At this age the head is not completely white like that of older birds. Here in the Galápagos, plumage seems more complicated. In some colonies all breeding birds have mostly brown heads with more or less white freckles. In other colonies, a majority of breeding birds had completely white heads. The naked facial skin around the yellow eye also varies in colour but breeding birds have at least some red around the eyes, even when the rest is greyish or even purplish.

On one side of Rábida there is a short, rather gentle walk on a red trail up to the cliff edge. From this cliff one has a beautiful view over the island and the sea towards Santiago. Whilst there, I watched a small compact flock of four Galápagos Doves flying in circles, higher and higher over the island, returning rapidly to the ground several times, and later joined by three more individuals. All seven flew even higher than before. I could only see them as small dots before they flew towards nearby Santiago, about 4 km away. It seemed they were afraid to fly too low over the sea. Flying higher helps them escape the patrolling frigatebirds. I followed them with my binoculars till they dropped down very rapidly over Santiago.

Other landbirds included three Large-billed Flycatchers near the coast and some rather dark coloured Mockers with broad, pale collars. I wondered if they would also fly over to the nearby Santiago as the doves had done. On a small island such as Rábida the population would soon 'evolve' if there were no contact with other populations. I noticed differences in the Mockers from Genovesa and St Cruz, and I remembered the very pale Mockingbirds I saw years ago on St Fé. It's strange that Pinzón, the island south of Rábida and between St Cruz and Isabela, has no Mockingbirds.

I think of a heron as a wetland species so it was peculiar to see them here in the Galápagos standing on bare lava, in typical hunched posture and, even more exotically, under a large cactus. The two here on Rábida were very pale, paler than we had seen anywhere else on other islands: they had no trace of chestnut under the black epaulets nor cinnamon thighs. They looked like pale European Grey Herons and not like **Great Blue Herons**, which of course they were.

Rábida has eight finch species (a large number for such a small island) compared with ten on nearby Santiago and only nine on the much larger St Cruz.

Next to Seymour, Rábida is one of the best islands for visitors to the archipelago to watch from a dinghy the two Galápagos pinnipeds side by side. Galápagos sealion has its origin in the northern hemisphere and is common on all islands. There are about 50,000 (1995) in the Galápagos, and they belong to a small subspecies, called *wollebacki*, of the widespread Californian sealion, *Zalaphus c. californicus*. Despite being smaller, a full-grown bull still weighs as much as three men, about 250–300 kg. The more slender and graceful female is only a third the weight of the male, about 80 kg. It's the females you see lying on the beach, on sand, amongst rocks, or even sometimes in lagoons, baking in the sun while the bull controls and guards his harem of up to 30 cows. Many bulls have no harem and gather in 'bachelor' colonies.

The smaller, more stockily-built Galápagos fur seal is less often seen than sealions, although the population is nearly as large. They are less tolerant of heat, preferring cooler water and more rugged coasts with plenty of places to shelter from the sun during the day. They are of southern origin and are closely related to the southern fur seal, *Arctocephalus australis*, which lives along the rocky shores of South America from Peru down to some sub-Antarctic islands, and also in cooler waters up to southern Brazil. The Galápagos fur seal, *Arctocephalus galapagoensis* (*Arcto* = bear, *cephalus* = head), is, despite its name, a sealion. They do look bear-like with their short head, and are often called 'sea-bear' in other languages (*Seebär* in German for example). They were once heavily hunted for their fur and nearly brought to extinction. Now they are protected.

A black fin just beside our dinghy. At first I thought it was a shark.

A large stranded whale, smelling strongly, lay on the red Rábida beach. I thought it was a humpback. Tony our guide was about to tell us which species it was when we saw a black fin in the water and further away another one. No, they were not sharks' fins. They are the typical fins of **pilot whales**, which were all around us in a compact school. Some leapt out of the water. They were rather small, 3-4 m long. Our dinghy bobbed about, water splashed all over us. Barnaby had to protect his camera. Then one surfaced like a submarine and this one was really large, much longer than our dinghy, perhaps 7-8 m. It was exciting to see these large mammals so close. We followed them easily and they didn't seem to fear us.

rounded fin

the false killer whale has a cucumber-shaped dorsal fin, bent backwards. The orca or killer whale's fin is long and points upwards

short rounded head

The slightly smaller, very similar, all-black false killer whale has a longer, more elegant head. The larger orca has white patches on its black body. Other whales are much larger, and the greyish dolphins smaller.

When seen clearly, the short rounded dorsal fin, positioned to the front of the pilot whale's back, makes identification easy. The round and rather heavy-looking head is also conspicuous. The old males in particular often look as if they are 'melon headed'. The elongated head of the females and immatures could be confused with that of false killer whale but the cucumber-shaped fin is positioned nearer the middle of the body. Pilot whales have long narrow sickle-shaped flippers, false killer and orca both have shorter, rounded flippers. (Pilot whales usually show only the front part of the heavy cigar-shaped body when they rise slowly to the surface, so only the first third is seen and the placement of the dorsal fin is difficult to judge.)

Pilot whales are still common in Galápagos waters but not so numerous as they once were. Schools of 5–20 can often be observed. We saw eight but there could have been more. One or two surface at a time and their fin or back is seen briefly. They dive again and swim close together in the same direction, so they are difficult to count. Is there a leader in the group? This gregarious habit (schools can be much larger than 20, over 100 have been observed) made them easy prey to whalers. Hunted for their oil, the frozen meat was sold as dog food. This inoffensive animal is now better protected but hunting still occurs, both legal and clandestine.

Dolphins are very well known for their acrobatics. False killer whales also vault but only in low flat curves, just clearing the water. **Pilot whales** leap only when very young, also in a flat arch, not emerging much from the water, and could be confused with false killers. However, young pilots are never far from their parents, staying in compact schools.

the nostril, called blowhole

A fully grown adult male pilot whale can be 8.5 m long and weigh 4 tons. Compared with the 20-m length and 60 tons of a fin whale (from the same Galápagos waters), the pilot is quite small. The female is even smaller at 6 m and about half the weight of the male. Dolphins are only about 2 m long and weigh 120 kg. Bottle-nosed dolphin is larger, at 3 m and up to 350 kg, so the pilot whale is still large compared with them. The similar all-black male false killer whale is around 6 m long and weighs 2 tons; the female is 4.5 m and weighs only 1 ton.

Only the first third of the cigar-shaped body is out of the water. The rather long dorsal fin and swollen bulbous forehead show this is a male. When older, the forehead can be even heavier and more conspicuous. They surface regularly, head first, to breathe and blast water about 45 m into the air. They can stay under water for nearly two hours and dive to 350 m.

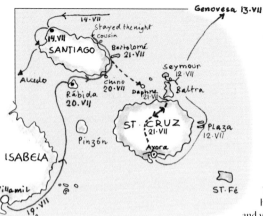

We had now visited about half the places we wanted to see. The green terra alta on St Cruz for landbirds; lagoons near Ayora and the Darwin Station (many finches); Plaza, Seymour and outlying Genovesa with different colonies of large seabirds on each island; the dry bushland on Santiago with tame doves and hawks; the long walk up to the well-vegetated Alcedo volcano on Isabela with its large tortoises and dry bushland landbirds; several coastal places on west Isabela, and Punta Espinosa on Fernandina with penguin, cormorant and pelican colonies; the red island, Rábida – and now to Sombrero Chino, the tourist island Bartolomé and, the day after, Daphne, the finch island. I would also have liked to have visited Pinzón, but this island is not open to visitors. We wanted to return to the terra alta on St Cruz because we had missed the rails, little secretive birds. St Fé, just opposite and visible from Ayora, was not on our itinerary. Barnaby had been there last year. For me, the most interesting bird on St Fé is the very pale Warbler Finch. Our plan was to visit the southern islands, Floreana, Española and San Cristóbal, with their mockingbirds, albatrosses and some other specialities.

From Rábida we sailed along the coast of Santiago towards Sombrero Chino, a small island just off the Santiago coast. The sea was calm and we saw very few birds the entire way. Before reaching the 'Sombrero', near Cabo Trenton, for the first time we saw a concentration of Masked Boobies. We had always seen them at sea, never more than five together; there were more than two dozen here. They may have been from the colony on the Islas Beagle, small islands lying south of Santiago.

These normally pelagic Masked were fishing close to the coast. They looked very noble in their silver-white plumage with golden yellow bill and jet black in their wings. Unusually there were no Blue-footed Boobies around. Some Magnificent Frigatebirds sailed above the Masked but did not come near the water. When groups of Masked flew south, some frigatebirds followed. Do they attack boobies only when they are near the colony?

The entrance to the 'Bay of Chino' is fantastic, with the large wide lava flows of Santiago to the left and on the right the evenly shaped Sombrero Chino, exactly like the 'Chinese Hat' of the island's name. There are no trees on Chino, just some low bushes growing mainly near the beach. The bay was as calm as a table top and a deep greenish blue, a colour I had never seen so brilliantly before. Barnaby and Tony wanted to dive into the clear water. We saw many fish and also some seals around our dinghy. I wanted to see which birds were on this island.

First there was a warbler on the beach, searching for food between the small marine iguanas. On the little track I watched many lizards for a long time. They were neither shy nor very colourful, small and different from the ones I had seen earlier on Rábida. A large dark hawk sat motionless like a statue on a lava block. It stayed there the entire time I was on the island like a decoration on top of the 'hat'. I found an Audubon's Shearwater colony in a wide open cave overhanging the sea, 7–10 m high. Flocks of 30–40 birds calling, but not loudly, flew in and out disappearing into small holes or crevices. There must have been hundreds. A few Elliot's Storm-petrels also flew into the same cave, perhaps they also breed there too. Lava Herons stood near the waterline undisturbed by the waves. A pair of Lava Gulls and lots of noddies patrolled the shore. Pelicans and Blue-footed Boobies fished between the boulders. It was peculiar not to find finches here. True, there are no bushes, only low shrubby vegetation, but I saw another Yellow Warbler, a bright male singing, while I watched the shearwaters.

Elliot's Storm-petrel 20 July 95 Sombrero Chino

Audubon's Shearwater Sombrero Chino

I was almost too close to these Audubon's when I sketched them from a rock a few metres above their colony as they flew in and out. It is better to keep at a distance when they are sailing over the waves to study the pattern on their underwings.

Several times, down here, south of the equator, I had difficulty orienting myself. At home, or travelling in Africa south of the equator, my bearings are usually clear to me. Here I had to study the map or ask our captain to be certain, and even then I could not believe that north was not south.

We left Cousin early in the morning and sailed south to Bartolomé, which we had passed yesterday in the narrow channel that separates this island from Santiago. Bartolomé is just over one square km and has some of the most fantastic scenery in the Galápagos. The 114-m summit, bare and moonlike, dominates the larger eastern part of the isle. The needle-shaped Pinnacle Rock on the smaller western part points north. Two bare islands are connected by a narrow green strip, a lagoon edged with white sandy beaches where marine turtles breed. We did not see any, but many turtle eggs lay empty on the white sand, possibly eaten by rats whose footprints were everywhere. It should be quite easy to eradicate rats on such a small island. We saw no finches in the green strip, just Yellow Warblers, and the only other landbird was a Galápagos Hawk that had flown over from nearby Santiago.

When we arrived at Bartolomé several tourist boats were anchored in the calm waters on the northern side. For most Galápagos visitors, this island with its unique landscape is a 'must', but since it is very small only limited numbers of visitors are allowed at one time. Everyone must keep strictly to the marked tracks; the lava is very fragile, the lagoon is small and care must be taken not to walk on the green sea turtle nests. There is rich sealife and good diving in the calm northern bay.

After a dry landing, there is a trail, at first over dusty tough lava, then partly over wooden steps up to the 114-m summit; an easy walk, not tiring. At the summit there is a panoramic view over the Galápagos. To the west, close by, is Santiago with its wild mountain formations, and Sullivan Bay, empty, with large wide black lava flows and a few white beaches with oasis-like green mangroves and other small patches of vegetation behind, protected by the large mountains. Towards the south, Pinzón, the closed island, and behind it, in the distance, when the weather is clear, the mountain and volcanos of Isabela. To the east, Daphne, the finch island, our next destination, with Seymour and Baltra beyond, both near Santa Cruz. While we were there a hawk came soaring over the narrow channel from Santiago. It sailed over our heads all the time we were on the summit. Another hawk hung over the black lava flow on Santiago.

Here the visitors' influence is clearly seen. To the right and left of the trail posts the first pioneer vegetation occurs but on the trail there is only dust. Of course the trail had been cleared of rocks, but uncontrolled walking would turn the whole island into a dusty trail.

hornitos

The view not only over the Pacific but over all the islands around, near and far, is fantastic. The immediate view is very dramatic. Down to the west, the smaller part of the island (marked on the right), Pinnacle Rock, pointing north with the narrow land bridge connecting the two parts of the island. The emerald green sea on the left and the blue bay to the right, changing colour with the light, were most impressive. The clear waters are a paradise for diving and snorkling. Up here one can also see how small the little green oasis is and how vulnerable it could be to the slightest disturbance. Down on the sandy beaches green sea turtles breed. It is essential to stick to the marked trail. Throughout the archipelago, trails are marked by small white posts (which do not spoil the views). So varied is this small island that the walk up to the summit is like a lesson in vulcanology.

On the cinder slopes, as here, tiquilia is the only plant to be found. Higher up there are a few scalesia and low tree-sized opuntias. Tiquilias are low silver-grey shrubs with small leaves. In the wet season they become a little, but not much, greener. Their flowers are tiny. The plants are spaced regularly, as if planted by man, forming here on Bartolomé a patchwork mat. One wonders how a plant can live in these dry conditions. The only other life I saw between the plants comprised a few insects and lava lizards. Life on Bartolomé is restricted to the small landbridge and around the shore.

Bartolomé is a good place to study different forms of lava. Most is crisp and tough, and even Pinnacle Rock is the remains of a much larger, now eroded, tough cone. Typical here are 'hornitos' (driblet cones, in English). These are like miniature volcanos formed by gas trapped in pockets under the flowing lava. In some places moisture turned into steam and the escaping gas bubbled up through the flowing lava to form even-shaped hornitos. They are seldom very high, mostly under 1 m and often occur in straight lines at regular distances, following the course of the lava. More occur on the black lava flow in Sullivan Bay across the channel on Santiago.

Amazing **lava cactuses**, growing in a cluster or clump, are often the only plant for miles on barren lava. The younger parts of the plant have bright yellow spines, the others are grey-green with a golden tinge. Old plants turn blackish when dying. To see their flowers you have to be up early. They open before dawn and by 8 am have already shrivelled.

Galápagos Penguins breed only on Isabela and Fernandina. Here on Bartolomé they can be seen all year round, mostly fishing in the bay between Pinnacle Rock and the landing stage or resting between the black lava boulders on the shore where, with all the holes and crevices, they could easily nest. Breeding has not been recorded here. Unlike their similar but larger South American cousins, Humboldt and Magellanic Penguins, Galápagos Penguins breed only in small colonies of a few pairs.

We left Bartolomé at midday and sailed southeast towards Daphne. The sea was rough and I felt unwell, but even worse, I worried that we would not be able to land on Isla Daphne Major. I had long dreamt of visiting the island, which is of special interest to me. Although called Major, it is only a small island. Just north of it is the even smaller Isla Daphne Menor. Both are nicely shaped crater tops, just poking their heads out of the sea. When we were close enough for a good view of the island the sea was still very rough, but less so than when we crossed the middle of the Canal de San Salvador. The island looked inaccessible. We turned slowly round to the southern side of the island and there the sea was a bit calmer. Tony thought we could land; at least we would try. There were seabirds everywhere, mostly Blue-footed Boobies, some Magnificent Frigatebirds and snowy white Masked Boobies with their jet black wingtips. Noisy tropicbirds chased around in groups of 3–4 in acrobatic flight around the steep cliffs. Swallow-tailed Gulls also sailed around including one juvenile, which until now, we had only seen a few of in flight. Noddies were numerous, some feeding their nearly full-grown chicks on the cliffs.

A juvenile Great Blue Heron hidden behind a bush. He scratched his head as if asking himself what we were doing there. Then he came out from cover and had a closer look at us.

The landing was not too difficult but we had to wait for the right moment to jump onto the rocks from our tossing dinghy. A small path leads from the shore up to the crater's edge, the only track one is allowed to take. The first bird we saw on landing was not a finch but a heron. I wondered what it was doing because there is no shore for fishing and the water surrounding the island is too deep to wade in, even for such a large heron. Since it was near the tourist trail, perhaps it was just a daily visitor like us. The highest point on the crater rim on Daphne Major is 120 m. The whole island, desert-like with only sparse vegetation and a deep wide open crater, is a paradise for seabirds. Steep cliffs all around the island, undercut by the waves, make it inaccessible. Boats can find no anchorage and dinghies cannot land. We needed a special permit (limited to a particular day and only given to small groups) to visit the island.

There are only four regular finch species on Daphne, but they were studied by Peter and Rosemary Grant, English scientists in the Department of Ecology and Evolution at Princeton University, for over 20 years. The Grants ringed, measured, observed and studied all the finches on the island and knew them individually. The population ranges, depending on the rains, between 200 and 1,000 individuals. I wanted to see these finches and also the conditions in which the Grants worked on this island, lonely even by Galápagos standards. We had seen the island twice before, the day we landed on Baltra and this morning from the summit of Bartolomé, lying far out at sea like a nutshell.

From the rim, the crater looks like an amphitheatre. On the flat guano-covered bottom are scattered hundreds of Blue-footed Booby nests. On sunny days, and this is nearly every day in the Galápagos, it must be very hot down there.

We walked up the trail to the rim of the volcano. It is rather steep in places and it's not always easy to walk on the loose and broken rocks. Many boobies had nested on the upper part of the trail and we had to avoid their long darting necks and pointed bills. So as not to disturb them too much, we had to walk around them, thus creating a new trail if many visitors do the same thing. In this way the sides of the trail are eroded very quickly; one reason to keep visitor numbers low. Except for *Opuntia* cactuses, some rather low Palo Santo trees and low shrubs like tiquilia and chamaesya as pioneer plants, there is not much vegetation on this island.

Once up on the crater's edge, there is a beautiful view down to the round and flat-bottomed crater floor where the boobies breed, with frigatebirds nesting on the bushes growing up the sides. The crater floor is the only really flat ground on the island. I wondered where the scientists had camped for such long periods. It was not possible down in the crater and there is no flat ground anywhere on the slopes. There is no shelter. In stormy weather it must be very windy and to fix a tent in this loose rough lava must be nearly impossible. Both Barnaby and I doubted whether we would like to stay in such a desert-like place for long.

A closer view of the typical white circles around each nest made by the droppings of the owners and their chicks. There must be a good layer of guano down in the crater. In years with heavy rains, the whole flat floor can be covered with water for a short time, a disaster for breeding birds.

This is also a good place to watch flying seabirds from above. This young Magnificent Frigatebird, on one of its first flights, shows the species' extremely long, broad wings, deeply forked tail and white head, which changes slowly to all black when in full adult plumage.

The bushes around the crater wall are covered with frigatebird nests (all are Magnificent). I wonder how the Blue-footed Boobies down on the floor manage to feed their chicks properly with these pirates around, but I saw no harassment.

Daphne really is 'tropicbird' island. We had seen these birds breeding on Plaza and Genovesa, but not in such numbers nor so well as here on Daphne. They are colonial nesters and the steep slopes of the crater must be very attractive to them. They make their nests in holes under overhanging ledges. Every pair jealously guards its nest site and serious fights often occur. Here on Daphne they were always quarrelsome and noisy, and we saw up to a dozen in display flights. They are most elegant with their silver-white plumage and long tail streamers, but also clown-like with their carrot-coloured bills. They breed all year round on Daphne, while on Plaza, not far away on the other side of Santa Cruz, they breed annually.

tail

a tropicbird's tail
and bill protruding
from the nest

bill

At first I thought it was
a dead bird lying behind
the rock. When I looked more
closely, the bird stared into my
eye. It was sitting on eggs, so I
slowly moved away to avoid
disturbing the bird

20/VII Daphne

Blue-footed Boobies nest down on the flat crater floor. Magnificent Frigatebirds make their flimsy nests, a poorly made platform of sticks and branches, held together mostly by their own guano, in the low bushes that grow in patches all around the crater wall.

The larger brilliant snowy white Masked Boobies nest on the crater's rim and on the steep outer slopes that lead down to the sea. Like their Blue-footed cousins, they also breed on the ground with a white guano ring around the nest scrape.

Masked Boobies always breed on cliffs or rocks, not on flat ground like Blue-footed, and they like space between their nests. They are the only booby species in the Galápagos to have an annual breeding cycle. Blue-footed breed almost continuously in their large dense colonies, each pair breed at seven- to nine-month intervals. Masked lay two large chalky white eggs and both parents incubate. Only one chick is reared to maturity. The stronger, generally the first born, will kill the younger and weaker sibling, improving its own chances of survival. The second egg is a kind of insurance in case the first gets damaged or the chick dies. We know this from other birds such as Golden Eagle, where two eggs are laid and one young fledges. Blue-footed lay two or even three eggs and could raise all the young. The tree-nesting Red-footed Booby lays only one egg, very rarely two, but often has great difficulties in raising just one chick.

Newly born Masked, like all booby chicks, are downy and grey-white. When the first dark primaries appear they look like dark-billed adults, but more doll-like. Blue-footed at this age are similar but have darker feet.

▲
The courtship display is a simple affair. The male, after landing in his territory, potters around without showing his feet to his mate (as Blue-footed males do). He lengthens his neck, points his bill to the sky, lifts his wings a little and whistles. Newly formed pairs at this stage are often rather aggressive. When they know each other well, the larger female comes close to the male, both bodies facing the same way, they look forwards, sideways, all rather stiffly and then fling their heads at each other and clash bills. It looks like they may bite each other but this is their way of 'kissing'. This can go on for hours. The female vocalizes continuously: raucous calls, quacks and even yells which can be heard over a long distance. This display looks quite aggressive compared with that of the more playful and courtly Blue-footed Boobies.

◄ A good looking young Masked Booby. At this age they look quite different from their parents and more like young Blue-footed, only smarter. The belly is whiter and Masked have a white collar while its cousin only has a white neck patch just above the mantle. Blue-footed also has the dark area spreading from the neck over the breast; this is the best way to identify them later when they can fly.

bill colour in all is variable

Medium Ground-finch

Small Ground-finch

Large Ground-finch

Cactus-finch

all have black bill when breeding

Three ground-finches and Common Cactus-finch breed on Daphne. All are closely related and of the same genus: *Geospiza*. They are separated by size and bill shape.

Common Cactus-finch is the most specialized of the four Daphne finches. It is never found far from cactuses, where it nests and finds food. When on the ground it looks like the other three species, more elegant and longer-billed.

The same female, showing her large, broad head with its massive but rather narrow bill, a perfect tool to open large, hard seeds, which none of the other three finches can tackle.

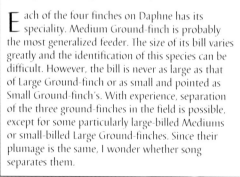

Large Ground-finch is by far the largest finch on Daphne. Here a female shows her enormous bill. The plumage in all three ground-finch species is identical.

Each of the four finches on Daphne has its speciality. Medium Ground-finch is probably the most generalized feeder. The size of its bill varies greatly and the identification of this species can be difficult. However, the bill is never as large as that of Large Ground-finch or as small and pointed as Small Ground-finch's. With experience, separation of the three ground-finches in the field is possible, except for some particularly large-billed Mediums or small-billed Large Ground-finches. Since their plumage is the same, I wonder whether song separates them.

A jet black male Common Cactus-finch with thick but elongated bill which turns from pale to all-black in the breeding season. When reverting to non-breeding plumage, the change starts at the base of the bill.

F rom high up on Daphne, our ship looked vulnerable on the almost black, wild water below. The coast around Daphne is so deep that we could not anchor, so the ship slowly drifted away from the coast. We had to signal our captain to approach the shore to meet our dinghy.

[handwritten map labels: Daphne, tourist trail, our dinghy, Seymour 12·VII, o Menor, o Mosquera, Daphne Mayor 21·VII, only with a special permit, 22·VII, here we found Galápagos tomatoes, ISLA SANTA CRUZ, Los Gemelos, Cerro Crocker, Plaza 12·VII, △ 768, △ 864, 10·VII, St Rosa, El Chato 22·VII, Caseta, farm land, Bellavista, TORTOISE RESERVE, AYORA 10-12 VII, 10·VII, places you can visit]

From Daphne we sailed to the Canal de Itabaca between Baltra and St Cruz. Having just seen ground-finches on Daphne, I wanted to watch them at the landing stage. All three species were present but I could not see any differences. St Cruz is most interesting. Here are found nearly all the habitats in the Galápagos including flat sandy shores, rocky cliffs, lagoons, slopes (to over 850 m), dry deserts, bare and empty or with fast-growing cactus, wet jungle and steppe-like grassland; untouched areas next to cultivated land, endemic plant communities next to areas with introduced trees and plants, and mixed areas where original plants have been destroyed by newcomers. Most native birds are found on St Cruz. Ten of the 13 finches live on this island, only Sharp-beaked is believed extinct here, but in Ayora we had seen a bird which could have been this species.

The top of a crater, just poking out of the deep black sea, only 32 ha of lava and nearly inaccessible, that's Daphne. Bare and desert-like from a distance, seabirds flying everywhere. It is a breeding bird's paradise: down on the crater floor, a large dense Blue-footed Booby colony, up on the crater walls in bushes (Daphne is not quite a desert) breeding Magnificent Frigatebirds. A large colony of Masked Boobies (well spaced nests) inhabits the slopes, mostly on the northeastern side. Red-billed Tropicbirds nest on the steeper western and southern slopes. Both Masked Boobies and the tropicbirds are quarrelsome. Audubon's Shearwaters breed on the steep cliffs along the waterline, next to Madeiran Storm-petrels and Common Noddies. We also saw some Swallow-tailed Gulls there. White-bellied Storm-petrels were dancing over the rough sea like butterflies. I don't know if they breed on Daphne. From August until April phalaropes stay in these waters, often in large numbers. When the sea is too rough to land it is always worth sailing around Daphne to watch the plentiful seabirds.

On the road from Canal de Itabaca to Ayora
on the other side of St Cruz, we stopped at
'Los Gemelos', the twins, two craters surrounded
by a dense *Scalesia* forest, one on each side
of the road. From the narrow track we had
an impressive view down into the crater,
overcrowded with vegetation. Here we watched
the fascinating **Vermillion Flycatcher** in its
bright red plumage, contrasting strongly with
its deep green surroundings. Several 'phlegmatic'
Vegetarian Finches searched for food in the trees.
They looked more at home than those we had
seen in the drier habitat below the Alcedo volcano
on Isabela. Here, up in the trees, they looked like
parrots. I heard a rail calling only a metre or
two from my feet but could not see the bird
in the dense undergrowth. The call sounded
like 'kick-kick-kick-koa'. Was this the 'Pachay',
the all-dark small Galápagos Rail? I watched
for a long time but did not see it. I should have
stayed longer here; like all rails they are curious
and will eventually come to look at you.
It depends on who can wait the longest!

From the moist green highlands we drove down to the dry and sleepy town of Ayora to buy fresh food for the next week. Barnaby wanted to take some pictures of the boatyard, a workshop on the road to the Darwin Station. Craftsmen were working slowly on two boats under the hot tropical sun. I don't know if they used local wood or not. One boat was just a frame, the other was nearly finished. One must be a good craftsman to build something like this in the open air. The boats looked more like works of art than seaworthy vessels.

At the roadside most of the plants and trees have been introduced, like this beautiful but poisonous climbing datura, locally called Trompeta del Angel.

Long-legged skinny cows of all colours, a mixture of different breeds. Is it worthwhile farming here?

We wanted to visit El Chato in the terra alta, where we could see giant tortoise and possibly one or even both native rails. To get close to the reserve we paid $20 to be driven over a private farm track for only 4–5 km; that's more expensive than a French motorway! We could see the influence of farming on the land, a steppe-like landscape with some bushes, unlike English cattle pastures. There were ground-finches everywhere and, near a farmhouse, a pair of Woodpecker Finches in some high trees. Vermillion Flycatchers displayed their territorial flight along the fences. Most common were the two newcomers, anis in the high reed-like grass, and Cattle Egrets with the cows. All these birds seemed to benefit from farming.

We passed through some open woodland invaded by guava trees which were laden with fruit. Though we did not see this, perhaps the fruit is eaten by Small Tree-finches. Foreign plants such as the aggressive guava could easily be a danger to endemic species; some are now well established on the terra alta and they are difficult or even impossible to control. They could easily overgrow the whole native forest.

I was amazed to see Galápagos Doves up here in the forest. We had watched them before on the coral pebble beach on Genovesa and in the dry desert-like habitats on Isabela and Daphne. Now, in this wet forest, like African Green Pigeons, they searched for food in the trees and on the dark forest floor where they looked like the Ruddy Quail Dove of the Greater Antilles. They were not so numerous up here, only in singles or pairs, unlike the hundreds we saw in the dry bush of Santiago. As the only dove in the Galápagos they use all habitats, and if left undisturbed the doves would evolve into different habitat-related species.

There is still some beautiful *Scalesia pedunculata* forest in the humid highlands of St Cruz, with trees up to 15 m high. Looking at the thick trunks of the *Lechosa* trees, it's difficult to believe they belong to the daisy and sunflower family. A composite with light seeds, they can colonize all the habitats in the humid zone more easily than 'real' trees with heavy seeds. There are now 15 different *Scalesia* species in the Galápagos, with about 20 different forms. In theory they are the plant equivalent of the Darwin's finches. Now protected by law, like all Galápagos endemic plants, their greatest danger is from guava, which on San Cristóbal has nearly overgrown the *Miconia robinsoniana*, a shrub growing in dense thickets 2–5 m high.

This Short-eared Owl, with bright yellow staring eyes, peering out of dark green vegetation in the dense *Scalesia* forest, reminds me of a Long-eared Owl in a northern hemisphere wood. Normally this cosmopolitan owl lives on moorland and heath. Here in the Galápagos, it has adapted to all habitats, breeding on the dry bare plateau on Genovesa and also in this dense vegetation. They hunt their prey, mostly birds, rats and mice, by day and night but are most active at dawn or in the early mornings. Their dog-like barking and yapping is mostly heard at night.

Leaving the farmland and walking through the *Scalesia* forest, we arrived in a large open space in the middle of which was a large shallow freshwater pool surrounded by luxurious vegetation. Giant tortoises were lying in the water. It was very hot so perhaps they were having their siesta. One was taking a mud bath at the edge of the pool. It was obvious from the trails leading into the forest that the tortoises come here regularly. There were also clear pig footprints in the mud and I found a wallow where they had taken their mud bath. Although feral pigs are not a danger to adult tortoises, they are to newly hatched and small young. Pigs eat everything. To control them on such a large and partly inaccessible island would be difficult if not impossible. A solution would be to import meat from Ecuador and not breed pigs anywhere on the islands.

Out of the dense vegetation I again heard the 'Kick-Keck-Kek-Koah' call, slightly different at the end of the phrase but similar to the call I had heard on 'Los Gemelos'. We waited motionless, and this time the mystery bird came out from the cover, a small all-dark, mouse-like **Galápagos Rail**. I just had time to make some quick sketches before it disappeared back into the thick vegetation, leaving footprints in the mud. For a rail, the toes were rather short. This was the only Galápagos Rail we saw during our entire visit.

There were Moorhens in the water next to the tortoise. They disappeared into the bushes when we arrived, but eight White-cheeked Pintails continued feeding in the typical dabbling-duck manner with their heads under the water. Perhaps the pond was shallow. There were three adult females with rather dull cheeks but large red spots on their bills, and five immatures looking even duller with brownish cheeks. I could not make out which of the three females was the mother. Five young seemed very few for three females since each can lay up to ten eggs. Barnaby breeds them in France where perhaps they have bigger clutches than in the Galápagos. This is often the case with island forms. There were no males (with their pure white cheeks), but this is normal. Only the females care for their brood, while males look for other females or group together in the lowlands. The ducks were not shy, only one flew up once, showing the green 'mirror' in her wings, and dropped down again between the sleeping giant tortoises.

A bird I really wanted to see was **Paint-billed Crake**, only discovered in the Galápagos in 1953. They are very secretive, but are seen more often than the smaller Galápagos Rail. Paint-billed is a bird of the farmland zones so perhaps we were too high up here in the forest. I wondered too if two small rails would live as neighbours in the same habitat. We failed to see Paint-billed during our stay (*see* p. 205).

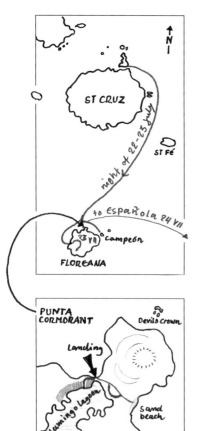

We left the Canal de Itabaca late in the afternoon, and sailed along the eastern coast of Santa Cruz. It was very mild and the sea was calm. We passed the two Islas Plaza at nightfall. Many Swallow-tailed Gulls passed our boat, dark silhouettes flying in one direction out to sea, taking no notice of our boat.

We arrived at the Floreana coast at 3 am after a very pleasant night and dropped anchor in the small bay at Punta Cormorant. I wonder how it got this name. Cormorants never come down to this southern island and only breed on the coasts of Isabela and Fernandina. There were four penguins fishing in the bay and they also breed on the two larger western islands. Otherwise, we saw only a few birds including six Brown Pelicans behind our ship, a lonely shearwater, one Galápagos Storm-petrel and some Magnificent Frigatebirds. Blue-footed Boobies were nesting in a scattered colony, quite different from the denser breeding sites we had seen before.

After a leisurely breakfast we landed on the brown beach which was speckled with greenish olivine crystals. A few lazy sealions were in the shallow water or lying on the beach with two flamingos strolling around. Just beyond this greenish glittering beach lies a large lagoon separated by a narrow strip of land with some bushes. We could smell the lagoon from a distance. There were four more flamingos in the lagoon and about ten stilts, some in immature plumage. We saw seven adult pintails, then a mother with four nearly full-grown ducklings feeding in the smelly, shallow water.

It was very calm here, even after some tourists from another boat arrived. We also visited the far side of the small spit. It's only a short walk, passing a dune with low bushes full of finches, but we saw only one warbler, a yellow-breasted female with a green crown. The beach here has nice white sand and is much longer and wider than at the landing stage. It's important to keep to the tourist track since sea turtles lay their eggs on this beach.

a dinghy   waiting tourist boats

Tourist boats waiting further out, away from the shallow coast, where even a dinghy can't get too close. You have to wade through the shallow water and be careful not to approach a territorial bull sealion when he also wants to go ashore. Normally the bull patrols further out in deeper water.

Female sealions in the water or on the beach are usually docile, except when with a new born pup. It is best to keep your distance, their teeth are very powerful. The two flamingos just strolled along the beach. It is a particular habit of Galápagos Flamingos to keep to small groups, and even singles are normal. They are different from the flamingos I know so well on the French coast, where flocks have at least 20-30 birds, usually even more when wandering away from their enormous breeding colony of several thousand pairs. Even when they are so tame their privacy should be respected and one should not approach closer than the boy in this photograph.

We had seen flamingos on Isabela, in the lagoons behind the small village of Villamil, where they kept their distance. They were not particularly shy there but less confident than on Floreana. Possibly they had learned in their long lives (flamingos can live up to 30 years) that man is not so harmless as large sealions. I wonder if there is any contact between flamingos on this outlying island and the more northerly islands.

We had seen flamingos far out at sea, flying the 30 km from Isabela to Santa Cruz. That's the distance between England and France. It is nearly twice the distance down here to Floreana. Flamingos are strong flyers. Why is a bird more reserved on one island and not the other? I had noticed this behaviour with Nordic waders on the coast of Namibia in Southern Africa, where Little Stints walked over my shoes, whilst a week earlier on the coast of Holland they flew off when I was 50 m away. Birds seem to know where and when they will not be molested. At home, a tame Raven eats from my hand but keeps its distance when I see the same bird some kilometres away from home – and I know it recognizes me!

The two here were really confident and we could observe them (only 3–4 m away) while they were having their siesta— standing on one leg. Another landed right next to us and displayed its large webbed feet.

Flamingos take all their food mainly algae, shrimp and water boat men from muddy water. They have a specially shaped bill that is unique in the bird world

when feeding, they hold the bill upside-down (unlike ducks) filtering small food out of mostly muddy water with special lamellas inside the bill. They prefer to feed in shallow lagoons but the long neck and feet allow them to feed in fairly deep water. When neccessary, they will swim and up-end to feed (like ducks)

Galápagos Flamingos have pale pink feet with bright pink joints. Colour is very individual. The related Chilean Flamingo has greyish legs with pink while the even more closely related Old World Greater Flamingo has all-pink feet and legs.

Most ornithologists believe that Galápagos Flamingos represent an outpost population of Caribbean flamingo. I think they are quite different. They are not so large, and I have not seen any so pink as a normal Caribbean flamingo. Their colour is closer to that of Greater Flamingo from the Old World. They differ also in their way of life. They are not seen in such large concentrations as any of the other five flamingo species worldwide. There are probably no more than 500 altogether in the Galápagos, spread over the lagoons on all the larger islands. They breed in about a dozen colonies with only a few pairs in each. This is an adaptation to the habitats of the Galápagos: small lagoons with limited food.

The flamingos here are not only a different subspecies from the Caribbean but, like most of the birds in the Galápagos, are moving to full species status. A population of about 500 birds means fewer than 200 breeding pairs since they first breed when about five years old. All Galápagos Flamingos must be very closely related and I am sure there is no contact with the Caribbean birds on the other side of Central America. Since their arrival in the Galápagos, a long time ago, they have been isolated from all other flamingo populations. Should a larger, deeper pink Caribbean flamingo find its way to these Pacific islands it would be quickly detected by observers.

The sign behind this feeding flamingo means: 'Never go behind it', even when the lagoon is dry. The flamingo population is small and vulnerable, and birds must be left alone. The flamingos can be observed from a short distance and must not be approached too closely.

typical conical nest mound made of mud →

when just born, the bill is straight but has the full curved shape when the bird is about 40 days old

legs dark

In their grey down they look like long-legged goslings. When there is not enough food in the lagoon, the parents will leave their half-grown brownish grey young alone to fend for themselves. They resemble their parents, a beautiful pink when about 3 years old

There was rich birdlife in the small trees, bushes and shrubs around the lagoon. Strangely, we saw only one Yellow Warbler but many finches. There were only a few Small Ground-finches, all females in their drab plumage; not one black male. Numerous Medium Ground-finches flew up and down while searching for seeds under the bushes or sitting above in the trees. Some had rather large bills and I took them for Large Ground-finches. Later I saw in my guide book that this species is extinct on Floreana.

There were three cactus-finches with the Mediums, also searching with their long bills under the bushes but not near any *Opuntia* cactus. Most amazing was a pale bird singing up in a tree like a Woodpecker Finch, a species not normally seen on Floreana. The bird flew into some bushes and disappeared. I could not follow it to see more detail. Once, from a distance, I heard a rather loud song which sounded like 'tschur-tschur-tschur' with a high-pitched 'wee-wee-wee' at the end. Was it a Woodpecker Finch or not? Since there were other visitors about, I wondered if someone else had seen or heard the bird that day but we could not stay longer to find out.

There were some small birds in a salt bush, busily turning and hopping around, often-upside down, like titmice.

I thought they were rather yellowish looking Warbler Finches until I saw clearly their short and conical bills. These birds were Small Tree-finches, all in female plumage, with not one dark-headed male amongst them, which would have given away their identity more quickly. It was odd not to see any Warbler Finches near the lagoon and only a few Small Ground-finches, yet over a dozen of the rarer Small Tree-finches.

We sailed along the coast of Floreana (Charles in English). Its official name of Santa María is no longer in use. Tony related some of the history of this island. In the early days, from the discovery of the archipelago in the late 1500s to the early 1700s, Floreana was visited mostly by pirates, who used it as a refuge, and later by whalers. There is fresh water on this island, which is rare in the Galápagos.

The real but dark history of Floreana began in 1809 when the marooned Irishman, Patrick Watkins, started the first settlement. He captured some visiting sailors and kept them as slaves to grow vegetables and breed animals to sell or barter for rum with visiting whalers. After two years he stole a small whaling ship and with five of his 'slaves' left the island. He arrived at Guayaquil in Ecuador alone.

After Ecuador officially annexed the archipelago in 1832 a small colony formed on Floreana, consisting mostly of political prisoners (but also others, including prostitutes). Many domestic animals and foreign plants were introduced to the island with terrible consequences. From 1926–27, Norwegian settlers in search of paradise tried to form a colony which eventually failed. You can still see the remains behind the post barrel. In 1929 the German era began.

A dentist (or doctor) from Berlin, Karl F. Ritter, with his friend Dore Strauch, tried to build a paradise, which became a hell for Dore. Three years later, Heinz and Magret Wittmer, with their first son, landed and settled in the highlands next to Ritter. Shortly thereafter a mysterious German-French baroness, Wagner-Bosquet, arrived with her two lovers and declared herself 'queen' of the island. She reigned with a pistol, wounding a visiting Danish sailor who became her third lover. The baroness and one of her lovers disappeared after a serious dispute and were never seen again. No remains were ever found. The Berlin doctor, a vegetarian, died of food poisoning from eating meat. Dore, who ended up in a psychiatric clinic in Berlin, wrote a book about her life on Floreana called *The Hell in Paradise*. Only Magret Wittmer and her son are still alive and lives with their family in Puerto Velasco Ibarra, the only village now on Floreana.

Up in the terra alta you can still see where the pirates carved out their first caves in the lava, and where the Wittmer family lived and built their house. Exotic trees of many kinds, like avocado and citrus species, grow there, and the land around and lower down is cultivated by people from the local village. A bus drives you up there, over a rather rough road, not very comfortable but quite enjoyable all the same. It's a very good place for finches as there is fresh water. From this site there are very good views over the island down to the sea, and you can understand why the first settlers, and the pirates, chose this area.

There are now several books about the early history of this island, including one written by Magret herself, which tell you the full story.

On Floreana you can also see the negative influence of human settlement on such a fragile environment. The endemic mockingbird is extinct, as is Large Ground-finch, and the once large colony of Dark-rumped Petrels is in real danger.

Passion flower, *Passiflora foetida*

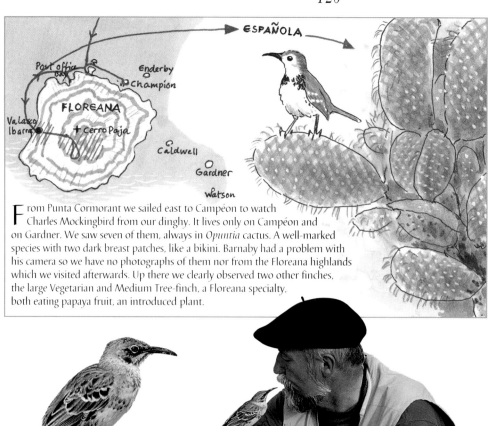

F rom Punta Cormorant we sailed east to Campéon to watch Charles Mockingbird from our dinghy. It lives only on Campéon and on Gardner. We saw seven of them, always in *Opuntia* cactus. A well-marked species with two dark breast patches, like a bikini. Barnaby had a problem with his camera so we have no photographs of them nor from the Floreana highlands which we visited afterwards. Up there we clearly observed two other finches, the large Vegetarian and Medium Tree-finch, a Floreana specialty, both eating papaya fruit, an introduced plant.

Our next visit was to Punta Suarez on Española (Hood), the albatross island. The first bird we saw was the large endemic Hood Mocker. We had not seen such tame birds as these Mockers anywhere else. Quite uninvited they came and settled on us. One used its bill to force open my mouth and look inside, piercing my tongue as if it was food. Then it flew off behind a rock. I saw it together with another searching for food on a sealion's placenta. Once more it returned to my shoulder, so I kept my mouth closed and it started to search in my pockets and then tried to undo my shoelaces, finally moving to my hand.

When we walked up the trail towards the albatross colony, we saw a very bright yellow-bellied flycatcher in a bush. At first I thought it was a female Vermillion, which is not usually found on Española, so I assumed it was a Galápagos Flycatcher, but when it turned around I could not see the two narrow wingbars typical of this species. Although the bill was rather small, the bird had the characteristically notched tail of Galápagos Flycatcher. Now, looking at the photos, I regret not spending more time with this little bird, but we wanted to see the albatrosses. On St Cruz and Isabela it was easy to separate the two flycatchers.

At first I thought it was the flycatcher's nest, clearly visible in the leafless bush, but, judging by its size, it must have been an old Mocker's nest.

When visiting a new island, it was always fascinating to watch the finches. Here they have the shape of **Small Ground-finch**, though paler and larger than on any other island we had visited. They were very numerous. In a small flock on low dry vegetation we spotted one that was much darker than the others and had a larger, longer bill. It looked to me like a Medium Ground-finch but there are no Mediums on Española. Besides Small Ground-finch there are only Warbler Finches and **Large Cactus-finch** (much larger-billed than the birds we had seen before on Genovesa).

We saw 25 small **Galápagos Doves** ▶ on the short 700-m walk to the albatross colony, mostly in groups of three or four, together with finches, searching for seeds under bushes and between the smooth lava boulders. They took no notice of us and carried on scratching about in the dry vegetation or on the ground with their long slightly curved bills.

◀ There were also many **Hood Mockingbirds**, or should we now call them Española Mockers since the island has changed its name. Apart from two together on the beach, we always saw single birds. They seemed to prefer to walk around rather than fly. As we walked, they followed us until chased away by the next territory holder. These Mockers were rather aggressive towards each other.

They were larger and paler than the two other Mocker species we had already encountered. Their legs are long and the bill is strong and long. The 'bikini' breast patch is larger than that of birds in the northern islands but much smaller and lower down the breast than in the fluffy Mockers we had seen on Campéon. Despite their numbers we did not hear any singing as on St Cruz. Perhaps it was outside the breeding season here on this southern island.

Many **Blue-footed Boobies** were sitting on their nests, situated both on and beside the trail, where there was open space without bushes. The boobies seem to prefer nesting right on the visitor trail where the ground is level and free from rocks. Most nests had large, rather quarrelsome chicks which pecked each other with their long bills while balancing by holding up their wings.

One adult stayed next to a trail post like a customs agent and would not let us pass, so we had to walk around the post on the forbidden side. A white chick, still downy, with its completely dark bill and mask was sitting right on the trail as if saying 'up to here and no further'. It held its wings open as though to block the way. This looked very uncomfortable to us, the wings twisted out from the bird, but we have seen chicks in even more peculiar positions.

'I am the greatest'

These short head feathers look
like seal's fur and they have
the same function, to
protect the bird when it
dives with high speed
into the water

The long strong 'piccador' bill
here belonging to a
large female

Its large blue feet give
this otherwise drab booby
a clown-like appearance.
The feet vary individually from
greenish turquoise through
bright blue to purple.

The usual clutch is two eggs
(*right*), laid about five days
apart, the first chick therefore
being much larger than the
second-born since young grow
quickly in the first few days.
When food is plentiful parents
will raise both chicks, sometimes
even three; if food is in short
supply the smaller chicks starve.

Any unprotected egg is attractive to Hood Mocker. They arrive immediately, peck at and even break the hard-shelled booby eggs to drink the contents – whether the egg is freshly laid, incubated or rotten.

It looks as if this booby was scratching its head and asking 'What can these two possibly be doing here?'

While some boobies had large chicks, others were still courting like this 'sky-pointing' male (*above*) in front of his larger female. The brightly coloured feet show up very well. They also use them when returning from the sea, saluting their partner on the nest with feet outstretched before landing. I wonder if they recognize each other by the colour of their feet?

Two and, in some clutches, even three eggs are incubated by both parents, alternating at about 15-hour intervals for around 41–42 days. The sitting or brooding bird lifts itself from time to time and bends its head to turn the eggs with the underside of its bill. This is necessary to regulate the egg's temperature and to avoid the embryo yolk sinking to one side; also to roll the eggs back to a comfortable position for the parent.

In the Galápagos, Waved Albatross only breeds here on Española, spread in colonies over the island. There are possibly 3,000 pairs. Another small colony of only a few pairs is found on the Isla de la Plata near the coast of Ecuador. They don't all breed every year, and in some disastrous years they fail to raise any young. They like to sit very close to each other, rolling the single egg around within the colony; none has a fixed nest spot and many eggs get lost or broken.

The huge, stout artificial-looking bill comprises a number of horny plates. The nostrils, resembling two short tubes, are on each side of the middle plate (called a culiminicorn). Young birds in the field are nearly indistinguishable from adults, having slightly duller coloured bills and all-white heads, unique for a young albatross.

nostril

The yellow bill has a waxy sheen and often a greenish lustre at the tip.

1 - *culiminicorn*
2 - *latericorn*
3 - *maxillary unguis*
4 - *ramicorn*
5 - *mandibular unguis*

an impressive hook

The male is larger than the female, (unlike Boobies, where the reverse is true). This pair (*top*) is 'bill-circling', part of the courtship, while the other two, both males, incubate eggs.

The forehead is somewhat flattened, eyebrows making a little 'roof' over the large dark brown eyes. This gives the albatross an almost childish, simple expression, unlike the fierce look of hawks and eagles.

L anding on Española is often quite difficult for the albatross, but taking off is even worse. There are boulders everywhere, large and small, and spiny bushes grow between them, over which the albatrosses have to run with their large webbed feet to gain enough speed to take off.

Waved Albatrosses have rather long thin feet and walk well on flat ground, but here, especially before taking off, they have to use their wings to keep their balance.

Galápagos Doves are opportunists. They are virtually everywhere, including the albatross colony, searching for seeds, and are not intimidated by these large-billed birds.

There were only a few pairs present when we visited the colony on 24 July. The same time last year, Barnaby had seen many more. There were no young, no real courting, just single birds sitting, possibly on eggs, and a few other listless adults amongst abandoned and broken eggs. Perhaps it was one of those disastrous years when no youngsters fledge.

An albatross can live for over 30 years. They start breeding when about 5–6 years old and pair for life. Courting starts in March when the males return to the colony. The first eggs, mostly of older pairs, are laid by mid-April, others lay their single egg as late as June. In January the last young leave the island, and from then until March, Española is albatross-free. They are all out at sea sailing and gliding between the Galápagos and Ecuador, some moving down to the coast of Peru.

When there is no suitable runway for them, they walk to the cliff edge, jump off while flapping their long wings heavily and 'swoop' into the air, turning to have a last look and sailing off in calm, majestic flight.

They look so clumsy on land but so elegant in flight, hardly ever flapping their wings, just gliding and sailing for hours, even days.

A Swallow-tailed Heron, a new Galápagos species? Is this the result of gene manipulation or evolution?

A young, Yellow-crowned Night Heron, still dark all over, and two Swallow-tailed Gulls at their favourite look out, where many seabirds rest (note the white-splattered boulder). There were many of these gulls on Española. Maybe they breed here on the low cliffs, or do they only rest here before flying far out to sea to fish?

The strong-billed, long-legged **Hood Mocker**, an opportunist like Galápagos Dove, hopping around amongst seabirds, always in search of food in an active but 'phlegmatic' manner.

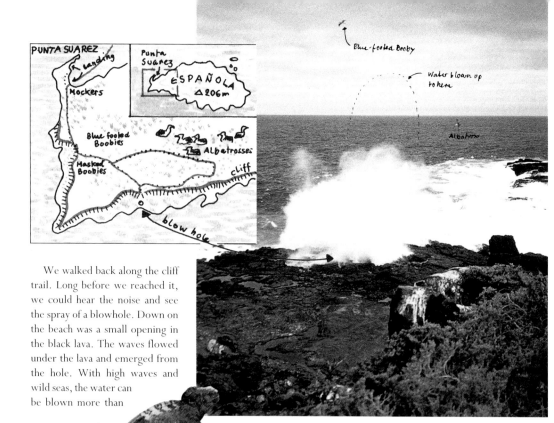

PUNTA SUAREZ

Punta
Suarez

ESPAÑOLA
△ 206m

Landing

Hockers

Blue footed
Boobies

Masked
Boobies

Albatrosses

cliff

blow hole

Blue-footed Booby

Water blown up
to here

Albatross

We walked back along the cliff trail. Long before we reached it, we could hear the noise and see the spray of a blowhole. Down on the beach was a small opening in the black lava. The waves flowed under the lava and emerged from the hole. With high waves and wild seas, the water can be blown more than

20 m into the air and foam spread all over the beach. We also had a very good view down to the black lava seafront crowded with red-flecked marine iguanas.

Marine iguanas are found on all islands and can vary in size and colour. On most islands they are greyish black with some paler grey or green spots. During the breeding season, males especially can have bright green, yellowish, orange or even red spots on their jet black skin.

Here on Española are the brightest of all marine iguanas, even during the non-breeding period. Some are more red than black, and we saw one with nice yellow spots and rings around its tail. It is a fantastic sight to see them in a large group on the black lava.

Masked Booby colony

On our return to the landing stage, we passed a low black cliff, flat on top like a table, where the aristocratic **Masked Boobies** nest. We had already seen them on Genovesa and Daphne in widely scattered colonies with considerable distances between the nests. Here they were more concentrated, mostly on the same cliff top, but not so dense as in a Northern Gannet colony, each pair keeping some distance from the rest. Their snowy white plumage showed well against the black lava.

We heard some females trumpeting but no whistling males. I could not see if the sitting birds had eggs. Unlike Blue-footed Boobies, which can breed at any time of the year, Masked have an annual breeding cycle which changes from island to island as we had observed on Daphne. I don't know when they breed here. Normally all Masked Boobies leave the island when not breeding. Unlike a Northern Gannet colony there was not the same coming and going. Life in the tropical Galápagos is more easy-going.

Galápagos Oystercatcher, like Masked Booby, prefers to keep at a distance from its neighbours, unlike European Oystercatcher, which is often concentrated in flocks of several hundred birds, especially at high tide; but they are very similar in appearance to American or European Oystercatchers with the long carrot-red bill and pied plumage.

From Punta Suarez, we sailed eastwards along the flat rocky coast of Española. The highest point on this island, possibly the oldest in the whole archipelago, is just over 200 m. The basalt lava on the southeastern side is the oldest rock on Española and the residue of an almost completely eroded volcano. We wanted to visit the long, wide sandy beach at Bahía Gardner. Before landing our panga dinghy on the beach, we visited the small Isla Gardner nearby.

A small flock of about 20 **Audubon's Shearwaters** was fishing near the rocky coast. We could watch them very closely from our dinghy as they swam in one small spot, often holding their wings high above them as they ducked their heads under the water, looking for prey. They were diving like ducks and were not under water for long. When they surfaced I could not see any catch in their bills but perhaps it was too small to see.

Blue-footed and Masked Boobies circled high in the air around the small island but, as on Punta Suarez, the frigatebirds were Great and not Magnificent as on most other islands. Until now we had seen large numbers of Great Frigatebirds only on Genovesa. There had been some on Seymour and a few on the southern coast of Isabela. Two *Buteo* hawks were sailing overhead, one chased a much larger pelican away from a rock in the sea and took its place. I had a good opportunity to sketch it while we had lunch. Obligingly it stayed on *its* rock.

A lonely Ruddy Turnstone in full breeding plumage searched for food among the rocks at the water's edge. Further away, and half asleep, were some Swallow-tailed Gulls, but not so many as on Punta Suarez. Mockers hopped about between but never close to the gulls, though they pecked at the tail feathers of a sleeping pelican.

The whole flock of shearwaters flew off simultaneously and carried on with their peculiar, and new to me, fishing technique. They looked dead, floating about with their heads under water for quite a while. Some were half submerged, upside-down, like dabbling ducks with just their rear ends and wingtips showing above water.

Near the shore, beside some resting sealions, an elegantly shaped **Wandering Tattler** with its long straight dark bill. We had already seen this migrant wader on many rocky and sandy beaches.

Another grey bird of similar size but with a decurved bill, a **Hood Mockingbird**, that has taken over the role of a wader here on this island.

The Mocker was not afraid of the sleeping sealions, while the tattler, nearby, kept close to the waterline. The Mocker walked around the sealion's head as if inspecting it closely.

Then he stopped in front of a sealion's mouth and with a short jump pulled something that looked like slime out of the seal's nose and swallowed it.

After Isla Gardner, we visited the broad sandy beach and dunes in Bahía Gardner. Sealions (many more than we had seen until now) were lying near the waterline. A single wader, which I identified as a Wandering Tattler, walked around them. Although there were many oyster-catcher footprints, we did not see any birds. A Whimbrel flew past, whistling. Small birds hopped around in the dunes amongst the dry vegetation and flat sand. They were Small Ground-finches and, amazingly, many Warbler Finches, behaving like ground-finches (on the ground too), only quicker in their movements. Most had reddish tails. Two were greyish, including their tails. I wondered if the reddish-coloured tails were stained. One found a large grub, which it held parrot-like, or more like a titmouse, with one foot, biting off little bits. In nearby spiny bushes two buzzed about like Goldcrests, a habit I had seen before.

Another Mocker was more interested in what looked like yellow plastic which it pecked at several times and then left lying on the white beach.

Warbler Finches were more numerous here than ground-finches and seemed large in comparison. A large-billed, very dark-coloured Española cactus-finch used its bill to push ground vegetation forwards, like a bulldozer, while a Warbler Finch behind it picked at the disturbed insects.

Large Cactus-finches are very interesting birds. Although called cactus-finches, they are not so closely linked to life in *Opuntia* as Common Cactus-finch on the other islands. Since there are no Medium nor Large Ground-finches on this island they take over their role. We saw them mostly feeding on the ground, usually in shade under trees.

However, two families of Mockers were even more interesting (*see* following pages).

It was as if some dry vegetation was marking the border between two family territories. From both sides, family members hopped up to this point and stopped.

Bending down, flicking its wings while the bird on the far side stood upright and froze. 4–5 family members on each side waited excitedly 2–3 m away.

The bird on the far side of the border returned to its group, which was very vocal and active. On this side the 'winner' stood at the border, frozen in an upright posture.

Then two birds from the other side returned, passed the dry vegetation and the 'winner' retreated a short distance towards its group where he stopped again, turned round looking at the two aggressors.

This display went on and on. Both groups became more and more excited, running around, calling loudly (mere bravado), jerking their long tails, dropping and spreading their wings. There was no direct body contact between the birds. Some in each group appeared to be more important than others.

The duration of the 'freezing' at the 'border' became shorter and shorter, and the borders were constantly changing. The distance between the groups seemed to be what mattered rather than the border line as I first thought.

They became more and more excited. Here opening both wings like a courting Sunbittern and looking very bold in the face of their opponents, all of them with long, stiff legs.

I could not tell which bird belonged to which group as they ran behind each other, chasing over the border, with-out pecking.

Again on the border where it all began; heavy wing-flicking, freezing, tail-jerking, calling, jumping, like boxers facing each other waiting for a weakness in their opponent.

Two birds, which seemed to be important, showed each other their broad breasts with dark 'bikinis', then jumped and grasped each other with their strong feet, rolling over in the sand. They didn't peck but only pulled each others legs. This happened so quickly, behind a bush, I nearly missed the action. All the others called excitedly but the fight was only between two birds.

Again 'freezing', showing each other their breasts. A third bird came from behind as if it wanted to push the two together, but the fight was over. They just stood there for a short while and then each group left in a different direction. All that was left in the arena was a long white-tipped tail feather which I still have.

During this skirmish there was one bird (possibly newly fledged and very short-tailed) between the two groups, begging for food, but it was ignored. Here it's running behind an adult.

'the broad breast with bikini This Mocking bird in the sand reminded me of similarly-shaped African Hoopoe Lark

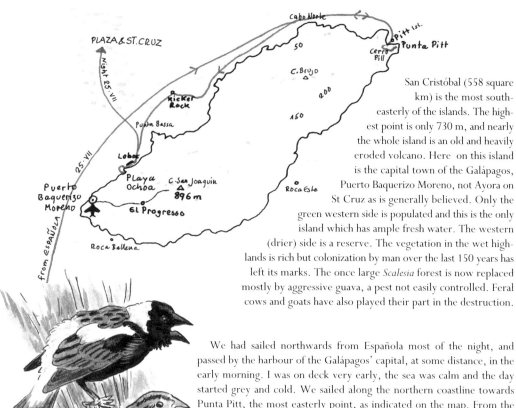

San Cristóbal (558 square km) is the most south-easterly of the islands. The highest point is only 730 m, and nearly the whole island is an old and heavily eroded volcano. Here on this island is the capital town of the Galápagos, Puerto Baquerizo Moreno, not Ayora on St Cruz as is generally believed. Only the green western side is populated and this is the only island which has ample fresh water. The western (drier) side is a reserve. The vegetation in the wet highlands is rich but colonization by man over the last 150 years has left its marks. The once large *Scalesia* forest is now replaced mostly by aggressive guava, a pest not easily controlled. Feral cows and goats have also played their part in the destruction.

We had sailed northwards from Española most of the night, and passed by the harbour of the Galápagos' capital, at some distance, in the early morning. I was on deck very early, the sea was calm and the day started grey and cold. We sailed along the northern coastline towards Punta Pitt, the most easterly point, as indicated on the map. From the deck, the land, which sloped gently down from the relatively low upland towards the coast, looked rather dry and boring, only the lower areas were covered with silver-grey leafless Palo Santo trees. When a warm wind wafted down from the hills over our boat we could smell the goats. I wondered if it was their work that left the land looking so dry.

There were few birds but many sea turtles in the water around us. Storm-petrels passed, too fast for identification. This changed once we had passed Cabo Norte and turned towards Bahía de Hobbs. Numerous Blue-footed Boobies, often in large flocks of several hundred, were fishing along the rocky coast, flying low in long lines over the waves or forming a compact flock higher in the air, out towards the open sea.

We dropped anchor at Punta Pitt. In the bay, fluttering around a small island like swallows, were hundreds of Galápagos Storm-petrels (possibly breeding here). Masked Boobies were breeding and we saw plenty of Swallow-tailed Gulls with chicks, some small and many nearly full grown. We landed on a small sandy beach amongst numerous sealions lying on the sand and under low bushes in the shade. Their strong odour was everywhere. We walked up a small trail between bushes full of finches, mostly Small Ground-finches, some Mediums, and in one bush, eight very dark Small Tree-finches. In a low bush, with four Medium and one Small Ground-finches, was another all-black bird with reddish brown undertail-coverts and a pointed bill that looked like a Sharp-beaked Ground-finch.

It was still cloudy, not very hot, and the walk up the ravine-like steep slope was very easy.

The North American Bobolink is a long-distance wanderer. They fly down in autumn from their breeding sites to winter mostly in northern Argentina. Only a few come regularly to the coast of Peru, but every year there are records from the highlands in the Galápagos, mostly from October to December, but occasionally July. It might possibly breed one day, but there are no records yet. The male in breeding plumage is unmistakable, and the females resemble no other Galápagos birds. Look out for them in the San Cristóbal highlands. (See also p. 261.)

The trail passed between some very dry, eroded rocks. Higher up there were some feral goats which behaved like wild animals. The whole scene reminded me of the dry southern slopes of the Spanish Pyrenées: same colours and same goats, except here they had differently shaped horns. I don't know if they are hunted here but when we approached they climbed higher up, disappearing behind rocks, always keeping out of gun range.

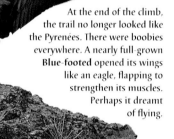

still something wrong
but what?

At the end of the climb, the trail no longer looked like the Pyrenées. There were boobies everywhere. A nearly full-grown **Blue-footed** opened its wings like an eagle, flapping to strengthen its muscles. Perhaps it dreamt of flying.

A pair of Blue-footed Boobies still courting. Others were breeding or already had chicks of different sizes. The differences in the sexes are clearly visible in this pair. The female has the larger pupil. In front, the male with cocked tail has a small 'staring pupil'. The male is relatively longer-tailed than the female. This may help him to fish in very shallow water near the coast for mostly smaller prey when the chicks are still young. Their feet are also different shades of blue (not a real difference between sexes). In most pairs I noticed that males had brighter coloured feet, not such a deep blue or purple.

Red-footed Boobies make their nests, which are often flimsy, in low bushes and shrubs higher up on the flat part at Punta Pitt. Nearly every individual has different coloured plumage. Only the bright red feet are common to all. Some are deep brown, others more greyish, some have golden brown or fawn-coloured heads, and some are almost brilliant white with black wings, like the larger Masked Boobies which breed here on the slopes adjacent to the cliffs. Most Red-footed were sitting on their tree nests, though some were still courting. They seemed to have a fixed season unlike Blue-footed which breed throughout the year.

At the end of the visitors' trail near the cliffs, there is a fantastic view over the sea. Below, deep red *Sesuvium* carpets the black lava. Both Frigatebirds, Great and Magnificent, sailed leisurely above this scene. Masked Boobies, like silver stars, flew in and out to sea from the lower cliffs. Blue-footed Boobies passed over us, often in hurried flight. There were only a few Red-Footed on the wing. They fly out later, fishing far offshore.

The red plants on the black lava look like an expansive piece of art. They are only bright red in the dry season. At other times of the year, when moisture is available, the whole picture changes as the *Sesuvium* turns green.

On our return, in the rocky part, another even younger Blue-footed Booby exercising its wings. The quills in the flight feathers show up very well while the body is still in down. The chicks grow very slowly: about 100 days from birth until they fly, and for the smaller Red-Footed Boobies, sitting on their flimsy nests, it is even longer, at around 130 days.

Passage

breach

Far out to sea, about 5 km off the coast of Bahía Stephens, is Kicker Rock, the curious remains of an old volcanic tuff cone, and a safe breeding place for many seabirds. Rising about 140 m out of the sea, it resembles a sleeping lion, hence the Spanish name, 'León Dormido'.

Since time was getting short for us and we had to be on St Cruz the following day, we did not stay long at Punta Pitt. As we sailed back along the coast of San Cristóbal in the opposite direction, I remained on deck watching seabirds. The weather was fine, the sun almost too strong. This morning we had seen albatrosses three times but now there was only one near Kicker Rock. Once again there were not many birds except mostly distant shearwaters and storm-petrels (apart from four Madeiran, the majority were Elliot's). After Punta Pitt, near Cabo Norte, we saw a flock of Galápagos Storm-petrels and then another at Kicker Rock, where, quite possibly, they breed.

Oddly we had not seen any tropicbirds near San Cristóbal and only a few **Brown Pelicans.** One immature was fishing near the shore in shallow water, diving from a great height (as seen in the photo). Blue-footed Boobies were the most common birds and there were more Masked Boobies than we had seen anywhere else. A few Red-footed Boobies were out at sea. I especially like to watch these elegant birds on the wing. Many Magnificent Frigatebirds hung in the air, and ten immatures, all with white heads, followed our boat for a while. It was just before lunch and Aurelio, our cook, was throwing scraps overboard. On Kicker Rock one frigatebird was sitting on its nest. There were no gulls or noddies to be seen along the coast and only one wader, a Whimbrel, which flew and called along the shoreline. Not one hawk sailed over the low hilly country of San Cristóbal (I believe they are extinct on this island).

Just for fun we sailed through the narrow passage between the high steep cliffs of Kicker Rock and then turned back towards the coast. We wanted to visit Lobos island. Some 100 m off the coast we watched an enormous flock of Blue-footed Boobies, more than we had seen before. Most were young birds with darker heads. It looked as though they were flying over a large shoal of fish, diving into the deep water, from a considerable height, and chasing the fish into shallower water near the rocky shores. Although near the shore, the boobies did not change their fishing

technique, still diving at great speed. I wondered how they avoided the rocks and getting stuck in the sand with their long bills. The water was no more than half a metre deep.

The smaller Red-footed Boobies never fish so close to shore and fly long distances to fish in deep water. Only when young will they play around in shallow water near the colony, sometimes catching a fish. They are still dependent on their parents for real food (even when the chicks are already on the wing), waiting for them to return from pelagic fishing grounds early in the morning or late in the evening. Masked Boobies are also deep-water fishers, but not Blue-footed Boobies. When watching them dive with speed from a great height into shallow water, one imagines they will never get out, but they do, and then fly up to dive again. The male weighs one third of the female, and with their long tails they are the real shallow-water experts.

During the first weeks after birth, the chicks are fed by their father. While the female guards the nest, he, nearly alone, is responsible for supplying the food. Later, the male leaves the family and the larger, heavier female takes over, single-handedly, fishing for larger prey, also near the coast but mostly in deeper waters. Blue-footed Boobies feed their chicks more often than do Red-footed boobies. The Blue-footed young grow more quickly and the parents can raise two or even three young, using less energy than Red-footed, which fish far out to sea and, like Masked Boobies, only raise one chick in a brood. The young of both Red-footed and Masked need longer to become fully independent.

These differences in fishing techniques allow the three species in the Galápagos to live close together, often on the same island, as we saw here on San Cristóbal. The central islands with deeper waters have mostly Blue-footed Boobies and a few Masked. On the outlying islands the Masked become more common, with Red-footed most numerous. From here they can fly to the more distant fishing grounds in deeper waters. Nest sites are also important in determining distribution, and Red-footed cannot live where large hawks are present.

▲ The shoal of fish must have turned back to deeper water. Some boobies followed but this time the fish were deeper, not just beneath the water's surface. Most birds remained near the rocky shore, others swam with their heads under the water, like dabbling ducks, and some dived from this position, but not very successfully. Many settled on the rocks, ▶ between sleeping sealions and a few pelicans that had not joined the boobies. The spectacle was over and calm returned.

We visited Lobos, a long low rocky island with patches of dense vegetation, mostly low bushes. The island is separated from San Cristóbal by a narrow channel. There was a Blue-footed Booby colony. Young birds sat in most open spaces but also under bushes. Many were still small but others were nearly full grown, in dark brown plumage with the typical pale neck patch and scalloped mantle. Frigatebirds sailed over the island but we did not see a single nest. There was a small colony of Magnificents across the channel on San Cristóbal.

An egret had left behind a beautiful silky feather but the bird was not there. A small heron that looked like a hybrid between a Lava and Striated Heron walked between the rocks catching insects. One pair of Lava Gulls and some noddies sat on large boulders. These birds, together with two Yellow Warblers, some Medium Ground-Finches and only two Small Ground-Finches, were all we saw on our short visit to Lobos.

▲
Part of the Blue-footed Booby fishing party after calm had returned. Some are still fishing between the rocks.

Chatham Mockingbird closely resembles Galápagos Mocker, which inhabits all the northern islands of the archipelago. We saw two only: a very shy bird near Punta Pitt and this one in a manzanillo or poison apple tree, on the white sandy beach at Ochoa, near Lobos island. The bird had a wounded leg and remained in the shade of the tree. It was not easy for Barnaby to take a good picture without a flash bulb (this is forbidden on the islands). The bird was shy, unlike the Mockers on Española, and more like those on St Cruz. Had they already learned to be wary?

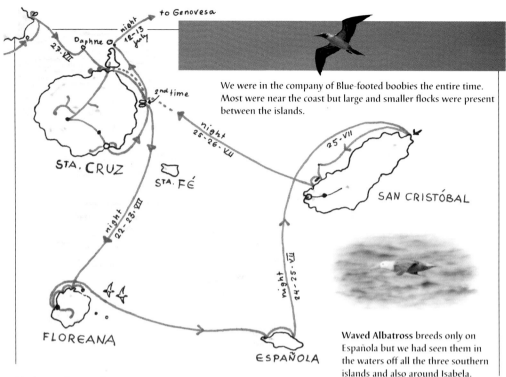

to Genovesa

night 12-13 july

Daphne

27.VII

2nd time

STA. CRUZ

STA. FÉ

night 25-26. VII

25-VII

SAN CRISTÓBAL

We were in the company of Blue-footed boobies the entire time. Most were near the coast but large and smaller flocks were present between the islands.

night 22-23. VII

night 24-25. VII

FLOREANA

ESPAÑOLA

Waved Albatross breeds only on Española but we had seen them in the waters off all the three southern islands and also around Isabela.

The longer distances between islands, such as St Cruz–Genovesa, St Cruz–Floreana or Española–San Cristóbal, were covered at night because it gave us more time on shore, but when sailing in more interesting waters, for instance around Isabela, we travelled by day, which was often very exciting, lying on the upperdeck and watching all the birds around us. There was usually too much movement in our small boat for Barnaby to use his camera and even identification with field glasses over large distances was not always easy. Frigatebirds, and sometimes storm-petrels, would follow us for a while.

Lying for hours in the bright sunshine, as I did during the afternoon along the coast of San Cristóbal, was very tiring for the eyes. I don't like wearing sunglasses because I prefer to see true colours. During the mornings when the sky was grey, or occasionally when we had fog, it was very relaxing but these were times when there were hardly any birds around. Now the sun was strong and birds were everywhere and I didn't want to miss a single bird, even small dots far off on the horizon. That evening I had a real problem with my eyes. It was very painful and I could do nothing about it, just wait. To avoid the same problem, wear sunglasses and enjoy your birds – even if this 'alters' the colour a bit.

It was around 7.30 pm when we left the coast of San Cristóbal and sailed northwest towards St Cruz. The sea was not calm but not too rough. Our captain, Marlon, said conditions would worsen as the sea in that part of the Canal de Santa Fé can be very rough. Although there was no strong wind, the waves rose higher and higher. I was still working in the salon (my eyes were painful), and now this. The heavy table moved around like a ball. It was almost impossible to walk. The ship rolled from one side to the other in the heavy swell; it was a real nightmare. We had not experienced such rough seas before. I felt unwell but luckily was not sick. Barnaby was never sea-sick. He comes from an island. I come from the Continent!

We were all happy to arrive in the channel between the two Plaza islands. At 2.00 pm we dropped anchor in a sea that was dead calm and we all had a good sleep, especially our captain. I wondered how he remained calm and navigated us here in such a rough sea.

After a good breakfast on deck, watching some Ruddy Turnstones on the rocks of Plaza Sur and hundreds of Swallow-tailed Gulls on the low cliffs of Plaza Norte, we visited the southern island again. Nothing had changed since our first visit. Again there was a large sealion on the landing jetty and we had to gently chase him away. He seemed familiar with that game. A large land iguana still guarded its cactus tree. It was just the same. I think this animal never moves, and is the most photographed beast in the Galápagos. Since Plaza is vis-ited by most tourists, everyone passes the cactus, and most take a photograph of the iguana. I wonder if it already has a nickname since it is so well known? Perhaps its son will take over when it dies; but I don't know how long the cactuses will last. We walked up to the steeper cliffs on the other side of the island.

Barnaby particularly wanted to take some more pictures of his favourite birds: tropicbirds. Plaza is the ideal island for this and that's why we returned. High up on the cliff with the birds flying below or level with you, and sometimes very close, is the perfect place for a photographer. The tropicbirds, with their shiny silver-white plumage and jet black markings, are very photogenic against the bright blue or black sea. They are always quarrelsome when in a group, fluttering and gliding up and down, often at high speed. This is the problem with them: they are so fast, you never know what their next movement will be. Good equipment is essential, but to obtain a satisfying picture of tropicbirds, patience is even more important.

▲
This is not the kind of picture Barnaby wanted to take but I think it illustrates the beauty of this species, their characteristic flight and elegant movements in the air.

◄ As I've mentioned, my favourite bird is **Swallow-tailed Gull**. After Genovesa, Plaza is probably the next best place in the archipelago to watch them closely. Like tropicbirds, they are very elegant in flight. I made some nice sketches of them (*see* pp. 214–215). Again, Barnaby was not satisfied with his pictures but I think they show this bird's flight 'pattern' clearly, the broad, straight open tail (*left*) and the forked 'swallow-tail' which gives them their name (*right*).

Swallow-tailed Gulls have large colonies on both Plazas. Usually their nests are on the steep lava cliffs, but some also nest near the upper rim, close to the visitors' trail, which makes watching them easy. Their nests are well spaced and never in dense colonies like northern gulls. All Galápagos birds like space. Chicks of all ages, always just one per pair, can be seen all year round. It's always worth looking for them on Plaza; but look carefully. As you see from the photograph (*left*) their pattern and colour camouflage them. Both parents take care of the chicks until they fledge when about 90 days old. During the day, parents with large chicks will stay (out of duty and mostly in pairs) somewhere in the colony. Only a few fly around, showing the characteristic silhouette against the deep blue sky.

Lava Gulls, unlike Swallow-tails are solitary birds, never nesting in colonies. They are seen mostly singly or in pairs, sometimes a family with one or two fledglings. I don't think they nest on Plaza. They need open lagoons or ponds along a quiet coastline where they can make their solitary nest. The young fledge when about 60 days old and look after themselves about two and a half weeks later when the Swallow-tails are still with their parents. The dark plumage camouflages them well against black lava boulders (like the adults seen in these photographs).

Near the landing jetty, once past the sealion guard, on the right are some large cactus trees with ever-present **cactus-finches**, like this all-black male.

Cactus-finches are of the same genus as the common Small Ground-finch, and are the same colour, but are larger, of a more slender build and longer-billed. They are perfectly adapted to live in the prickly *Opuntia* cactuses where they spend most of their lives. They feed on cactuses, nest in them and are never seen far from them. Only at Cormorant Point, on Floreana (under bushes and in the Darwin Station (drinking water)) did I see any some distance from cactus.

The bulky, cup-shaped, roofed nest (with a side entrance hole) is always built in prickly pear cactus. The territorial male builds several nests for his female to choose from. The nest is then lined with soft material, such as white seabird feathers, before eggs are laid. This is similar to the habits of our northern hemisphere Wren, where the male also builds several nests and the female makes her choice and 'decorates' the inside. When one sees this prickly world in which they live, one wonders how they can manoeuvre amongst the sharp spines and even stand on top of them in search of food. They take the nectar from the cactus flowers with a specially adapted tongue. They also eat the seeds and ripe fruit as well as catch any edible insect that comes near the cactus. Their life is 'cactus'.

It was about 10.30 am when we left the Plazas to sail north along the St Cruz coast. The sea was not especially calm but appeared so compared with last night. I was still careful with my eyes but stayed on deck watching seabirds most of the time. Except for some Audubon's Shearwaters, there were only a few birds over the waves. Single Elliot's Storm-petrels passed some tropicbirds and Brown Pelicans, but most surprisingly there were no frigatebirds and only a few Blue-footed Boobies, usually common in coastal waters. A bonus sighting was a large black-winged gull, leisurely flying south low over the waves, in search of food. I watched it for some time and identified it as a Kelp Gull, which, until now, had only been recorded once in the Galápagos.

.We passed the Itabaca Canal, where, as expected, noddies and Blue-footed Boobies were present, and anchored off the St Cruz coast, near Caleta Tortuga. In our dinghy we visited the large sheltered lagoon which is surrounded by broad green mangrove. Beyond, the land, dry and grey with Palo Santo trees, rose to the green jungle of the terra alta, now partly obscured by fog. There were many Pacific green turtles in the shallow water of the lagoon as well as golden and leopard rays which seemed to fly under the water with their large wing-like fins. Mockingbirds and warblers sang in the mangrove. Lava Herons flew low over the water, quick and agile, showing the yellow or orange feet; in one the pale silver back was clearly visible. The call is a rather harsh and aggressive 'rack-rack'. Here again some birds were possibly Striated Herons, not in breeding plumage, but in the evening light identification became more and more difficult.

Some sat low on the mangrove roots stabbing at small prey. Even sealions were barking between the trees; a very tranquil scene.

There was a small heron in the dense vegetation but I could not identify it with its greyish head and brown striped breast. Was it a young Lava or Striated Heron, or was it a hybrid?

(*Opposite page*) **Brown Pelicans** and some **Great Blue Herons** had a scattered colony in the mangroves. Here all the pelicans on their tree nests were in full breeding plumage, white heads with a golden tinge and bright chestnut necks. The Blue Herons looked rather dull with only short black aigrettes, a pale washed-out version compared with the beautiful continental Blue Heron.

A large, beautiful pink Galápagos Flamingo waded in the shallow water at the edge of the mangrove. We watched it for a long time, studying its every detail while it fed. It paid no attention to us and Barnaby was able to take these excellent photographs.

An immature Great Blue Heron, not so pale as the adults seen in the mangrove earlier but still rather dull.

On the left, the resting heron looks more like a scarecrow than a photogenic bird. Moving along the beach, with a large lava bank behind and the light too strong against the sea, did not help.

After the lagoon at Caleta Tortuga, we visited the white sandy beach of Las Bachas. We arrived at high tide. An immature Great Blue Heron was standing on its long strong feet in the water. When Barnaby approached it with his camera it was not afraid and just walked further into the sea to catch a small fish and then moved slowly out to the beach. It stood looking rather listless and bored, then moved further away along a black lava bank, catching small things here and there, possibly insects. Then it slept for some time. We nearly lost interest but suddenly, like a ballerina, it danced towards the water again. Here Barnaby got his shot at the right moment, the photo opposite, on page 153, which won the 'Runner Up' prize in the 15–17 year old group in the 'British Gas Young Wildlife Photographer of the Year 1996' competition.

While sitting on the crown of a dune, in the warm white sand, watching some seabirds fishing around a small island and sketching the whole scene, a peculiar pelican appeared among the other birds.

pure shiny white

I got excited when I saw this pelican. It looked so different from the hundreds we had seen until now, much paler and larger, with a completely white head and neck. Was it a Peruvian Pelican? I watched very carefully, taking note of every detail, and then realised it was not a Peruvian, just a large pale Galápagos Brown Pelican. When it flew up, the pale panel on its wing was not diagnostic as it is in Peruvian. Or was this a non-breeding Brown Pelican visitor from the Continent? (I did not see the pale streaks on its belly as on continental birds.)

For our last night in the Galápagos, we sailed back to the large lagoon we had visited before and anchored near the shore. From a distance we saw numerous large white birds fly down from the highlands and settle on the mangrove, now dark green in the shadows. They looked like white candles on a Christmas tree. At first I thought they were Great Egrets, but on looking closely with my binoculars, saw they were all Cattle Egrets. Only in one mangrove tree were there some 20 larger Great Egrets together in the same place.

Cattle Egret must now be a very common bird on St Cruz. I counted more than 150 of them, and many more were sitting beyond the trees out of view, with still more flocks arriving. Was this the roosting place for all the St Cruz Cattle Egrets? Do they also breed here? This newcomer is now possibly more common than its larger cousin, Great Egret. Are these birds, now found on all larger islands, the offspring of the few birds that found their way to the Galápagos in the 1980s? If so, they have been very successful. Or perhaps there have been several invasions. Seeing this large flock coming to roost safely in the mangrove was a very symbolic moment for me on our last evening. These were the birds that made us think of visiting the Galápagos again after Barnaby had told me he had seen so many of them in 1994.

Will other birds, plants, insects and mammals find their way naturally (not brought by man) to the islands? Although, I suppose, man is part of nature so creatures brought by humans could be regarded as 'natural'. If Europeans had never found their way to the Americas Cattle Egrets would never have had the right conditions in which to settle and colonize. Local birds probably could not exploit the new conditions so well as this 'foreign' species. And once established on the Continent, they had no difficulty in finding these islands where there are plenty of cattle both on farms and living wild.

Changes in bird populations are occurring all the time worldwide. Some birds expand their distribution in a very short time, for example Collared Dove, which has spread across Europe and into China and Japan. The cause of such dramatic range extensions is not fully understood.

Nights come early and quickly in the tropics. Now the lagoon was dark and the Cattle Egrets had settled down for the night. With the last light, I could still see their white bodies against the nearly black leaves. The sun disappeared rapidly over the ocean in a beautiful sunset, specially made for our last evening in the islands. Far out on the horizon, in the dark sea, against the orange sky, we saw Daphne, 'the finch island', which we had visited a week before. The clear black silhouette looked like a sleeping animal and I thought of all the interesting birds we had seen there. Some of them spend their entire lives on this island, which now looked so tiny, a world of its own.

Aurelio wanted to make us a special last supper on board and cleaned a large fish on deck. Immediately some pelicans invited themselves and waited for their share. Sealions playing around our boat barked loudly but they were not interested in the scraps thrown overboard. I had noticed this before, unlike the ever-hungry pelicans, they like to fish for themselves. A Lava Gull, like a dark ghost, settled on our dinghy and waited for something. These slate-black gulls are not so bossy as the

larger northern gulls. They are not really shy but like to keep at some distance.

I stayed on board and watched birds flying past in the last light, mostly shearwaters and some noddies. We had seen so many things in these wonderful islands, now being on deck for the last evening, the time seemed to have passed so quickly. We had visited all the most interesting islands, except for Pinta and Marchena, which are not open to visitors. We did not have time to go to nearly inaccessible Darwin and Wolf, the two most northerly, outlying small islands. Barnaby had visited St Fé the year before, but we did not visit it this time.

Out of the 59 Galápagos breeding birds, we had seen 56. We were not lucky with Marsh Owl or Painted Rail or perhaps the rarest of all, Mangrove Finch, although we looked hard for it. Is it now extinct? Why should this be, to me the mangroves had not changed since I saw them the first time? For the regular avian visitors from the northern hemisphere it was not the right time of the year. These are usually seen in the Galápagos from September until March/April, though we still saw 11 species of wader including two plovers. A bird I thought was a Purple Martin could have been a misidentified Galápagos Martin. Of the many 'accidentals' in the Galápagos bird list we saw two, a Black Storm-petrel and a Kelp Gull. Altogether we had seen 66 species. I sketched them all, while Barnaby had photographs of most of them.

It is always nice to go somewhere and see all that you wanted to, even though we missed one rail and one finch. More important for me is to really observe the birds' behaviour in their natural habitats, and the Galápagos islands are ideal for this. Nowhere else in the world are the birds so confident and so approachable. Most of the time you don't even need your binoculars. We really had a wonderful time on the enchanted isles, with every day bringing new experiences for both Barnaby and myself. While still on board, a large bird flew over our boat and landed nearby in shallow water. It was nearly too dark when Barnaby took his last shot that evening of this Great Blue Heron.

Tony, our guide. For us he was the best guide we could have had during our visit.

Hermann

Marlon, our captain and a park warden, who sailed us around all the islands and found his way, even in the roughest sea, and his brother, Roland, who helped with everything on deck, and also steered our boat whenever the captain took a rest.

Peter, who looked after our cabin and dived for lobster.

Aurelio, our cook, who made the best 'Chivo', good lobster, and on the last day even pale blue ice cream for Barnaby (out of nothing!).

Roland
Barnaby, photographer

The *Espanola* carried a crew of four and was equipped for eight passengers, but Barnaby and I enjoyed the comfort of having her to ourselves. The boat was 40 feet long with a beam of 12 feet, and displaced 26 tons, cruising at 9 knots. The sea was generally very calm, but twice, on long night crossings in the open sea, we all wished we had been ashore! We both enjoyed the entire trip because the atmosphere on board was always friendly, even when we kept the *Espanola* and her crew waiting far beyond the time we had scheduled for our return. There was just so much to see on every island. Barnaby and I felt there could be no finer team to accompany us on any future visit to these enchanted isles.

THE PHOTOS

THE SKETCHES AND DRAWINGS

pure silver
snowy white

strong
bill

jet black

strong feet

greyish
cast on tail

I was a young teenager on my two trips to the Galápagos and made mistakes an experienced photographer would have avoided. I should have paid more attention to scenic shots to give proper perspective to some of the islands. Two rolls of film were completely blank when developed. For insurance, I should have used both cameras to record pictures of the most interesting sights, especially since we seldom went back to the same location and there was no way of knowing how the pictures would turn out until we returned to London.

On the first trip I lost a case containing most of my film. This could have been a disaster, but I was able to buy film at the tourist boutiques on Santa Cruz. Film is only available on a few islands such as Santa Cruz, San Cristóbal and perhaps Isabela and Floreana. It is of course much more expensive, and it can be difficult obtaining special films. It is wise not to pack all your film in one case in the event of loss or damage.

On my second trip I brought enough film. As a precaution, bring more than you expect to use. If you run out on one of the more remote islands it could be several days before you find any stores. Extra batteries for each camera are a must.

My equipment consisted of one camera, a Canon EOS 500, and two zoom lenses, a 25–75 mm and a 75–300 mm. It is easy to get close to most of the birds and animals to photograph them. The 75–300 mm lens is therefore sufficient for most normal shots. A small compact camera would have been useful. My equipment was fine for most normal photography, although I would have liked a longer lens or a 1.4x converter for the Canon for certain shots. I brought two filters, a polarising filter and a UV filter that I used on all occasions because of the bright light conditions. I took a tripod and used Fujichrome Sensia 64, 200 and 400 film. I find the quality amazing. I used 200-speed film for most of my shots. There is no need to take flashbulbs, and their use is forbidden anyway.

All the sketches in this book, with few exceptions, were made during this visit to the Galápagos islands. We failed to see Painted Rail and Short-eared Owl so I used sketches made on my first trip. Woodpecker Finch was 'on strike', and wouldn't use a tool this time, so on page 249 I used a page out of my old field sketchbook. The layout of the sketches and the writing of text I undertook at home.

Unlike a photographer, I don't need much equipment, and light is not so important to me either. Some paper and pens is all I need. I use a smallish, easily held sketchbook, so that the wind doesn't interfere with my drawing. For the last four years I have preferred to work with felt pens when I can, and even for the basic colours I use a range of 'Tombo' felt pens. Only when there is time or I want more detail do I open my water-colour box. I prefer to watch birds for a long time and sketch their behaviour and movements; it is less important for me to make a 'perfect' picture. Some sketches therefore look a little rough, but with field notes jotted around them I can work on them again at home. In the Galápagos, with a few exceptions, the birds are not very colourful; but the great advantage for an artist is that they are not shy. On Española, a Mockingbird even came and sat on my pen while I was sketching him. A Large-billed Flycatcher on the Alcedo walk took a fly which had landed on my hand. Some birds are very easy to sketch, such as frigatebirds or boobies; they often just sit around and don't move too much. I prefer to sketch active and 'busy' birds such as Warbler Finch. Since the birds are so tame, I only used binoculars and didn't take a telescope, it would have been heavy to carry and little use on the moving deck of a boat.

So equipment for sketching is pretty minimal, but what you do need are good observational skills and a great deal of patience!

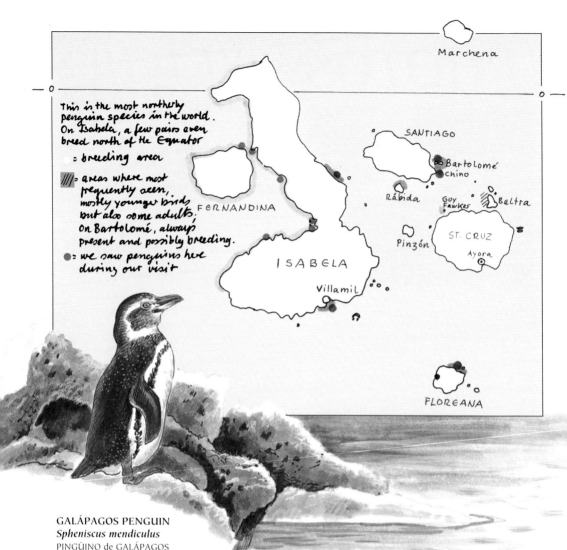

This is the most northerly penguin species in the world. On Isabela, a few pairs even breed north of the Equator

○ = breeding area

///= areas where most frequently seen, mostly younger birds but also some adults; on Bartolomé, always present and possibly breeding.

● = we saw penguins here during our visit

Marchena

SANTIAGO

Bartolomé
chino

Rábida

Guy
Fawkes

Baltra

FERNANDINA

Pinzón

ST. CRUZ

Ayora

ISABELA

Villamil

FLOREANA

GALÁPAGOS PENGUIN
Spheniscus mendiculus
PINGÜINO de GALÁPAGOS

This is a very small penguin, only 53 cm long, about 37 cm in height, and weighs approximately 2 kg (compare with the large Emperor Penguin, which weighs 45 kg and has a length of 115 cm). Only Little Penguins from Australia and New Zealand (40 cm long) are smaller.

The similar, larger Magellanic Penguin (70 cm), which breeds in small areas along the Chilean coast, is possibly the closest relative of the Galápagos P. The related Humboldt P. (65 cm) breeds mostly on the Peruvian coast, but non-breeders occasionally wander to the Gulf of Guayaquil. Magellanic P. has been found in New Zealand waters. Such wanderers may have reached the Galápagos where they have evolved into smaller birds. A wandering Galápagos P. has been trapped on the Panama coast.

The world population of these little 'clowns' of the Galápagos is no more than 1,500–2,500 birds, and it's possible the population has never been larger.

Breeding colonies are found only around Fernandina and on the west side of Isabela, from Caleta Iguana near Punta Cristóbal in the south up to Cabo Berkeley; but some pairs breed ever further north, above the Equator up to Punta Albemarle. They like the colder waters in this part of the Galápagos, where their preferred food of small fish and crustaceans abound. Breeding colonies are small (a few pairs), but up to 40 pairs have been observed. Before breeding starts, the birds moult, which takes about two weeks. They usually pair for life, but partner changes are more frequent than in other penguin species. The nest is made under rocks in small holes, crevices or burrows. They lay two eggs normally, and both parents incubate and take care of the chicks (in most cases only one survives), for about 40 days. Two, even three, broods are possible in a year. After breeding, the young birds and some adults disperse and are then also seen on other islands (*see* map above).

Non-breeders spend most of their time in the water but will come ashore to preen their feathers, and are then often seen sitting on rocks asleep. The non-breeding groups are mostly small, 2–7 birds, but when the water temperature drops below 23°C, groups of over 20 can be seen fishing together. On land they look rather funny, but they are not shy. In the water their movements are more elegant and they can swim very fast but are afraid of divers because of their resemblance to sealions, their worst enemy, so keep your distance.

cheeks paler

grey breast

15.VII Isabela, Playa Negré
first penguin seen, swimming
around, but only for a short while

pink

breast-band
not complete
imm.

juv

16. July Fernandina

cheeks
pale

some yellow
pink

no sharp
separation,
colour
intergrades

second breast-band
in adults

normally wings cover this
band indicated by the
red line

penguins often seen
swimming half submerged or
sometimes with just their head or bill
out of the water

woolly

brown

all black

grey

some pink
on bill

red
eyes

light grey

16. July Fernandina
see also p.206 oystercatchers

male iguana

18 July Isabela Elizabeth Bay ▷
two sitting on a small lava rock
near the shore. Moulting head
feathers. They looked more like
childrens' toys than real birds,
especially the bird on the right which
resembled a hedgehog. Both are immature birds

big heads

taking off looks very difficult but landing is even worse, especially on land with blocks of lava everywhere. Legs streched out, they look like a landing aircraft

SANTIAGO

Rábida

FERNANDINA

30

40

ISABELA

Pinzón

ST. CRUZ

1

2

this number next to the red dot indicates how many we saw

SAN CRISTÓBAL

1

2

1

2

FLOREANA

about 10

many

ESPAÑOLA

only island where they breed in the Galapagos

WAVED ALBATROSS
Diomedea irrorata
ALBATROSS DE GALÁPAGOS

When Barnaby visited Española in 1994 there were many more albatrosses breeding or with chicks. This year, 24 July 1995, there were only 17 birds in the colony. Of course there were many more pairs on the rest of the island, which is not open to visitors. Was this already a sign of El Niño? Egg-laying is at its peak in the first two weeks of May but there were no chicks around either. Normally by the end of March the first male albatrosses arrive in the colonies and establish their territories. When females arrive they mate quickly and the females lay their single egg on the bare ground. Both parents brood for 60 days and take care of the chicks for another 170 days. While the parents are away at sea searching for food, the chicks gather together in nursery groups. On return, the parents find their chicks by calling. When the chicks are larger, food is only given once a week, later only every second week. The large amount of food (up to 2 kg) given consists of an oily liquid of digested fish and squid. Once the chicks are 'fledged', they depart to return to start breeding when they are four to six years old.

While sailing from Bahia Elizabeth on Isabela, towards Punta Moreno, the sea was very calm. There was a line of albatrosses sitting on the water. At long distance, they looked like black dots, and with binoculars like toy ducks. Their white heads were clearly visible. There were six in one line, then 15 in another. 18 July

paler

legs

golden yellow shine

mustard yellow

blue-grey feet

? I could not see the underwing pattern in this bird 19 July near Los Cuatro Hermanos

Sometimes it looks as though they have a small pointed crest

Take-off was a lot of work. There was no wind and perhaps that's why it took even longer. Quite difficult to sketch them, especially the underwing pattern. They were too far away for a photo

See also nest pages

Galápagos Ecuador 0° La Plata

blue = non breeding distribution

When visiting Española between January and March you will not see any Waved Albatrosses. This is the non-breeding season and the birds are all at sea. At this time of year they roam the colder waters of the Humboldt Current together with younger birds which spend all the year in the fish- and squid-rich waters off the coast of Ecuador and Peru. This is the only albatross species now living in tropical waters. All others go further south or, in the Pacific, further north, up to the Hawaiian islands. The adults breeding on Española will fly far out to sea, often staying 1–2 weeks away from their nest or chicks in search of food. Nearly all of the approximately 12,000 pairs of Waved Albatross breed on Española. Only a few have been found breeding on the Isla de la Plata off the mainland of Ecuador. By December, when the young birds are adult-sized and already similar in plumage to their parents (which is not the rule in most albatross species), they will fly out to sea and stay there for the next 4–6 years before returning to breed, mostly in the colonies where they were born.

eye-brow

In a good year there are Waved Albatrosses everywhere on Española. Next to them, breed Blue-footed Boobies, and in the nearby bushes Great Frigatebirds in their flimsy tree nests. But now, in July, it was different. There were no chicks and only a few adults sitting on their single large white egg, which weighs about 285 g. Other birds were just sitting around and when they stood up there was no egg visible. In one pair, where the male appeared much larger, the birds were sitting in front of each other striking one another's bills. Another pair behind them, standing upright, was doing the same. A very large, possibly male bird, stood on the 'trail' looking through us, as if we were not there. I could sketch him and all the other birds easily. When looking straight at us, the broad eyebrows showed up well (I think they are broad to protect the birds' eyes against the strong sun). The whole atmosphere was calm, even a bit melancholy, quite different from my first

one pair was still courting, but appeared listless. All the others were either breeding or just sitting around

♂?♀

About 4 - 5 m from us one bird was rolling its egg. The egg was stained with reddish-brown dust

one bird walked with rather clumsy gait over large lava blocks towards the cliff. This was quite an effort and sometimes it sat down. It was not easy for the bird. At the edge of the cliff, it jumped and flew off, sailing away after a few wing beats

visit to Española years ago at the end of March when the colony was full of courting birds.

Unlike many other albatrosses, which build large cup-shaped nests, Waved have no nests. They never stay for very long in the same place. While we were there, one moved its egg some distance (between its legs). The birds can move the egg as much as 50 m, but not all in one day. I could not understand why they did this as it is quite a risk for the egg. It could easily fall into a crevice and be lost. Many eggs do get lost in this way, and many are abandoned. On the edge of this colony there was a Blue-footed Booby sitting on one of its own eggs and a large albatross egg which it had 'adopted'. One egg in a crevice was split open and mockingbirds, which are very agressive on this island, were drinking from it; the contents already smelled horrible. I don't think that Waved Albatrosses discern any difference between their eggs and those of other pairs. If they lose one, they will adopt an abandoned egg quite happily.

There is a wet landing on a long, white sandy beach, where sealions and very tame mockingbirds are always present. The marine iguanas are black with red patches. Sometimes Large Cactus-finches can be seen on the short walk which passes a Blue-footed Booby colony, just before the albatrosses.

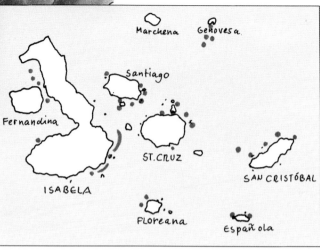

AUDUBON'S SHEARWATER
Puffinus lherminieri
PUFINO

Possibly, next to Blue-footed Booby, this shearwater was the seabird sighted most frequently near all the islands we visited. Often they were in large flocks, unlike Dark-rumped Petrel which we only saw singly, except when we were out at sea near Punta Veintimilla, Isabela, when we saw three together.

DARK-RUMPED PETREL
Pterodroma phaeopygia
PATAPEGADA

Of the six rare Galápagos species to be seen, two are highly endangered: Dark-rumped Petrel and the Mangrove Finch (p.246). The petrel has three different populations on the islands, and these breed at different times of the year. The birds from each colony are slightly different in colour and size. Floreana birds are the largest; those from St Cruz are the smallest. Unlike the shearwater, which breeds in fairly safe cavities in sea cliffs, the petrel makes burrows in the highlands so the eggs, chicks and adults fall easy prey to introduced predators such as rats, cats and dogs.

Dark-rumped Petrel *Pterodroma phaeopygia* is declining seriously at both its breeding stations, in Galápagos Islands (to Ecuador) (nominate *phaeopygia*), and in Hawaii, Hawaiian Islands (to U.S.A.) (race *sandwichensis*) (King 1978-1979). The species breeds on at least four islands in the Galápagos, but suffers there from predation and habitat loss produced by rats, cats, dogs, pigs, burros and cattle; these problems are now subject to rectification (Coulter 1984, Coulter *et al.* 1985, Cruz and Cruz 1987). In Hawaii, some 430 pairs nest largely in Haleakala National Park and are at risk from a variety of introduced mammals (Simons 1985, Stone *et al.* 1988).

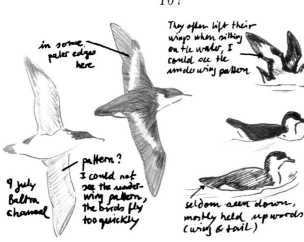

in some, paler edges here

They often lift their wings when sitting on the water, I could see the underwing pattern

flying low over water with legs dangling   15 July near Isabela

A flock of over 25 was fishing next to our dinghy, often holding their heads under the water and also diving
24 July - Islet Gardner near Española

pattern? I could not see the underwing pattern, the birds fly too quickly

9 July Baltra channel

seldom seen down, mostly held upwards (wing & tail)

they open their tails before flying in to a hole under an overhanging lava cave on a small islet in Bahia Gardner   24 July

wings stiff as though vibrating

9·VII Channel Baltra / St Cruz (the first) 2-3 flying past. They look rather brownish in bright sunshine
11·VII One in Puerto Ayora, St. Cruz
12·VII sailing along the east coast of St Cruz many seen, always 2-4 together flying past our ship. Then near Baltra, in the north, even more, flocks of 15-20, some sitting on water with noddies.
13·VII Many seen, flocks of 50-60 together, before Genovesa
14·VII Only one small flock (8) before Caleta Bucanero
15·VII Hundreds (Playa Negra, Isabela) swimming, fishing. In the evening an endless stream of hundreds flying past towards Cowley
16·VII many in small flocks near Isabela/Fernandina, also in the Canal Bolivar.
17·VII Only a few near Lago Beagle, Isabela
18·VII Near Punta Moreno, Isabela flocks of 20-30, in the evening, even larger flocks swimming, fishing
19·VII Sailing towards Rábida, hundreds near Los Cuatros Hermanos, often seen fishing in company of noddies many flying past

20 VII Only a few near Rábida, but on the same day hundreds flying in and out offshore on Sombrero chino
21 VII Before Bartolomé, only a few
23 VII Only a few at sea while sailing towards Floreana
24 VII Flocks 8-25 Punta Suarez and Bahia Gardner, Española
25 VII A few near San Cristóbal
26 VII A few near Plaza and some more in the Channel of Baltra (Canal de Itabaca)

26 July Canal de Itabaca

in some, paler edges — long, narrow, stiff
like a black triangle
long
strong
rather long tail

12 July Sailing from Plaza to Seymour, one, larger than Audubon's, very black and white, stiff-winged, typical head pattern

Back was brownish with a grey shine
paler
Neck clearly separated by pale colour from black head cap

16 July near Fernandina one bird, paler than bird on 12 July

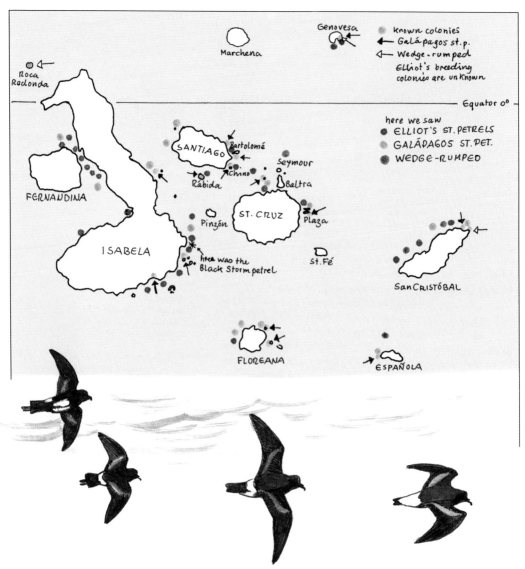

Known colonies
← Galápagos st.p.
⊲ Wedge-rumped
Elliot's breeding
colonies are unknown

Equator 0°

here we saw
● ELLIOT'S ST. PETRELS
○ GALÁPAGOS ST. PET.
● WEDGE-RUMPED

Marchena
Genovesa
Roca Redonda
SANTIAGO
Bartolomé
Seymour
Rábida
Chino
Baltra
FERNANDINA
Pinzón
ST. CRUZ
Plaza
ISABELA
here was the Black Storm petrel
St. Fé
SanCRISTÓBAL
FLOREANA
ESPAÑOLA

● **ELLIOT'S STORM-PETREL**
Oceanites gracilis
GOLONDRINA de TORMENTA
de ELLIOT

○ **GALÁPAGOS STORM-PETREL**
Madeiran Storm Petrel
Oceanodroma castro
GOLONDRINA de GALÁPAGOS
Golondrina de Madeira

● **WEDGE-RUMPED STORM-P.**
Oceanodroma tethys
GOLONDRINA de TORMENTA
de GALÁPAGOS

The three very similar storm-petrels breeding in the Galápagos, are very, very difficult to separate in the field. All are small, nearly the same size, and all are black with a white rump. But there are some details which can help indentification. They are always on the move, and these movements, or the 'jizz characters' as birdwatchers say, will help you to separate them.

Elliot's is the smallest and most like Galápagos Storm-petrel, but the tail is shorter and square-ended; feet show beyond tail. White belly is often not visible in the field. The white, very narrow rump goes around the side of the belly. 'Walks' over the water, follows boats, often close to the shore.

Galápagos has a dark appearance with a slightly forked tail, white rump-band, and narrow, rather large pale brown panels on the wing, only visible at close range. Flight buoyant, even shearwater-like, with shallow wingbeats. Does not normally follow boats.

Wedge-rumped also very dark with a large rump-patch, almost reaching notch of tail and down to flanks. Pale upper wingbars only visible at close range. Wings are long, narrow and pointed, often held slightly forward. Mostly feeds at night and comes to breeding grounds during the day.

brownish panel easily visible

head darker

legs

squarish tail

dancing next to our boat. Wing and belly pattern easily visible, long legs extending beyond tail
12 July north of Plaza

ELLIOT'S

bouncing, dancing over the water, often behind our boat

pale panel on underwing

white, not always visible

The white belly is not always easily visible. The clear wing bar and square white rump are better field marks.
18 July Bahia Elizabeth Isabela

Rump from above
some have dark marks here
13 July before Genovesa

fork not always visible in the field

19 July, Villamil to Rabida always one or two following our boat

brownish

rather large, pale brown mirrors

16 July / 10.30 hrs

short legs

When tail is spread no fork visible

pale upperwing panel

forward angle

13 July Genovesa

pale underwing panel

white

wings held bowed and slightly forward

sailing from Isabela to Fernandina calm, fantastic sailing with many storm petrels. Two species

a light silvery shine

pale wing bar

head darker than back, which is a dark grey

tail rather long & forked

dark

rounded

dark

silvery

darkest

I identified the bird as a BLACK STORM-PETREL Oceanodroma melania or was it a Markham's Storm-petrel? O. markhami?

On 19 July 1995, when sailing from Villamil / Isabela towards Rábida, near Cabo Nepera de Vado, there was a very dark storm-petrel flying in a straight direction, past our boat. Later it turned back again in a straight line, all the time keeping nearly the same height above the water, never dipping down to feed. It had rather strong wing beats, looked very dark and larger than the other three species I had seen till now in the Galápagos. There was no sign of any white on the rump, but a pale wing bar was present; its under wings were all dark

13 July, Genovesa,
a tropicbird sitting on its nest in a
hole on a lava cliff. Body in the
shade and tail hanging outside in
the sunshine, like a decoration. The
bright red bill is clearly visible even
in the shade

RED-BILLED TROPICBIRD
Phaethon aethereus
RABIJUNCO ETERES, in Galápagos also called Avetropical, Piloto ...Contramaestre

Worldwide there are only three species in the tropicbird family, of these, Red-billed has the most limited distribution, but it does have three subspecies. The subspecies *mesonauta* breeds on the American side of the tropical Pacific (incl. Galápagos), the Caribbean and Cape Verdes; the nominate *aethereus* on S. Atlantic islands, and *indicus* in the Red Sea, Persian Gulf and Gulf of Aden. After breeding they are all highly pelagic, flying far from their breeding areas. They are mostly solitary, but when food is plentiful they can concentrate in large flocks. Their preferred food is medium-sized flying-fish, smaller herring-like fish, and also squid.

The Red-billed subspecies, *mesonanta*, breeds in the Galápagos. It is very interesting that in most colonies breeding goes on all year round while on Plaza there is an annual breeding cycle between August and February.

Nesting sites on Plaza are plentiful and from the high cliffs you can easily watch the beautiful aerial display of this most elegant Galápagos seabird, often just below you.

On Genovesa they will breed all year round. There are plenty of nesting sites on the cliffs and being so far out at sea it is also an ideal island for the tropic birds, except there is more competition for food with the large Red-footed Booby colonies.

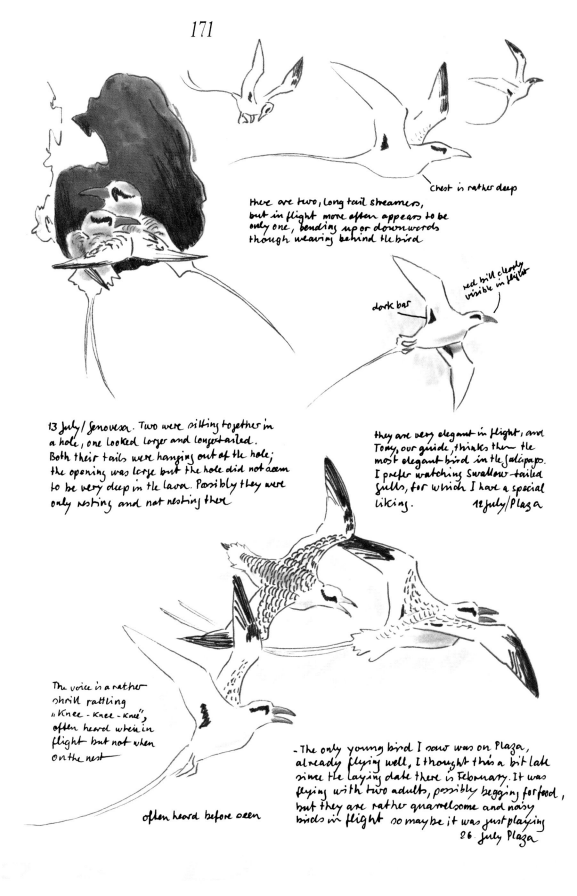

chest is rather deep

there are two, long tail streamers,
but in flight more often appears to be
only one, bending up or downwards
though weaving behind the bird

dark bar

red bill clearly
visible in flight

13 July / Genovesa. Two were sitting together in
a hole, one looked larger and longer-tailed.
Both their tails were hanging out of the hole;
the opening was large but the hole did not seem
to be very deep in the lava. Possibly they were
only resting and not nesting there

they are very elegant in flight, and
Tony, our guide, thinks them the
most elegant bird in the Galápagos.
I prefer watching Swallow-tailed
gulls, for which I have a special
liking.   12 July/Plaza

The voice is a rather
shrill rattling
"knee - knee - knee",
often heard when in
flight but not when
on the nest

often heard before seen

- The only young bird I saw was on Plaza,
already flying well, I thought this a bit late
since the laying date there is February. It was
flying with two adults, possibly begging for food,
but they are rather quarrelsome and noisy
birds in flight so maybe it was just playing
26 July Plaza

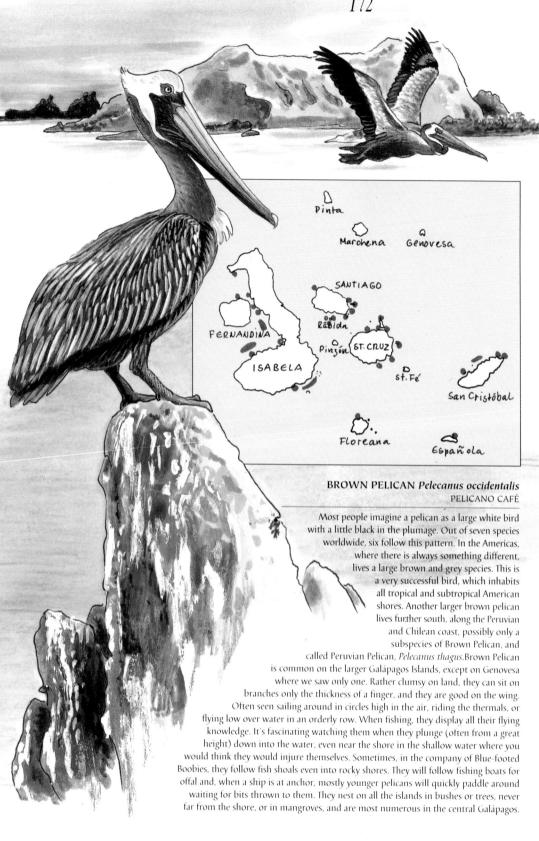

BROWN PELICAN *Pelecanus occidentalis*
PELICANO CAFÉ

Most people imagine a pelican as a large white bird with a little black in the plumage. Out of seven species worldwide, six follow this pattern. In the Americas, where there is always something different, lives a large brown and grey species. This is a very successful bird, which inhabits all tropical and subtropical American shores. Another larger brown pelican lives further south, along the Peruvian and Chilean coast, possibly only a subspecies of Brown Pelican, and called Peruvian Pelican, *Pelecanus thagus*.Brown Pelican is common on the larger Galápagos Islands, except on Genovesa where we saw only one. Rather clumsy on land, they can sit on branches only the thickness of a finger, and they are good on the wing. Often seen sailing around in circles high in the air, riding the thermals, or flying low over water in an orderly row. When fishing, they display all their flying knowledge. It's fascinating watching them when they plunge (often from a great height) down into the water, even near the shore in the shallow water where you would think they would injure themselves. Sometimes, in the company of Blue-footed Boobies, they follow fish shoals even into rocky shores. They will follow fishing boats for offal and, when a ship is at anchor, mostly younger pelicans will quickly paddle around waiting for bits thrown to them. They nest on all the islands in bushes or trees, never far from the shore, or in mangroves, and are most numerous in the central Galápagos.

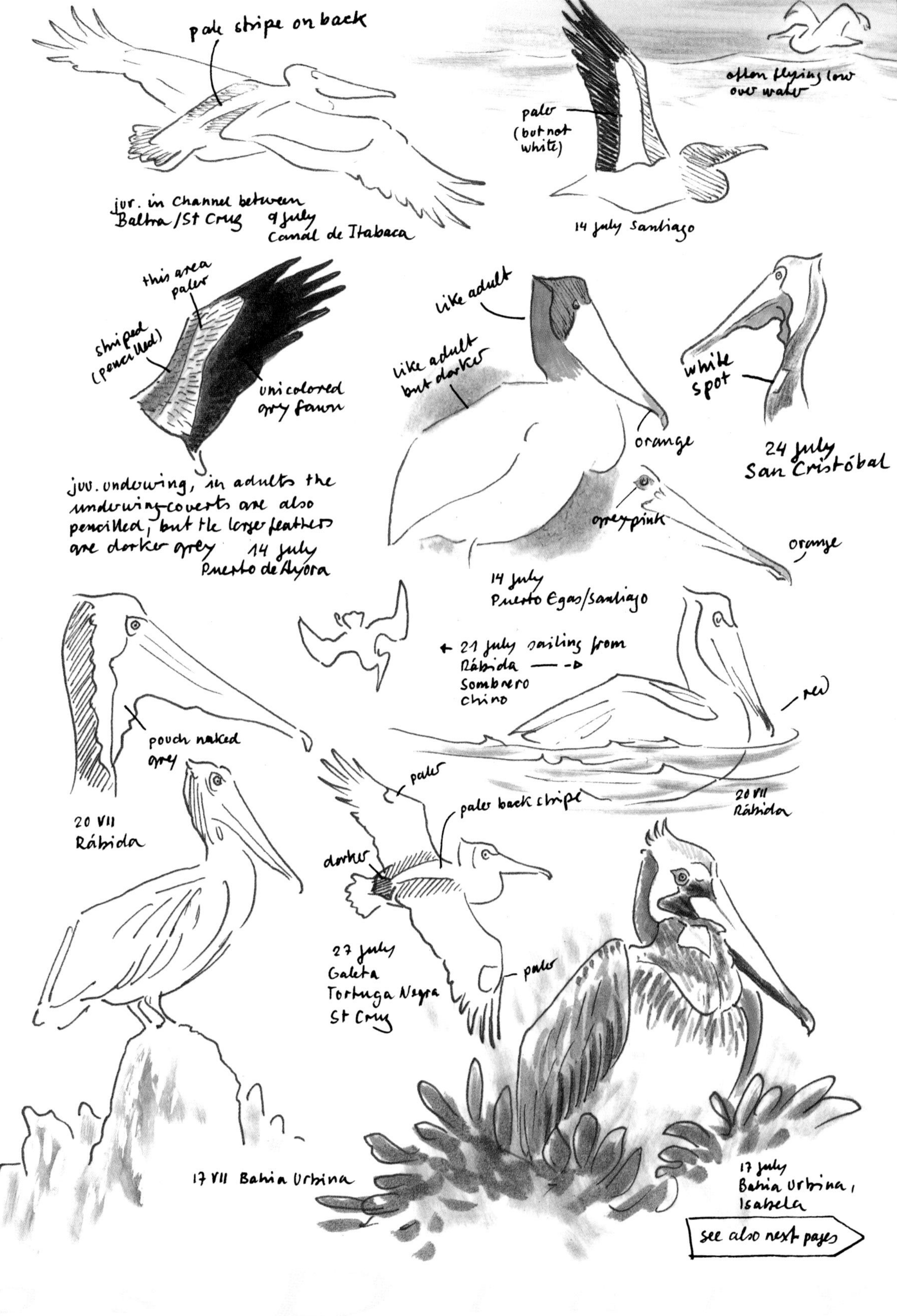

pale stripe on back

jur. in Channel between
Baltra/St Cruz   9 july
Canal de Itabaca

paler
(but not
white)

often flying low
over water

14 july santiago

this area
paler

striped
(pencilled)

unicolored
grey fawn

juv. underwing, in adults the
underwing-coverts are also
pencilled, but the larger feathers
are darker grey   14 july
Puerto de Ayora

like adult

like adult
but darker

orange

grey-pink

14 july
Puerto Egas/Santiago

white
spot

24 july
San Cristóbal

orange

pouch naked
grey

20 VII
Rábida

← 21 july sailing from
Rábida
——▷
Sombrero
chino

red

20 VII
Rábida

paler

paler back stripe

darker

27 july
Galeta
Tortuga Negra
St Cruz

paler

17 VII Bahia Urbina

17 july
Bahia Urbina,
Isabela

see also next pages ▷

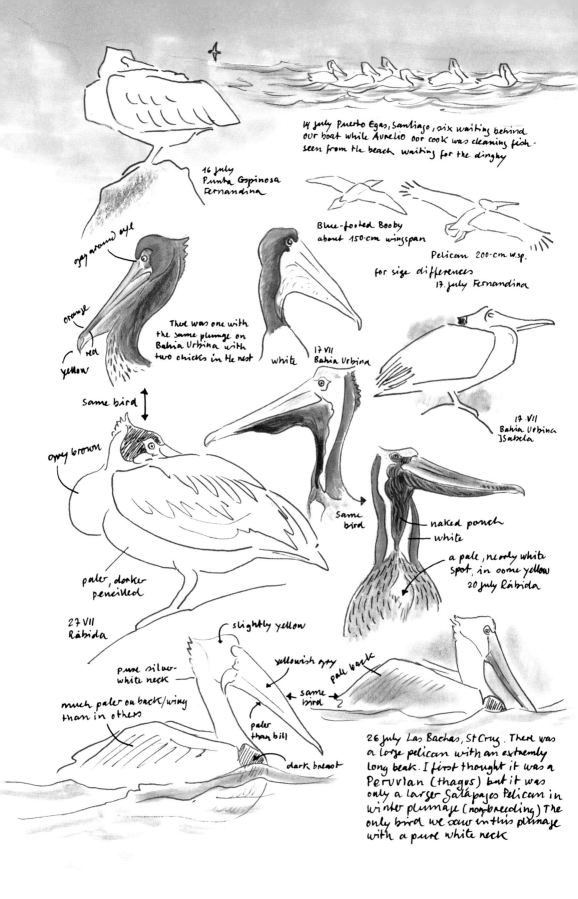

16 July
Punta Espinosa
Fernandina

14 July Puerto Egas, Santiago, six waiting behind our boat while Aurelio our cook was cleaning fish. seen from the beach waiting for the dinghy

Blue-footed Booby about 150·cm wingspan

Pelican 200·cm w.sp.
for size differences
17 July Fernandina

grey around eye

orange
red
yellow

There was one with the same plumage on Bahia Urbina with two chicks in the nest

white

17 VII
Bahia Urbina

17·VII
Bahia Urbina
Isabela

same bird

grey brown

paler, darker pencilled

27 VII
Rábida

same bird

naked pouch
white

a pale, nearly white spot, in some yellow
20 July Rábida

slightly yellow

pure silver-white neck

much paler on back/wing than in others

yellowish grey

pale back

same bird 2

paler than bill

dark breast

26 July Las Bachas, St Cruz. There was a large pelican with an extremely long beak. I first thought it was a Peruvian (thagus) but it was only a larger Galápagos Pelican in winter plumage (non-breeding) The only bird we saw in this plumage with a pure white neck

head mottled black/white

pale, nearly white spots

bill pale grey

grey

pouch paler than bill

white down like fur

pencilled reddish

17 July Bahia Urbina, a juv. with wings already feathered

one feeding adult had greyish-blue rim around eye not pink

chick

they always feed only one chick at a time

adult feeding the bill of the chick is seen through the adult's pouch

chick

Barnaby took a photo of this - see under 17 July in the Photo section (p. 78)

17 July Bahia Urbina, Isabela, on 1 m high saltbushes, a colony of about 50 nests, more than normal. Some already breeding but still with dark heads or dark mottled with white. In most nests there were two chicks, in some only one. Many young birds already flying, these were mostly fed by white-headed adults. It is possible they breed earlier

adult with two chicks
on a ledge,
10 july Ayora harbour

landing on a ledge
Ayora 10 july

BLUE-FOOTED BOOBY
Sula nebouxii
PIQUERO PATA AZULES

female   male

the largest colony
we saw here

Marchena

Genovesa
only a few pairs

SANTIAGO

FERNANDINA

Rábida.
Pinzón

ST. CRUZ

small
colony

ISABELA

a few
breeding

SAN CRISTÓBAL

FLOREANA

a large colony
ESPAÑOLA

The female is strongly built and larger than the male. Her eye seems to have a larger black pupil, but this is a black pigmented ring around the iris which makes the pupil appear larger and gives her a different appearance. Like the immatures, she has a nasal, hoarse, duck-like voice, whereas the male produces a plaintive whistle. Some males seem to have brighter coloured blue feet of different shades, even tending toward violet, but this is not reliable in establishing the sex.

THE seabird you will see all the time. But this is not the most numerous booby. There are more Red-footed Boobies, most common on Genovesa, where Blue-footed is rare. Red-footed are more pelagic, while Blue-footed is an inshore feeder. The nominate Blue-footed, *S. n. nebouxii*, breeds on islands along the coasts of Mexico, Ecuador and Peru. In the Galápagos, where some 75% of the world population breeds, they are larger and brighter, and are the subspecies *S.n. exisa*. They breed mostly in large colonies on flat ground, such as in the crater on Daphne, but small colonies are also found on cliff ledges, such as the one in Ayora harbour. Mostly they lay 1–3 eggs but sometimes more. After breeding, which occurs all year round, birds disperse further out to sea. Young birds, ringed as chicks in the Galápagos, have been recorded on the mainland coast of Ecuador.

"sky pointing"

tail

see also pages 180-181

pale

12 cm

the head feathers are sprouting

mustard-grey

← same chick →

an older chick, looks at first glance like a Masked Booby

first feathers growing

a happy, well-fed chick sitting comfortably in bright sunshine. They can assume the funniest positions, often laying down as if they were dead

oil gland

a fat downy chick fed by the father wing feathers are growing

24 July Española

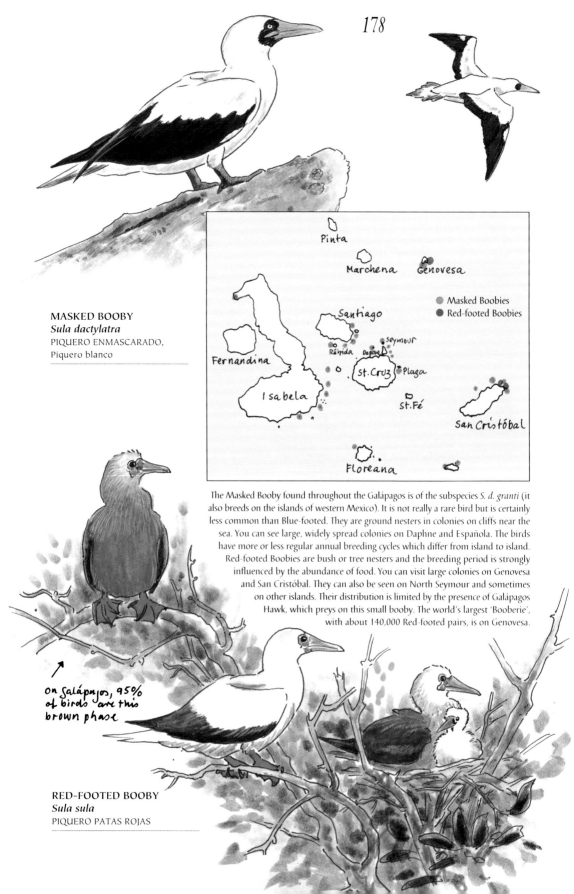

MASKED BOOBY
Sula dactylatra
PIQUERO ENMASCARADO,
Piquero blanco

Map labels:
Pinta
Marchena · Genovesa
● Masked Boobies
● Red-footed Boobies
Santiago
Fernandina
Rábida · Daphne · Seymour
St.Cruz · Plaza
Isabela
St.Fé
San Cristóbal
Floreana

The Masked Booby found throughout the Galápagos is of the subspecies *S. d. granti* (it also breeds on the islands of western Mexico). It is not really a rare bird but is certainly less common than Blue-footed. They are ground nesters in colonies on cliffs near the sea. You can see large, widely spread colonies on Daphne and Española. The birds have more or less regular annual breeding cycles which differ from island to island. Red-footed Boobies are bush or tree nesters and the breeding period is strongly influenced by the abundance of food. You can visit large colonies on Genovesa and San Cristóbal. They can also be seen on North Seymour and sometimes on other islands. Their distribution is limited by the presence of Galápagos Hawk, which preys on this small booby. The world's largest 'Booberie', with about 140,000 Red-footed pairs, is on Genovesa.

On Galápagos, 95% of birds are this brown phase

RED-FOOTED BOOBY
Sula sula
PIQUERO PATAS ROJAS

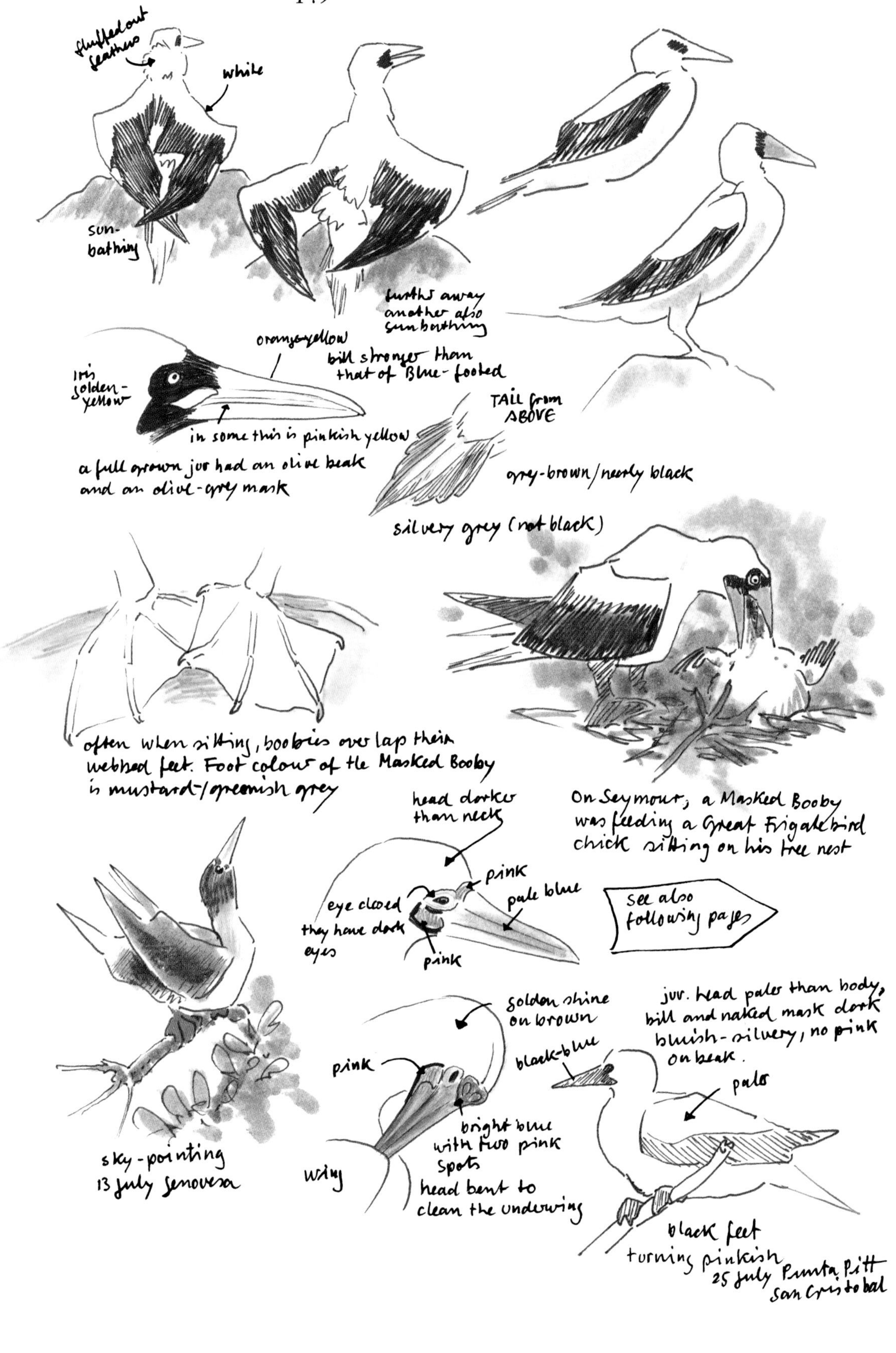

fluffed out feathers

white

sun-bathing

further away another also sun-bathing

bill stronger than that of Blue-footed

orange-yellow

iris golden-yellow

in some this is pinkish yellow

a full grown juv had an olive beak and an olive-grey mask

TAIL from ABOVE

grey-brown/nearly black

silvery grey (not black)

often when sitting, boobies over lap their webbed feet. Foot colour of the Masked Booby is mustard/greenish grey

head darker than neck

pink

pale blue

eye closed they have dark eyes

pink

On Seymour, a Masked Booby was feeding a Great Frigatebird chick sitting on his tree nest

see also following pages

golden shine on brown

black-blue

pink

bright blue with two pink spots

head bent to clean the underwing

juv. head paler than body, bill and naked mask dark bluish-silvery, no pink on beak.

pale

sky-pointing 13 July Genovesa

wing

black feet turning pinkish
25 July Punta Pitt San Cristobal

Brown Pelican   Blue-f. Booby
differences in shape and size

A few pelicans can often be seen with
Blue-footed Boobies sitting on low lava rocks
Sometimes 50-60 boobies together, joined by
a single Blue Heron

head paler

long

pale

white
triangle

white

Blue-footed Booby

tail
paler than
rest

white

back mottled,
head always
paler

dark head,
this is a juvenile

often they dive
very close to the shore in shallow
water between lava blocks. Before
touching the surface, they close
their wings and open their long
tail.

the blue feet are
not always seen in flight,
except when landing; in
juv. they are all dark

◁ before landing, the bird
greets its partner on the
nest, showing its bright
blue feet.

short
legs?

white dropping
marking a circle
around the nest

tail spread before
landing

Masked & Red footed
all sketched on
Genovesa 13 July

Masked, before landing,
over its nest, holding wings in a V

like albatrosses, Masked and
Blue-footed swim well (unli
frigate birds) We did not see a
Red-footed Booby on the water

BLUE-FOOTED BOOBY

The mid-sized Galápagos booby. Mostly brown above, white below with a 'streaky' head and broad white patch at the hindneck and back. Tail dark with a paler centre. The adult male is of lighter build and has a proportionally longer tail (not a good field mark) which allows it to dive in shallow waters. The juvenile has a dark head and tail; the neck patch is smaller, back dark, mottled paler and with a white patch. The underwing pattern at all ages is similar but less defined in the juvenile. The juvenile is easily confused with juvenile Masked Booby, but see differences in the underwing.

MASKED BOOBY

Largest Galápagos booby. This snow-white large seabird with black wings is easy to identify. The bright yellow beak and its size separate it easily from white-phase Red-footed Booby. In the Galápagos, Masked's tail is not all black (subspecies *granti*) but silvery-white with darker edges. The dark juveniles have a white neck-collar, which is missing in Blue-footed, and an all dark back with only a narrow pale crossbar on rump. See also the different underwing pattern, compared with the similar Blue-footed. Immatures have an even wider neck-collar and white in the upperwing.

RED-FOOTED BOOBY

This is the smallest species in the gannet/booby family. The white phase, rare in the Galápagos, has a darkish tail which separates it from the large Masked. The common brown phase (95% of those found in the Galápagos) and the brown, pale-headed also have dark tails. The local subspecies is *S. s. websteri*. All adults have greyish bills (yellow in Masked). The juveniles of all phases are dark chocolate-brown, slightly paler on the underside and have dark bills. Moult into adult plumage is slow. The red feet, especially in the white phase, are a good field mark; they are drab yellow in younger birds.

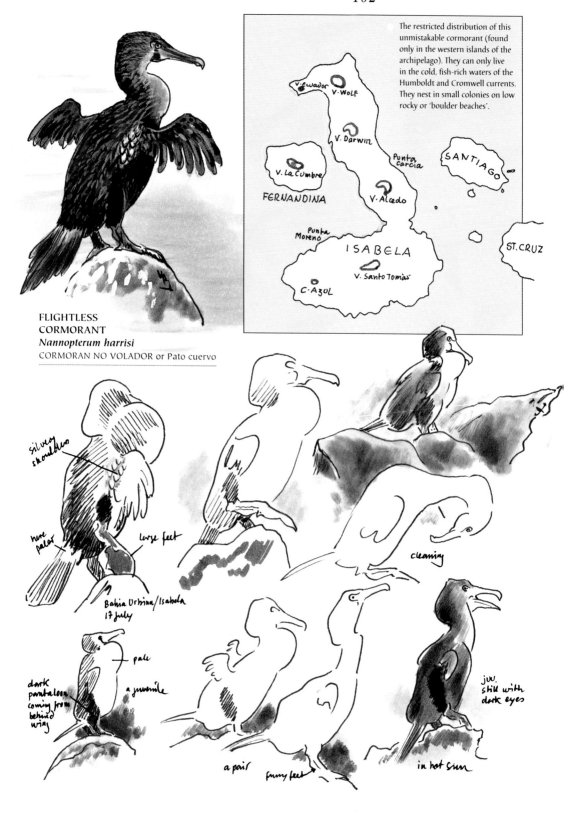

The restricted distribution of this unmistakable cormorant (found only in the western islands of the archipelago). They can only live in the cold, fish-rich waters of the Humboldt and Cromwell currents. They nest in small colonies on low rocky or 'boulder beaches'.

V. Ecuador
V. Wolf
V. Darwin
Punta Garcia
SANTIAGO
V. La Cumbre
V. Alcedo
FERNANDINA
Punta Moreno
ISABELA
V. Santo Tomas
C. Azul
ST. CRUZ

FLIGHTLESS CORMORANT
Nannopterum harrisi
CORMORAN NO VOLADOR or Pato cuervo

silvery shoulders

nice pales

large feet

Bahia Urbina / Isabela
17 July

cleaning

pale

dark pantaloon coming from behind wing

a juvenile

juv. still with dark eyes

a pair

funny feet

in hot sun

male sitting on nest

female cleaning her back

chalk-white droppings

Punta Morena / Isabela
18 July

on nest, breeding

with chick

cleaning

incredible, but it was like this

a pair displayed and walked along like penguins

When one of the pair returns from fishing at sea it always brings a present for his or her mate, otherwise the sitting bird will NOT leave the nest or even let the partner come near

a bird sitting next to this had some yellow on the underbill and its body was more brownish with greyer wings and a pale throat

all black including bill and dark eyes imm.?

tail hanging in water

They swim very low in the water, often only the head is visible

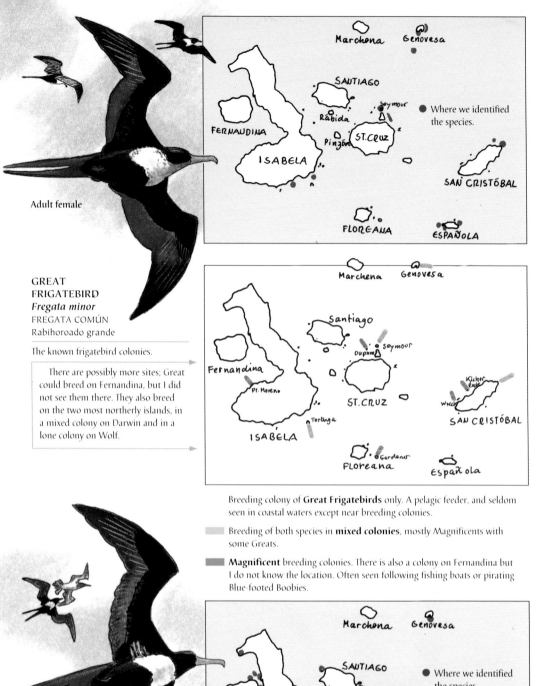

GREAT
FRIGATEBIRD
Fregata minor
FREGATA COMÚN
Rabihoroado grande

The known frigatebird colonies.

There are possibly more sites; Great could breed on Fernandina, but I did not see them there. They also breed on the two most northerly islands, in a mixed colony on Darwin and in a lone colony on Wolf.

● Where we identified the species.

▬▬ Breeding colony of **Great Frigatebirds** only. A pelagic feeder, and seldom seen in coastal waters except near breeding colonies.

▬▬ Breeding of both species in **mixed colonies**, mostly Magnificents with some Greats.

▬▬ **Magnificent** breeding colonies. There is also a colony on Fernandina but I do not know the location. Often seen following fishing boats or pirating Blue-footed Boobies.

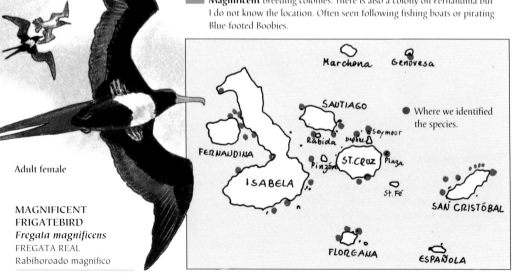

Adult female

MAGNIFICENT
FRIGATEBIRD
Fregata magnificens
FREGATA REAL
Rabihoroado magnifico

● Where we identified the species.

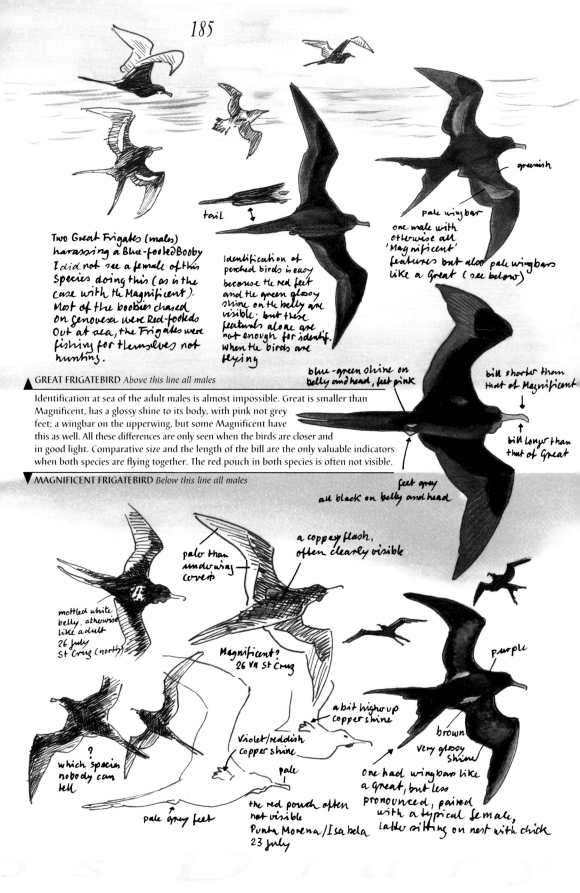

185

Two Great Frigates (males) harassing a Blue-footed Booby I did not see a female of this species doing this (as in the case with the Magnificent). Most of the boobies chased on Genovesa were Red-footeds Out at sea, the Frigates were fishing for themselves not hunting.

tail

Identification of perched birds is easy because the red feet and the green glossy shine on the belly are visible. but these features alone are not enough for identif. when the birds are flying

greenish

pale wingbar

one male with otherwise all 'Magnificent' features but also pale wingbars like a Great (see below)

blue-green shine on belly and head, feet pink

bill shorter than that of Magnificent

bill longer than that of Great

▲ GREAT FRIGATEBIRD *Above this line all males*

Identification at sea of the adult males is almost impossible. Great is smaller than Magnificent, has a glossy shine to its body, with pink not grey feet; a wingbar on the upperwing, but some Magnificent have this as well. All these differences are only seen when the birds are closer and in good light. Comparative size and the length of the bill are the only valuable indicators when both species are flying together. The red pouch in both species is often not visible.

▼ MAGNIFICENT FRIGATEBIRD *Below this line all males*

feet grey
all black on belly and head

a coppery flash, often clearly visible

paler than underwing coverts

mottled white belly, otherwise like adult 26 July St Cruz (north)

purple

Magnificent? 26 VII St Cruz

a bit high up copper shine

brown

Violet/reddish copper shine

very glossy shine

pale

which species nobody can tell

One had wingbars like a Great, but less pronounced, paired with a typical female, latter sitting on nest with chick

pale grey feet

the red pouch often not visible Punta Morena/Isabela 23 July

All Great Frigatebirds on this page

on immature male,
some had a dark band
across the belly (possibly
the nest stage towards adult
plumage), the red pouch not
visible on all
13 July Genovesa

pouch

jur. like
Magnificent
but a rusty
shade on head,
some, possibly older,
had white heads

white

chick

13 VII Genovesa

female with
chick on a
flimsy nest

panting
in bright, hot
sun on a rock

brown

white

♀

beak

juvenile laying on a rock
ledge sunbathing
13 July Genove[sa]

red eye-ring,
blue in Magnificent

white

brownish

silvery

♀ sitting on a lava boulder
taking a sunbath
13 July Genovesa

187

just some white on belly like a belt

white head brown back

pale panel

a female with a very patchy belly

20 July Chino

some fawn (brown) here

some immatures have 'whitish' areas here

feet dark red

the pale feet are sometimes visible

See also Masked Booby (p 179)

18 July Bahia Elizabeth

25 July Punta Pitt San Cristobal

shows variation in breast of juveniles and immatures possibly age-related

pouch

12·VII Seymour

a Masked Booby fed a Frigatebird chick and then stayed beside it, as though keeping guard. There was no aggression towards the chick. Why was a ground nester doing this?

male, on 'guard' with a downy chick

same male as below; a female is sitting next to the male. The female flew off sometime later

female has red feet and a blue eye-ring
(red in Great Frigate female)

waiting again on nest for a female   27 July Genovesa

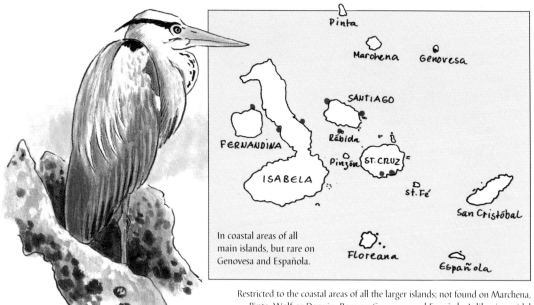

In coastal areas of all main islands, but rare on Genovesa and Española.

GREAT BLUE HERON
Ardea herodias
GARZA AZULADA or Garza Morena

The largest heron in the Galápagos. The endemic subspecies, *A. n. cognata*, looks like a pale, washed out version of the brighter North American subspecies. A quiet bird, its voice is seldom heard and seems easy to overlook despite its size. Birds can become very active when fishing, mostly alone on shorelines or in mangroves.

Restricted to the coastal areas of all the larger islands; not found on Marchena, Pinta, Wolf or Darwin. Rare on Genovesa and Española. It likes intertidal zones, mangroves and saltwater lagoons. We only saw nests in big bushes or trees hanging over water, but it is said that it also nests on cliff ledges. Nests are used again in different breeding seasons and become rather large, compact constructions of branches with a finish of smaller twigs. Breeding occurs in any month of the year. Two to three bluish eggs are laid, and both parents incubate for about 28-30 days. Chicks are fed by both parents, mainly with fish, but lizards, young marine iguanas, young birds, mice and young black rats are caught too.

a juvenile, all yellow underbill upper bill very dark

chest crest

pink white   yellow

stripes dark grey

no crest

short crest

adult

back is darkish grey with some white spots on the wings

white spots

salmon pink

A breeding bird (both sexes are alike) not shy at all. I made this sketch at a distance of a few metres on the beach at Las Bachas 26 July Northern Santa Cruz

yellow like the soles of their feet

a juvenile 26 July Las Bachas

It looked to me as if it was walking over its own feet

a pale greyish pink

this bird appeared
very pale, as
though faded

Once at Playa de los Alemanes, a Great Blue Heron
was sitting in a bush nest to a Great White Egret.
It looked much larger and heavier, but very pale.
This was too far away for Barnaby's camera
10 July Santa Cruz

Compared with a baby
European Grey Heron this
little 'hedgehog' must be
about 10 days old

The nest, with one chick, was much larger than
a pelican nest nearby. Even this breeding
adult, like all the Blue Herons we saw, had a
very short occipital crest   16 July Punta Espinosa
                                        Fernandina

Wading in shallow
water

moving very slowly
while fishing near
the beach

Walking along the shore at Las Bachas,
a juvenile started to spread its
feathers for a sunbath. I walked
away and it opened its
wings completely

with their large
feet, they make
distinctive footprints
in wet sand along
the shore

26 July 96

In the lagoon at Caleta Tortuga,
there was a well-feathered chick
looking at us, standing upright alone
in its nest.

neck is very long

Great Egret is more often seen around lagoons in the inter-tidal zone than in the grassy 'terra alta' where Cattle Egret is more common. You will often see them fishing, even in deep water, something that cattle Egrets never do

26 July Caleta Tortuga, St Cruz

short

heavier body short wing beats, rather rapid = Cattle Egret

10 July St Cruz beyond the Playa de Los Alemanes, a Great Egret was sitting with a Blue Heron in a bush. They looked around a bit when we arrived then both sat motionless, half asleep, for quite a while. The size difference was easy to see

long all black

flight slow, deep wing beats = Great Egret

I did not see them flying together, but in any case Great Egret is much 'longer', a bit 'spiny' looking, with its long legs. Cattle Egrets, mostly seen in flocks, are more heavily built and shorter

Genovesa
Marchena
SANTIAGO
FERNANDINA
Rábida
Pinzón
ST. CRUZ St Fé
SAN CRISTÓBAL
ISABELA
FLOREANA
ESPAÑOLA

GREAT EGRET
Casmerodius albus
GARZA BLANCA

Great Egret is not so common as the larger Great Blue Heron or smaller Cattle Egret. It is found only on the larger islands, Fernandina, Isabela, St Cruz, Floreana and San Cristóbal, where it is mostly restricted to the coastal areas but will also feed inland. They take small fish, also lizards, grasshoppers and other insects, but will also catch small birds or mice. They breed in small colonies in mangroves near the shore. A normal clutch is two eggs. Both parents incubate and take care of the chicks. After breeding, the long display plumes on the back (called aigrettes) are lost.

Anywhere where cows or horses
graze in the 'terra alta' you
will find Cattle Egrets, often in
large flocks of 20-30 birds. But they don't
breed up there. Their colonies are down on the coast.

12. july Plaza Sur. A Cattle Egret slowly approached
a peaceful feeding group of four small Ground-
finches. With a quick snap it caught an all
black male and swallowed it. Is this a new
habit developed on the Galápagos?

The egret was a bit worried,
dancing around, while the
wings of its prey covered both
its eyes. It couldn't see a
thing

from catching to swallowing
it took about two minutes

After it caught the finch,
which was still alive,
the egret hammered
it against the ground with its
beak. Something dropped down,
feathers or a leg, and the
egret swallowed its prey

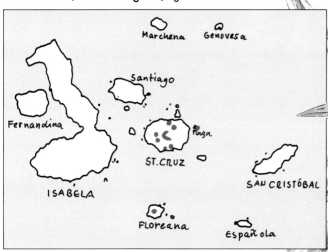

Marchena Genovesa
Santiago
Fernandina
Plaza
ST. CRUZ
SAN CRISTÓBAL
ISABELA
Floreana
Española

This newcomer, originally from Africa, was first recorded in the Galápagos
in 1964; since 1986 it has been known as a breeding bird and is now common
on the four islands with cattle farms: St Cruz, San Cristóbal, Floreana and southern
Isabela. The presence of cattle has allowed the bird to become established. Cattle
Egrets also visit Santiago and possibly other islands, but the wild roaming goats,
donkeys 'etc. in the bush are not so attractive as cows on grazed farmland. Cattle
Egrets are also attracted by sealions lying near the shore (as we saw on Playa), and
also by the large tortoises up near farmland on St Cruz.

CATTLE EGRET
Bubulcus ibis
GARZILLA BUEYERA

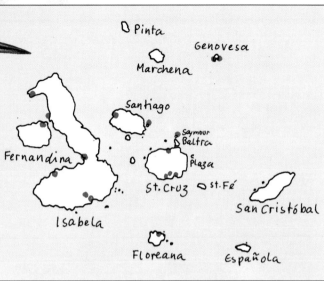

LAVA HERON
Butoroides sundevalli
GARCITA de GALÁPAGOS

This bird is an all-dark, lava-coloured, small heron. Depending on the light, its plumage has a silvery glow like old lava, but also a green on violet sheen. The bill is shiny black. When breeding, the legs become orange or red; out of breeding season they are silvery grey. The immature Lava Heron looks like an immature Striated Heron, but is darker. Lava and Striated Herons are difficult to separate in the field, and their voices are alike.

Lava Heron is endemic to the Galápagos. It is not very clear whether it is a full species, a subspecies or a colour morph of Striated Heron (found worldwide). Lava Heron is found in the intertidal zones of all the islands, even the small ones, not only on lava but also in the saltwater lagoons where it nests, alone, using lower branches when in mangroves, and spaces under rocks in areas of lava. It is not a colonial nester as are most other herons, and defends its rather small territory against all intruders. When conditions are right, it will nest two to three times in a year, and rear two to three chicks.

STRIATED HERON
Butorides striatus
GARCITA VERDOSA

Same size, same bill and leg colour as Lava heron, brighter and at a distance paler looking, never so dark as Lava Heron, even in the shade.

The distribution of Striated Heron is very peculiar in the Galápagos. Striated is only found on the larger islands: Fernandina, Isabela, St Cruz and San Cristóbal, but also on Pinta. Possibly a newcomer. Only recently known as a breeder in the Galápagos. No detail is known about its breeding on the islands and it seems not to vary from Lava Heron. Striated is found over most of tropical South America, not only along the coasts. The so called Green Heron lives further north as far as the Great Lakes in North America. Intermediate individuals occur on many Galápagos islands. Either the two species hybridize or they are just the same species with the dark Lava form being more common. Immature Striated are paler than same-aged Lavas. Some, possibly older, have unstreaked bellies.

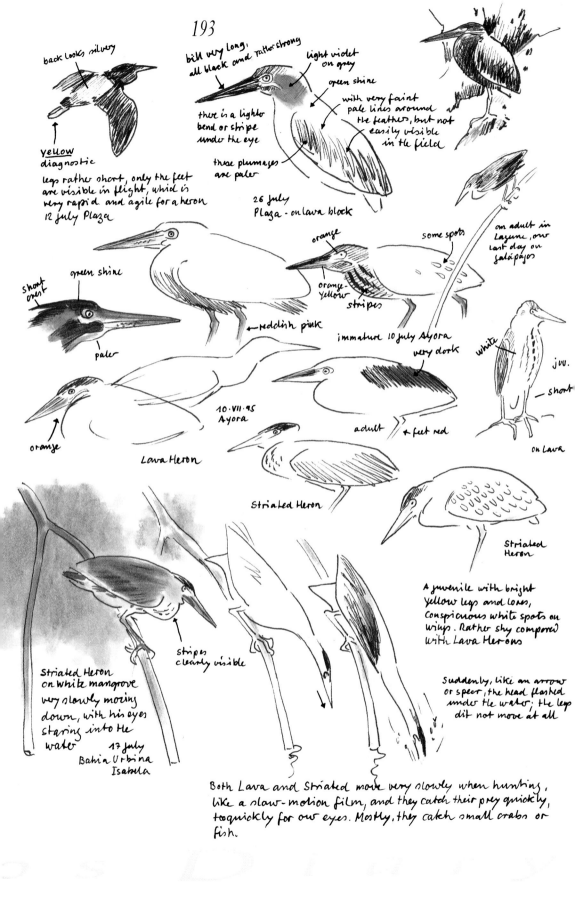

back looks silvery

yellow diagnostic

legs rather short, only the feet are visible in flight, which is very rapid and agile for a heron
12 July Plaza

bill very long, all black and rather strong

light violet on grey

green shine

with very faint pale lines around the feathers, but not easily visible in the field

there is a lighter bend or stripe under the eye

these plumages are paler

26 July
Plaza - on lava block

some spots

on adult in Lazune, our last day on Galápagos

short crest

green shine

paler

orange

reddish pink

orange

orange-yellow stripes

immature 10 July Ayora
very dark

white

juv.

short

10·VII·95
Ayora

adult

feet red

on Lava

Lava Heron

Striated Heron

Striated Heron

A juvenile with bright yellow legs and lores, conspicuous white spots on wings. Rather shy compared with Lava Herons

stripes clearly visible

Striated Heron on white mangrove very slowly moving down, with his eyes staring into the water
17 July
Bahia Urbina
Isabela

Suddenly, like an arrow or spear, the head flashed under the water; the legs did not move at all

Both Lava and Striated move very slowly when hunting, like a slow-motion film, and they catch their prey quickly, too quickly for our eyes. Mostly, they catch small crabs or fish.

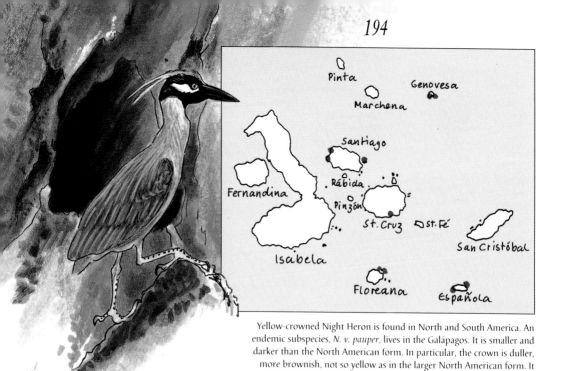

Yellow-crowned Night Heron is found in North and South America. An endemic subspecies, *N. v. pauper*, lives in the Galápagos. It is smaller and darker than the North American form. In particular, the crown is duller, more brownish, not so yellow as in the larger North American form. It breeds on all the islands, except the most northerly, Wolf and Darwin. During the day, it stays mostly in the shade, becoming active at dusk. We saw them often in Ayora, together with Lava Herons, under the street lights near the harbour. They were most common on Genovesa. We saw none on Fernandina or Isabela, although they occur on both islands. They hunt mostly for insects but will also catch rats, as I saw in Ayora. Their main food is crustaceans and they fish less than Lava/Striated Herons. They will breed all year round, the nest made between mangrove roots or under a lava block and well hidden. Both parents incubate the three to four eggs.

YELLOW-CROWNED NIGHT HERON
Nyctanassa violacea
GUAQUE

crown grey
brown in the middle

13 July Genovesa. Yellow-crowned are very common on this island We saw many, often hidden away under a rock or in a hole, or between vegetation. They looked very dull, not bright as in the United States; the crown especially is often grey with some brown intermixed Only one adult had a yellow crown (a very pale straw colour). None was shy when we passed, they stayed where they were and I could sketch them easily

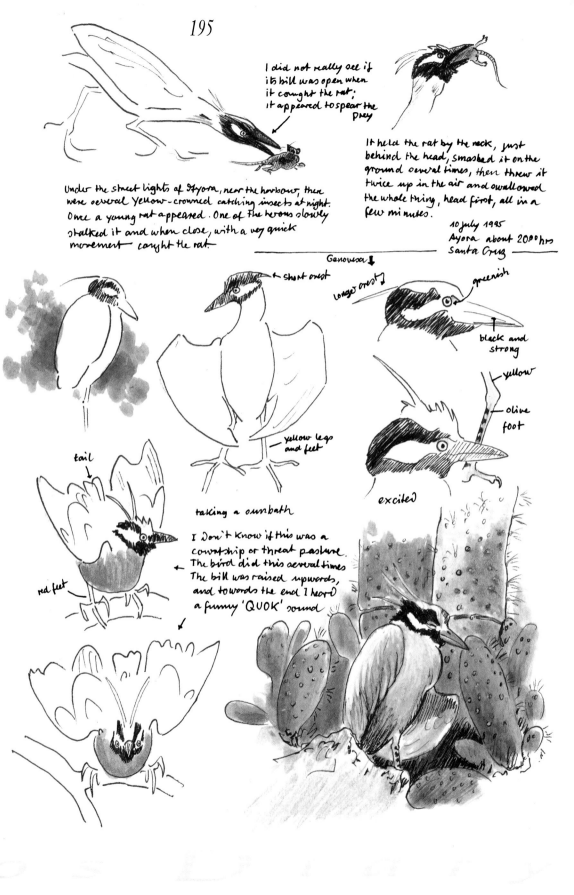

I did not really see if its bill was open when it caught the rat; it appeared to spear the prey

It held the rat by the neck, just behind the head, smashed it on the ground several times, then threw it twice up in the air and swallowed the whole thing, head first, all in a few minutes.

Under the street lights of Ayora, near the harbour, there were several Yellow-crowned catching insects at night. Once a young rat appeared. One of the herons slowly stalked it and when close, with a very quick movement — caught the rat.

10 July 1995
Ayora about 20:00 hrs
Santa Cruz

Genovesa

short crest

longer crest

greenish

black and strong

yellow legs and feet

yellow

olive foot

excited

tail

red feet

taking a sunbath

I don't know if this was a courtship or threat posture. The bird did this several times. The bill was raised upwards, and towards the end I heard a funny 'QUOK' sound

On the map above (Galápagos): here we only saw footprints in the mud — Santiago — Rábida — St.Cruz — ISABELA — two flying — Villamil — Punta Cormorant — FLOREANA

On the lower map: USA — Florida — MEXICO — Carribean Isl — VENEZUELA — Galápagos

GREATER FLAMINGO
Phoenicopterus ruber
FLAMENCO

The flamingos found in the Caribbean and Galápagos are Greater Flamingos, the same species breeding in southern Europe, Africa and 'western' Asia. The birds found in the Caribbean are a much deeper red than birds elsewhere. There are possibly some 80,000 birds in the Caribbean, but it's difficult to count them since they are rather erratic in their breeding haunts. Large colonies one year can be vacant in others.

It is difficult to understand how the flamingo reached the Galápagos from the Caribbean, but other birds, such as the finches, could also have come from there. There are three similar finch-like species in South America but they are found in the high Andes. In the Galápagos there are no more than about 500 flamingos in total (some counts say 350, others 200). In some ways Galápagos flamingos are different from those in the Caribbean: paler in colour, and breeding in very small colonies of only a few pairs.

These are the 12 places where it is easiest to see flamingos, and it is also here where they breed. They need shallow, salty lagoons for mud rich in shrimps and water-boatmen which, together with minute crabs, are their main food. They are rather nervous birds and should never be disturbed near the colonies as they easily desert their nests if unsettled.

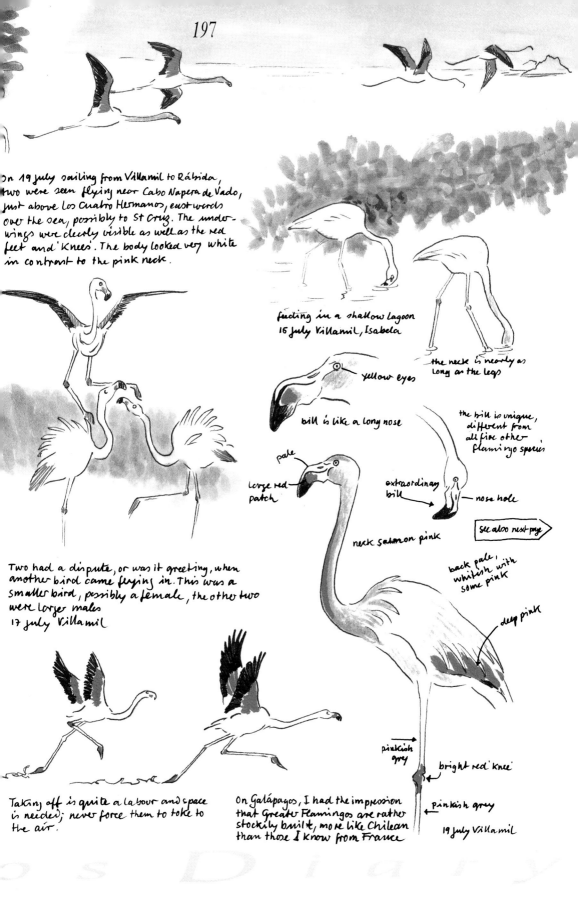

On 19 July sailing from Villamil to Rábida, two were seen flying near Cabo Napera de Vado, just above Los Cuatro Hermanos, east-wards over the sea, possibly to St Cruz. The under-wings were clearly visible as well as the red feet and 'knees'. The body looked very white in contrast to the pink neck.

feeding in a shallow lagoon
15 July Villamil, Isabela

the neck is nearly as long as the legs

yellow eyes

bill is like a long nose

the bill is unique, different from all five other flamingo species

pale

large red patch

extraordinary bill

nose hole

see also next page

neck salmon pink

back pale, whitish with some pink

deep pink

Two had a dispute, or was it greeting, when another bird came flying in. This was a smaller bird, possibly a female, the other two were larger males
17 July Villamil

pinkish grey

bright red 'knee'

Taking off is quite a labour and space is needed; never force them to take to the air.

On Galápagos, I had the impression that Greater Flamingos are rather stockily built, more like Chilean than those I know from France

pinkish grey

19 July Villamil

At the large lagoon of Villamil/Isabela, flamingos are
often seen in the company of pintails, Whimbrels,
plovers and turnstones. On the smaller ponds, just
outside Villamil, single flamingos were feeding next
to moorhens. They seem to be a bit shier there than the
birds we saw later on Floreana, possibly due to some
shooting

Pintails are strong and swift fliers. Near Villamil,
they often fly from one pond to another. The green
mirror with the pale tail is a very good distinguishing
feature in flight. Only during northern winters is
there a chance of seeing another duck species, the
North American Blue-winged Teal

Marchena   Genovesa

Santiago

⬛ = only visitor
◧ = regular

Fernandina   Rábida

Pinzón   St. Cruz

Isabela   St. Fé

San Cristóbal

Floreana   española

WHITE-CHEEKED PINTAIL
Anas bahamensis
ANADE GARGANTILLO
In Galápagos, PATILLO

Wherever there is open water you can observe this small, beautiful pintail, in the
highlands as well as on lagoons along the shoreline or even on temporary pools.
When the rains are plentiful, they even move up to Genovesa and down to Española where
they are not normally found. They make their nest in thick vegetation, always
near water. Up to 10 eggs are laid and incubated for around 25 days by the female,
which also cares for the ducklings. These can swim and dive from their first day. They
also feed on their own; mostly on insects to start with, but soon on all kinds of water
plants. When food is plentiful they grow very quickly, eating all day long, but they
fly only well when about 2 months old. Often the family (mother with youngsters)
stays together till the next breeding, after heavy rains. Often they are absurdly
tame for a duck compared with White-cheeks on the Continent.

As shown on the map, there are three subspecies of White-cheeked Pintail. The largest and brightest lives in the West Indies, the nominate form. The South American subspecies, *rubrirostris*, is smaller and slightly duller coloured. The Galápagos pintail (subspecies *galapagensis*) is the smallest and dullest. In particular, the females can look rather drab and dull, but some older males can be as bright as the South American pintail. The Galápagos subspecies is also the most isolated and restricted of the three, but still very common. There are around 1,000 pairs, but natural disasters can quickly alter this figure. All island birds are vulnerable to these localized disasters. When the shallow large crater lake collapsed on Fernandina in 1968 and fell about 300 metres, over 1,000 pairs of pintail were killed. The more frequent rain occurring during an El Niño phenomenon may allow numbers to rise again even on Fernandina. The brighter, larger South American form of White-cheeked Pintail is very popular and widely bred in capitivity in Europe and the United States.

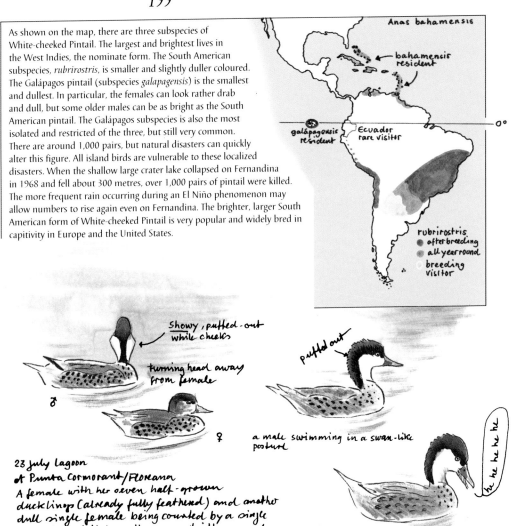

Anas bahamensis

bahamensis resident

galápagensis resident

Ecuador rare visitor

0°

rubrirostris
● after breeding
● all year round
○ breeding visitor

Showy, puffed-out white cheeks

turning head away from female

♂

♀

puffed out

a male swimming in a swan-like posture

In this posture, I heard a very thin whistle

he he he he

23 July lagoon at Punta Cormorant/Floreana
A female with her seven half-grown ducklings (already fully feathered) and another dull single female being counted by a single male. I didn't hear the same whistles as made by Barnaby's pair of Continental subspecies which he keeps in France

a sharp line between white cheeks and chocolate neck

large spot

Larger all colours brighter
♂

no sharp separation cheek — neck

small red spot

smaller duller darker colours
♀

The sexes are separable in the field, especially when seen together. Males look much brighter longer-tailed. Young birds are still duller than females

this looked very pale and showy

long and pointed

both primaries were on one side, the tail was not between them

Male courting. It seems to me they stay longer in this position when courting than the similar Northern Pintail, Anas acuta
23 July Floreana

GALÁPAGOS HAWK
Buteo galapagoensis
GAVILÁN de GALÁPAGOS

Once common on all islands, except Genovesa, Wolf and Darwin. Now extinct on Floreana, and perhaps also on San Cristóbal due to human disturbance and persecution. On St Cruz there are now only 2–3 breeding females with three males and some younger birds, but on nearby St Fé they are still common. The total Galápagos population is probably no more than 250 birds. A powerful predator, like a small eagle. Young marine iguanas, young sea turtles, Red-footed Boobies and adult landbirds as well as native and introduced rats are their prey, but the hawks also scavenge stranded fish, goat or other carcasses and the placenta of sealions. The female, which holds a large territory, often mates with up to four males. All help to rear the brood of 1–3 chicks and defend the territory against intruders. They are not very social birds, but can congregate outside the breeding season around a carcass.

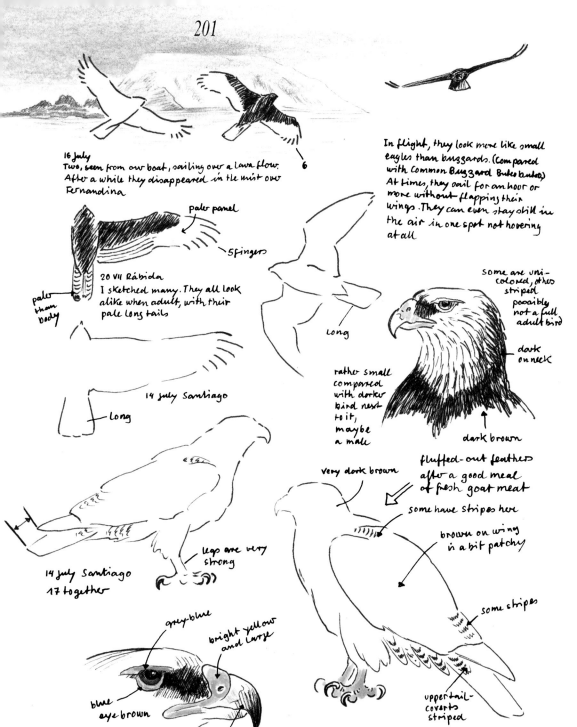

16 July
Two, seen from our boat, sailing over a lava flow.
After a while they disappeared in the mist over
Fernandina

6

In flight, they look more like small eagles than buzzards. (Compared with Common Buzzard Buteo buteo) At times, they sail for an hour or more without flapping their wings. They can even stay still in the air in one spot not hovering at all

paler panel

5 fingers

pale than body

20 VII Rábida
I sketched many. They all look alike when adult, with their pale long tails

some are uni-colored, others striped possibly not a full adult bird

dark on neck

Long

rather small compared with darker bird next to it, maybe a male

dark brown

14 July Santiago

Long

Very dark brown

fluffed-out feathers after a good meal of fresh goat meat

some have stripes here

brown on wing is a bit patchy

legs are very strong

14 July Santiago
17 together

grey-blue

bright yellow and large

some stripes

blue eye brown

strong bill

uppertail-coverts striped

The rims around the eyes were not yellow, as often stated in the literature. I saw them very close up (less than a metre) They were all blue or grey-blue

The feet are very strong for a buzzard (hawk) it's more eagle-like in all aspects. It looked to me like a dark White-tailed Hawk from Mexico or Texas, Buteo albicaudatus

see also next page

o s D i a r y

Over a lava field (Alcedo track)
three hawks were courting.
They showed their talons to
each other and then flew off
to a big tree. Seen from
more than 800 - 900 m. away
15 July
Isabela

Early morning near Fernandina, a
large ship, the Galápagos Explorer,
at anchor, all still asleep, I heard
a cry. At a distance a hawk flew
past, all dark, no wing panel visible,
or was this only the morning light
that gave this effect?
Disappeared in the mist
17 July 1995

24 July in Bahia Gardner, Española, one pair
in the Bay, flying around over rocks and
islets. They disappeared, and after an hour
one appeared again, flying with heavy
wing flaps towards a rock where a sitting
booby flew away. The hawk settled
down, cleaned its feathers a bit and then sat
motionless for quite a while. Its silhouette
showed dark against the sky when we were
sailing away. The other hawk did not
come back

really a
small eagle

14 July
Santiago

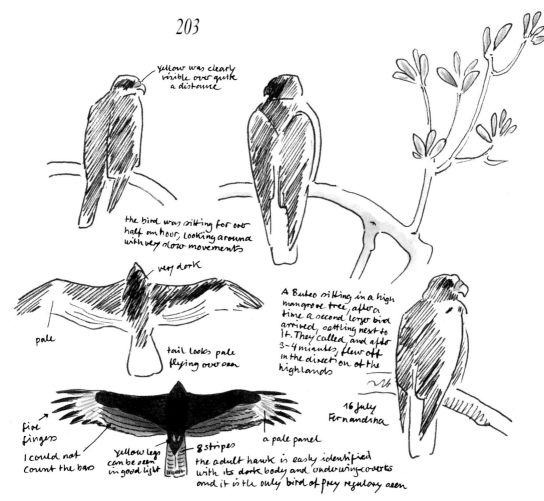

yellow was clearly visible over quite a distance

the bird was sitting for over half an hour, looking around with very slow movements

very dark

pale

tail looks pale flying over sea

A Buteo sitting in a high mangrove tree, after a time a second larger bird arrived, settling next to it. They called and after 3–4 minutes, flew off in the direction of the highlands

16 July Fernandina

five fingers

I could not count the bars

Yellow legs can be seen in good light

8 stripes

a pale panel

the adult hawk is easily identified with its dark body and underwing-coverts and it is the only bird of prey regularly seen

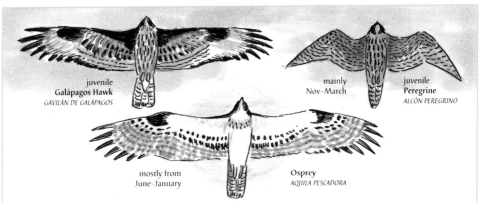

juvenile
Galápagos Hawk
GAVILÁN DE GALÁPAGOS

mainly
Nov–March

juvenile
Peregrine
ALCÓN PEREGRINO

mostly from
June–January

Osprey
AQUILA PESCADORA

Two more raptors occur in the Galápagos. These are visitors from North America, seen mostly along the coast. Both have worldwide distribution and are potential breeders in the archipelago. The larger Osprey could be confused with a young endemic hawk but the body and underwing-coverts are clear, with black patches on the carpal joints.

The Ospreys' habit of diving, talons first, into the sea to catch fish, their only food, separates them as well. Peregrine Falcon could also occur inland but stays mostly along the coast where there is more prey to be caught in flight. The wings are long and pointed. Flight is rather slow with some glides, very fast and powerful when hunting. The young bird has a rather dark body, the adult is paler. Both are dark from above.

The little 'mouselike' Pachay is not really rare, but is difficult to find. Once very common, now declining, it is no longer found in the lowlands and mangroves but only in the highlands of the larger islands. Since about 1983 there have been no records from Floreana, and on San Cristóbal where it was very common, it is now rare. On 11 July we looked for this rail near the Cerro Crocker\ on St Cruz, but failed to find it. Again in the highlands on St Cruz on 22 July, driving past a cattle ranch, I noticed great changes in the area since my last visit to the Galápagos. Later, we walked through dense vegetation towards El Chato. Once a small bird crossed our track like a mouse, it was too quick for identification. Arriving at some shallow pools there were three Moorhens, pintails and some large tortoises. After sitting quietly, while the rest of our party went to the next pond, I saw my only Galápagos Crake, long enough to sketch it. It was mostly hidden in dense vegetation only 2 m from my feet.

GALÁPAGOS CRAKE
Laterallus spilonotus
PACHAY

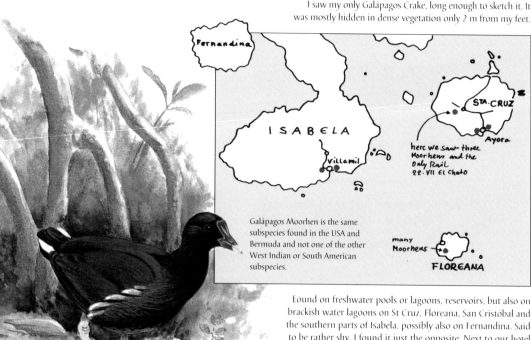

Galápagos Moorhen is the same subspecies found in the USA and Bermuda and not one of the other West Indian or South American subspecies.

COMMON MOORHEN or GALLINULE
Gallinula chloropus
GALLINULA

Found on freshwater pools or lagoons, reservoirs, but also on brackish water lagoons on St Cruz, Floreana, San Cristóbal and the southern parts of Isabela, possibly also on Fernandina. Said to be rather shy, I found it just the opposite. Next to our hotel in Ayora there was a lagoon, more salt than brackish water, where a pair with three full grown young was present all the time. Later, two more adults appeared. On the first day, 9 July, they were rather shy, and it was impossible for Barnaby to photograph them. But the next day I sat still on a lava block (not hidden) to sketch them. They searched for food nearly under my feet. I have never seen this happen in Europe. Near Vilamil, on Isabela, they were very common on the small ponds, very near the village. Again less shy than in Europe. On Floreana, up in the highlands, overlooking the country from Asilo de la Paz, there were some ponds at a distance where we saw dark birds swimming with paler ones. These could only have been Moorhens with some pintails.

short & strong legs

then it stopped looked around it was like a little ball

After squeezing, a little very dark crake ran out of the vegetation. I did not see any white spots on the back and it looked tail-less.

it disappeared into the vegetation and at once looked out again. I saw the red eyes

and then came out of the vegetation and searched for about 1-2 minutes for food. It had no white spots on the back. Possibly a young bird.

15 cm ⟹
Size
⟸ 20cm

Both crakes are endangered, not yet really rare, but difficult to find. Mostly silent, this time we did not hear them at all. The Galápagos Crake is smaller than the larger ground-finches

Paint-billed Crake
Neocrex erythrops
Gallareta

We had no luck with this beautiful little bird. I saw it years ago and made some sketches. There were none in 1995 at the same place, but we did not stay very long. This crake is slightly larger than the endemic Galápagos Crake

when swimming, pumps head

white

white under tail-coverts, highly visible, especially when in the dark lagoon vegetation

some had more orange bills, not so deep red

white

brown

legs: tibia red, then olive yellow like the European subspecies

pumping

front shield

yellow

orange red

19 July Villamil

The young birds still had green bills, except one whose shield appeared with some red. The legs were more greenish, and without red on the tibia.

tibia

stripes buff

greenish

pale near white

pale

When an adult found a kind of worm, a full grown young bird approached and the adult left it for him.

AMERICAN OYSTERCATCHER
Haematopus palliatus
OSTRERO

Unmistakable. A rather chunky, chicken-sized, black and white shorebird with a long, strong heavy bill. Not very shy, and when seen close up, the back is not black as in European Oystercatcher, but brown. The pale eye is conspicuous. In the Galápagos subspecies, the lower breast border between the black and white is often irregular and is not sharply separated as in the North American subspecies.

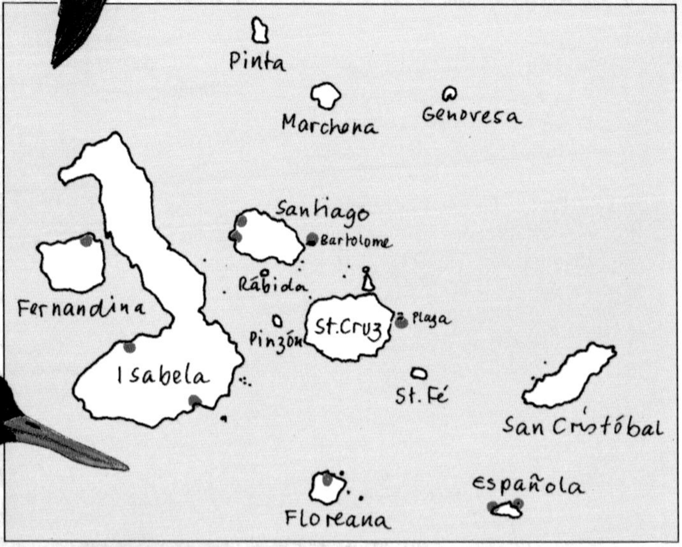

Pinta

Marchena   Genovesa

Santiago
Bartolome

Fernandina   Rábida

St.Cruz   Plaza
Pinzón

Isabela

St. Fé

San Cristóbal

Floreana   española

Found around all islands on rocky and sandy shores, also on intertidal pools and saltwater lagoons. An endemic subspecies, *H. p. galapagensis*, of the widespread North and South American species.

yellow Warbler

Tattler

16 July Punta Espinosa, Fernandina.
All these different species were lying or sitting
together on black lava, as if they were on
Noah's Ark. A little Yellow Warbler was
searching for food between them,
without fear.

eyes conspicious

long & strong

not a sharp separation (line)   preening

dark
white
flecked

16. July

Punta Espinosa
Fernandina

pale eyes

nearly as red as in adult

lower third dark

pale fringe

I did not notice that the younger birds
had longer bills as so often seen in
European Oystercatchers

'crest'

one, possibly a younger bird,
had darker eyes, nearly no
eye-ring and a
pinkish grey bill,
with one-third
dark

← Not a sharp
separation
(also in most adults

red

the bill seems to be
stronger and longer
than in European
Oystercatchers

its legs were grey
(pale)

umbra

rounded

rather
long
tail

carrot-red
bill

black

seems asleep
(but eyes open)

pointed
like a
small
crest

14 July
Puerto Egas
Santiago

leg very pale

no hindtoe

adult

white not
always visible

pale flesh
(pinkish grey)

Once saw three together, then again another three
two adults, one juv/imature →

① **SEMIPALMATED PLOVER**
Charadrius semipalmatus
CHORLITEJO

10 July/95 one at Playa de Los Alemanes, St Cruz
14 July Puerto Egas, Santiago, 16 birds
19 July Villamil, Isabela, four on the lagoon

② **GREY PLOVER**
Pluvialis squatarola
PLAYERO CABEZÓN

14 July two at Playa Espumila
and One with six tattlers at
Puerto Egas / Santiago

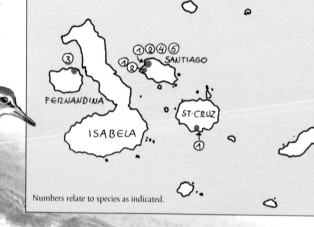

Numbers relate to species as indicated.

③ **SPOTTED SANDPIPER**
Actitis macularia
CORRELINO

16 July at Punta Espinosa, Fernandina,
one bird among tattlers
flying away alone

breeding
plumage

non-breeding
plumage

④ **SANDERLING**
Calidris alba
PLAYERO COMÚN

14 July at Playa Espumila / Santiago,
there were two Sanderlings and one
Western Sandpiper between 16
Semipalmated Plovers and five
tattlers

⑤ **WESTERN SANDPIPER**
Calidris mauri
PLAYERO OCCIPITAL

typical

14 July
Puerto Egas, Santiago,
one was sitting with a group
of six tattlers on lava blocks near
water. When a hawk appeared, all flew
off together and settled down again
a bit further away, again on lava

When the birds flew off, the black
axillaries were clearly visible on
the otherwise white underwings,
which are dark in tattlers.

heavy bill

changing into
breeding plumage

only a yellow base
not orange

orange feet

orange

Two Grey Plovers at Playa Espumila on Santiago showed
the extremes of colour in this species. One was nearly
white, somehow looking bleached out, and the other
was mottled with some black on belly and breast

19 July
Lagoon at
Villamil,

one was in full breeding plumage,
the other only partly. It was chased
away by the full breeding bird,
which behaved territorially.
They could breed here one day.

trailing edge

16 July Punta Espinosa,
Fernandina.
When the Spotted Sandpiper flew off
to feed again, between some other
lava blocks near water, wings looked
rather stiff and rounded with a
little white wing bar. The white trailing
edge was clearly visible

small
wing bar

— rounded

Long

slightly
down curved
with a rather
fine, pointed
tip

Strong

It was not the best time of the year to see all
the North American waders that normally spend
the northern winter, some from August onwards,
in the Galápagos islands. Nearly 30 species
have been observed, some of them only once,
others regularly and often in large numbers.
One species, on 14 July Ist Cruz, moved away
so quickly and unexpectedly I had no
time to identify it.

for its size, compared with the nearby
Sanderlings, and with its strong slightly
curved bill, I took it for a Western
Sandpiper. Semipalmated Sandpiper,
Calidris pusilla, is very similar, only
a fraction smaller and shorter-billed
(only a few records from the Galápagos)

● WILLET
Catoptrophorus semipalmatus
PLAYERO ALIBIANCO

WHIMBREL

● WANDERING TATTLER
Heteroscelus incanuses
ERRANTE

all three species

SANTIAGO

FERNANDINA

Rábida

Seymour

ST. CRUZ

ISABELA

FLOREANA

ESPAÑOLA

12 VII — Two on <u>Seymour</u>, conspicuous, strong yellow legs searching for food among Swallow-tailed Gulls in a fur seal colony

14 VII — five in <u>Puerto Egas</u>, Santiago, a second flock of four and thereafter another five, possibly the same with two Sanderlings and a Grey Plover. This morning there were also two on <u>Play Espumila</u>

16 VII — <u>Punta Espinosa</u>, Fernandina, once saw two then three and later 12 on lava near water

19 VII — One on sandy beach at <u>Villamil</u>, Isabela

20 VII — Two on beach between sea lions, then one single, <u>Rábida</u>

21 VII ● One in the bay near <u>Roca Cousin</u>/Santiago
  ● <u>Canal de Itabaca</u> one on the <u>St Cruz</u> side then two on the other side on <u>Baltra</u>

24 VII — One flying over a lava field and one on the sandy beach between sea lions, <u>Bahia Gardner</u>

26 VII ● One near the landing place, searching between boulders along the shore, <u>Plaza Sud</u>
  ● One on the sandy beach at <u>Las Bachas</u> St Cruz and then again in the lagoon on mud, possibly the same bird which was before on the sandy beach

WHIMBREL
Numerinus phaeopus
ZARAPITA

10 VII — Two singles at different places, one with stilts on <u>Playa de los Alemanes</u>, St. Cruz

14 VII — One on the lava coast, <u>Puerto Egas</u>, Santiago

16 VII — <u>Punta Espinosa</u>, Fernandina, twice, one near tattlers but keeping alone, The second bird was very pale, calling, high-pitched like a European whimbrel

19 VII — One on sandy beach in the harbour at <u>Villamil</u>

23 VII — One on the lava coast near the <u>Post bay</u>, Floreana

24 VII — Bahia Gardner, Española, one flying past our boat, calling

26 VII — on the sand beach at Las Bachas near the lagoon, calling. When we came back later from the lagoon it was still there and a second bird had joined it.

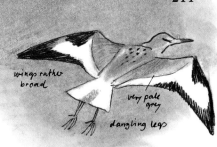

wings rather broad

very pale grey

dangling legs

some white trailing

shorter neck

The bird was not particulary quick but it was difficult to make sketches in such a short time

16 July Punta Espinosa, Fernandina. walking along the path towards the northern side to see cormorants, a rather large, broad winged bird flew up between the rocks. At first I thought it was a godwit but seeing the pale tail showing well against the black lava, I identified it as a __Willet__ the only one we saw on our trip.

It called, a shrill and loud 'Kip Kip', dropped down between lava and flew up again later. This time I clearly saw its underwing and there was no more doubt about its identity. A rather long stay for this species from North America

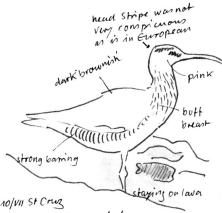

head stripe was not very conspicuous as is in European

dark brownish

pink

buff breast

strong barring

staying on lava

10/VII St Cruz
not shy, but was alert when we came too close, but it did not fly away. It looked rather buff compared with the birds I had seen in Britain and France and dark on its back. It was the American subspecies hudsonicus

darker than the rest of the upperwing

underwing buff

buff

wing shoulder longer

24 July near Bahia Gardner, Española a bird was flying past the ship, the dark buff underwings clearly visible as well as the dark rump which is white in European bird.

white

unicolour

20 July Rabida
Tattlers !!!

strong bill

strong legs mustard yellow

24 July Gardner Bay
running like sanderlings before the tide on the sandy beach, long-necked they look very elegant, rather small head, and long body when at rest like those here

darker

July is not the best months for North American waders in the Galapagos. But some also stay when others are on their breeding haunts in the North. The most common is the Tattler and Turnstone. They are present all year round in small numbers. This changes towards the end of August when large flocks of Northern Phalaropes arrive and at the same time many other waders, some regular, others only as rare vagrants

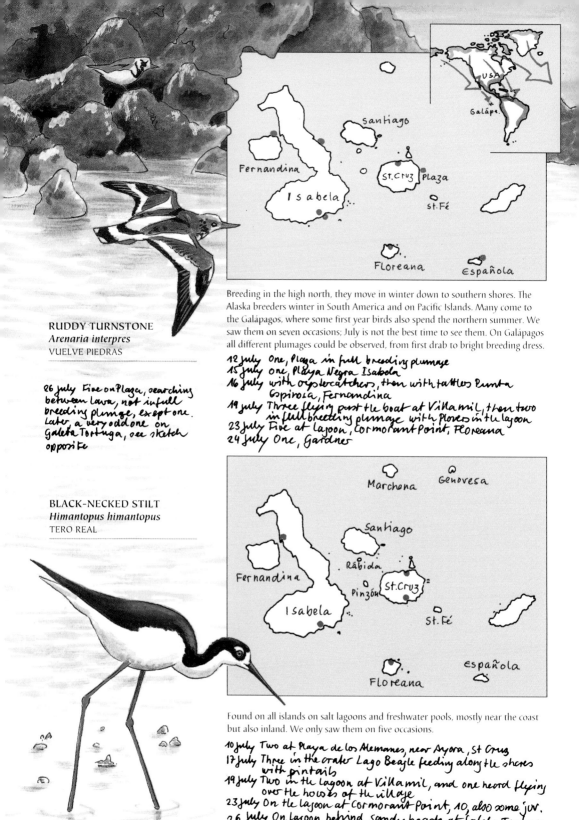

RUDDY TURNSTONE
Arenaria interpres
VUELVE PIEDRAS

26 July Five on Plaza, searching
between lava, not in full
breeding plumage, except one.
Later, a very odd one on
Galeta Tortuga, see sketch
opposite

BLACK-NECKED STILT
Himantopus himantopus
TERO REAL

Breeding in the high north, they move in winter down to southern shores. The
Alaska breeders winter in South America and on Pacific Islands. Many come to
the Galápagos, where some first year birds also spend the northern summer. We
saw them on seven occasions; July is not the best time to see them. On Galápagos
all different plumages could be observed, from first drab to bright breeding dress.

12 July One, Plaza in full breeding plumage
15 July one, Playa Negra Isabela
16 July with oystercatchers, then with tattlers Punta
Espinosa, Fernandina
19 July Three flying past the boat at Villamil, then two
in full breeding plumage with plovers in the lagoon
23 July Five at lagoon, Cormorant Point, Floreana
24 July One, Gardner

Found on all islands on salt lagoons and freshwater pools, mostly near the coast
but also inland. We only saw them on five occasions.

10 July Two at Playa de los Alemanes, near Ayora, St Cruz
17 July Three in the crater Lago Beagle feeding along the shores
with pintails
19 July Two in the lagoon at Villamil, and one heard flying
over the houses of the village
23 July On the lagoon at Cormorant Point, 10, also some juv.
26 July On lagoon behind sandy beach at Galeta Tortuga

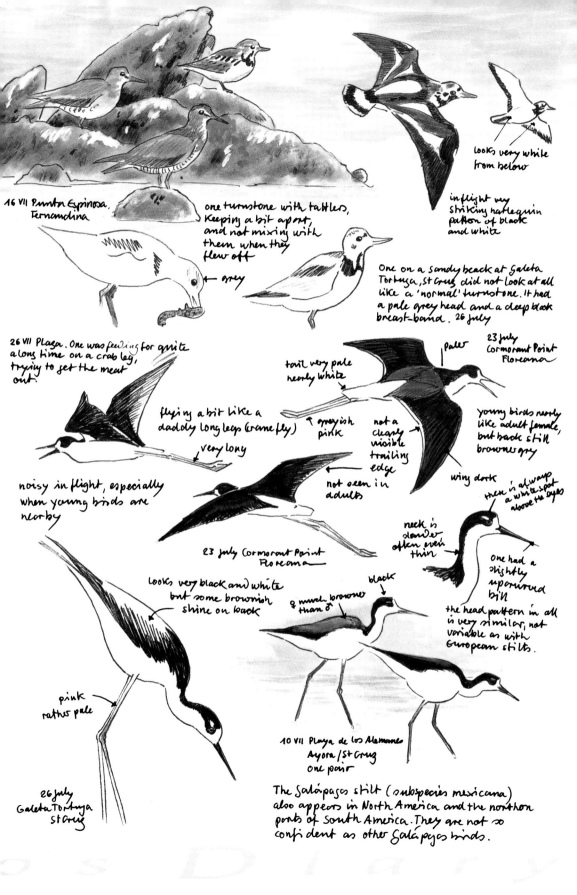

16 VII Punta Espinosa, Fernandina

one turnstone with tattlers, keeping a bit apart, and not mixing with them when they flew off

← grey

looks very white from below

in flight very striking harlequin pattern of black and white

One on a sandy beach at Galeta Tortuga, St Cruz did not look at all like a 'normal' turnstone. It had a pale grey head and a deep black breast-band. 26 July

26 VII Plaza. One was feeding for quite a long time on a crab leg, trying to get the meat out.

flying a bit like a daddy long legs (cranefly)

tail very pale nearly white

greyish pink

not a clearly visible trailing edge

not seen in adults

very long

pale

23 july Cormorant Point Floreana

young birds nearly like adult female, but back still brownisgrey

wing dark

there is always a white spot above the eyes

neck is slender often even thin

One had a slightly upcurved bill

noisy in flight, especially when young birds are nearby

23 July Cormorant Point Floreana

looks very black and white but some brownish shine on back

black

♀ much browner than ♂

the head pattern in all is very similar, not variable as with European stilts.

pink rather pale

26 July Galeta Tortuga St Cruz

10 VII Playa de los Alemanes Ayora / St Cruz one pair

The Galápagos stilt (subspecies mexicana) also appears in North America and the northern parts of South America. They are not so confident as other Galápagos birds.

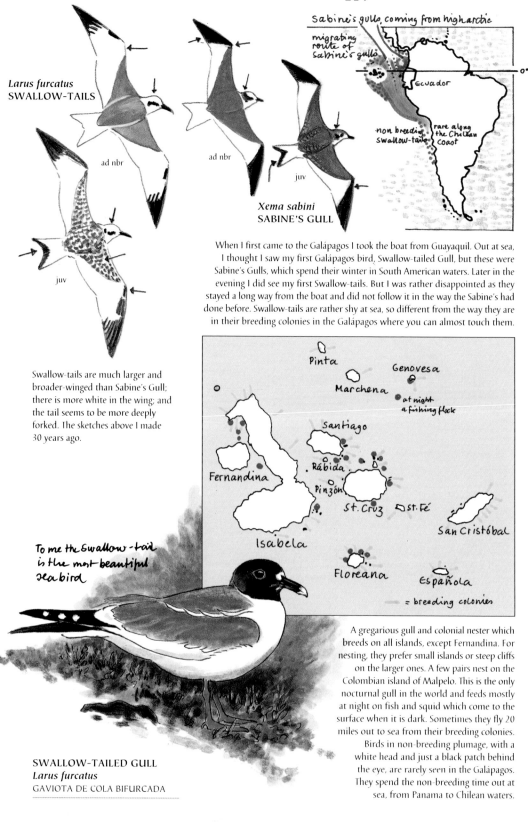

Larus furcatus
SWALLOW-TAILS

ad nbr

ad nbr

juv

Xema sabini
SABINE'S GULL

juv

Sabine's gulls coming from high arctic

migrating
route of
Sabine's gulls

Ecuador

0°

non breeding
swallow-tails

rare along
the Chilean
coast

When I first came to the Galápagos I took the boat from Guayaquil. Out at sea, I thought I saw my first Galápagos bird, Swallow-tailed Gull, but these were Sabine's Gulls, which spend their winter in South American waters. Later in the evening I did see my first Swallow-tails. But I was rather disappointed as they stayed a long way from the boat and did not follow it in the way the Sabine's had done before. Swallow-tails are rather shy at sea, so different from the way they are in their breeding colonies in the Galápagos where you can almost touch them.

Swallow-tails are much larger and broader-winged than Sabine's Gull; there is more white in the wing; and the tail seems to be more deeply forked. The sketches above I made 30 years ago.

Pinta

Genovesa

Marchena

at night
a fishing flock

Santiago

Rábida

Fernandina

Pinzón

St. Cruz   St. Fé

San Cristóbal

Isabela

Floreana

Española

= breeding colonies

To me the Swallow-tail
is the most beautiful
seabird

A gregarious gull and colonial nester which breeds on all islands, except Fernandina. For nesting, they prefer small islands or steep cliffs on the larger ones. A few pairs nest on the Colombian island of Malpelo. This is the only nocturnal gull in the world and feeds mostly at night on fish and squid which come to the surface when it is dark. Sometimes they fly 20 miles out to sea from their breeding colonies.

Birds in non-breeding plumage, with a white head and just a black patch behind the eye, are rarely seen in the Galápagos. They spend the non-breeding time out at sea, from Panama to Chilean waters.

SWALLOW-TAILED GULL
Larus furcatus
GAVIOTA DE COLA BIFURCADA

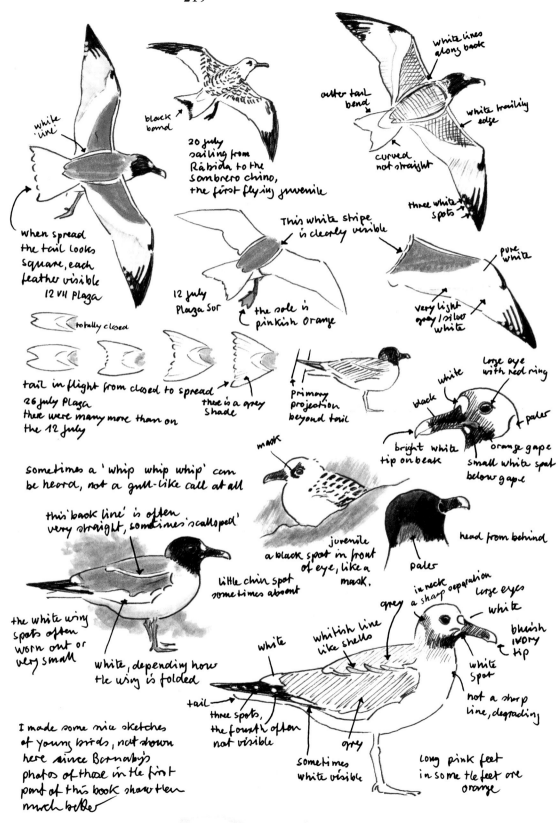

white 'line'

black band

20 july sailing from Rábida to the Sombrero chino, the first flying juvenile

white lines along back

outer tail bend

white trailing edge

curved not straight

three white spots

when spread the tail looks square, each feather visible 12 VII Plaza

This white stripe is clearly visible

pure white

12 july Plaza Sur

the sole is pinkish orange

very light grey / silver white

totally closed

tail in flight from closed to spread

26 july Plaza there were many more than on the 12 july

there is a grey shade

primary projection beyond tail

large eye with red ring

white

black

paler

bright white tip on beak

orange gape

small white spot below gape

mask

sometimes a 'whip whip whip' can be heard, not a gull-like call at all

this 'back line' is often very straight, sometimes 'scalloped'

juvenile a black spot in front of eye, like a mask.

head from behind

paler

little chin spot sometimes absent

the white wing spots often worn out or very small

white, depending how the wing is folded

white

whitish line like shells

grey

in neck a sharp separation

large eyes

white

bluish ivory tip

white spot

not a sharp line, degrading

tail

three spots, the fourth often not visible

grey

sometimes white visible

long pink feet in some the feet are orange

I made some nice sketches of young birds, not shown here since Barnaby's photos of those in the first part of this book show them much better

LAVA GULL
Larus fuliginosus
GAVIOTA de LAVA

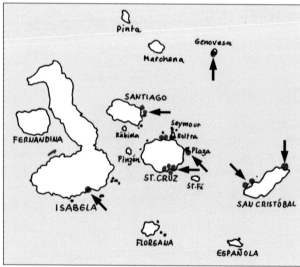

➤ It is most likely that you will see Lava Gulls here.
● Where we saw them

9 VII one adult in Ayora harbour
10 VII a juvenile in same harbour, one pair on Playa de los Alemanes and later another pair in the harbour
11 VII three flying over our hotel / Ayora later one juv. two ad. in the harbour and later one calling near hotel
12 VII a pair on Plaza
13 VII one pair on Genovesa, calling typically gull-like 'klee ow'
18 VII one pair followed our boat for some time settling on the dinghy, near Punta Moreno, Isabela
19 VII a pair at Bahia Villamil on our boat, one had an injured leg, this one been later again in the harbour
20 VII in the evening one on our dinghy near Roca Cousin, Santiago
21 VII one pair on our boat, Bartolomé
22 VII one in Canal de Itabaca, then one in Ayora, and again, later, another pair in the Itabaca channel
25 VII a pair on Punta Pitt, one pair with young on Isla Lobos, one pair on Play Ocha, all San Cristobal
26 VII a pair on Plaza, then one at Las Bachas which followed us to Galeta Tortuga. Next morning
27 July it was still there following us to Itabaca, to say 'Adios'

Unlike the Swallow-tail, Lava Gulls remain all year in the Galápagos. They are seen mostly along shores or in saltwater lagoons but also in harbours or in large seabird colonies. Rarely are more than two birds seen together; they also nest singly, and breeding occurs throughout the year. Swallow-tails lay one egg, Lava Gulls two. Opportunistic scavengers along the tideline or in harbours, they take dead fish that have been washed ashore, marine invertebrates, sealion placentas, newly born marine iguanas as well as sandworms and seabird eggs. They follow fishing boats or come to sit on tourist boats and wait for waste. There are about 300-400 pairs in the Galápagos, the entire world population.

bend

a pale patch on rump

white eye-ring (broken)

red inside bill

flying away

pale

bend

tail

adult

9 july Ayora

some pale edges on wing

pale uppertail-coverts with a dark line in centre

juv. 9 july

25 july Isla Lobos, one pair with an juvenile, which I believed, seeing the short wings, could not fly. It was all dark with a paler chin and some pale edges to the wing feathers, a very brownish look. the normally tame adult was here shy and nervous

paler chin

juvenile

it looked like a Lava Heron

white

three spots

ad 10 july Ayora

the spots are pale grey not white and are this shape

funny behaviour, I saw this in three different individuals. This here on 26 july Las Bachas, St Cruz

13 july 95 Genovesa

Looking at his feet

white

breast darker than belly

about the size of a European Black-headed Gull, rounder and a bit larger

white

eye in adult a mustard/yellow colour

white

on the neck the hood is clear cut

this area before the eye is a bit paler

red but often not clearly visible

Some have no white spots on their primaries (possibly worn off)

very pale grey, nearly white

not a sharp line of colour separation

some red on gape

tail

grey

not a sharp colour separation

primary projection

26 july Plaza

black and rather long

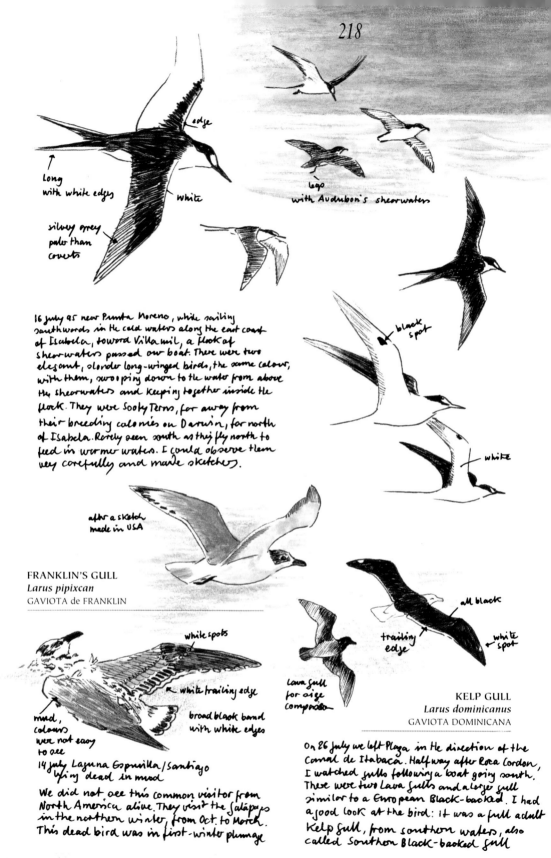

218

edge

long
with white edges

white

silvery grey
paler than
coverts

legs
with Audubon's shearwaters

black
spot

white

16 July 95 near Punta Moreno, while sailing
southwards in the cold waters along the east coast
of Isabela, toward Villamil, a flock of
shearwaters passed our boat. There were two
elegant, slender long-winged birds, the same colour,
with them, swooping down to the water from above
the shearwaters and keeping together inside the
flock. They were Sooty Terns, far away from
their breeding colonies on Darwin, far north
of Isabela. Rarely seen south as they fly north to
feed in warmer waters. I could observe them
very carefully and made sketches.

after a sketch
made in USA

FRANKLIN'S GULL
Larus pipixcan
GAVIOTA de FRANKLIN

white spots

white trailing edge

broad black band
with white edges

mud,
colours
were not easy
to see
14 July Laguna Espanilla/Santiago
lying dead in mud

We did not see this common visitor from
North America alive. They visit the Galápagos
in the northern winter, from Oct. to March.
This dead bird was in first-winter plumage

all black

trailing
edge

white
spot

Lava Gull
for size
compared

KELP GULL
Larus dominicanus
GAVIOTA DOMINICANA

On 26 July we left Playa in the direction of the
Canal de Itabaca. Halfway after Roca Cordon,
I watched gulls following a boat going south.
There were two Lava Gulls and a large gull
similar to a European Black-backed. I had
a good look at the bird: it was a full adult
Kelp Gull, from southern waters, also
called Southern Black-backed Gull

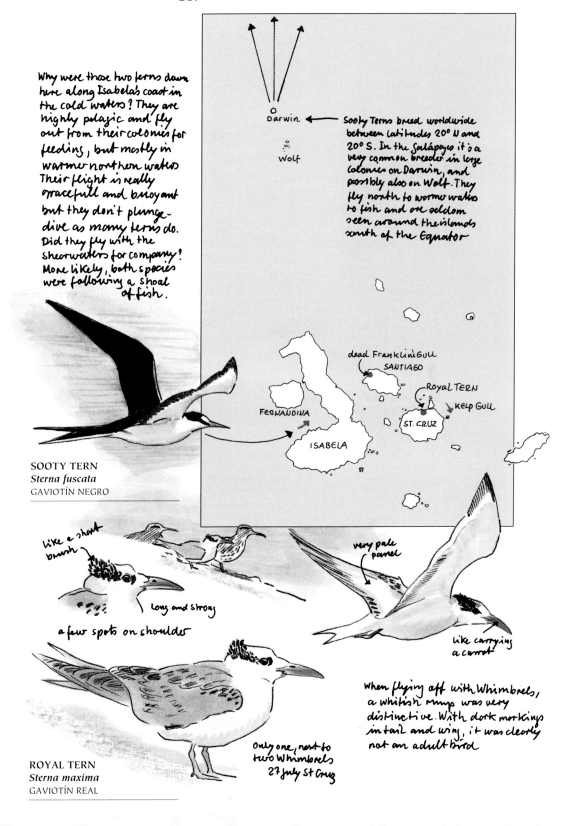

Why were those two terns down here along Isabela's coast in the cold waters? They are highly pelagic and fly out from their colonies for feeding, but mostly in warmer northern waters. Their flight is really gracefull and buoyant but they don't plunge-dive as many terns do. Did they fly with the shearwaters for company? More likely, both species were following a shoal of fish.

Sooty Terns breed worldwide between latitudes 20° N and 20° S. In the Galápagos it's a very common breeder in large colonies on Darwin, and possibly also on Wolf. They fly north to warmer waters to fish and are seldom seen around the islands south of the Equator

Darwin

Wolf

dead Franklin's Gull
SANTIAGO

Royal TERN

Kelp Gull

FERNANDINA

St. CRUZ

ISABELA

SOOTY TERN
Sterna fuscata
GAVIOTÍN NEGRO

like a short brush

long and strong

a few spots on shoulder

very pale panel

like carrying a carrot

ROYAL TERN
Sterna maxima
GAVIOTÍN REAL

only one, next to two Whimbrels
27 July St Cruz

When flying off with Whimbrels, a whitish rump was very distinctive. With dark markings in tail and wing, it was clearly not an adult bird

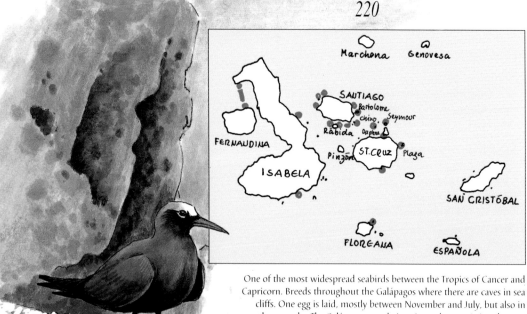

One of the most widespread seabirds between the Tropics of Cancer and Capricorn. Breeds throughout the Galápagos where there are caves in sea cliffs. One egg is laid, mostly between November and July, but also in other months. The Galápagos population, *A. o. galapagensis*, is sedentary, unlike that in the Caribbean which moves south after breeding.

The only dark brown seabird in the Galápagos, with a paler cap in adult birds. Much smaller than the all dark grey Lava Gull, with a slender build, but still heavy for a tern. Juveniles are all dark brown and could be confused with the all dark juveniles of Sooty Tern. Both have mantle and wings tipped with white. Sootys have forked tails. The immatures are all dark to begin with and gradually develop a pale cap. The tail is wedge shaped, the bill rather long, and legs short.

COMMON or BROWN NODDY
Anous stolidus
GAVIOTÍN CABEZA BLANCA

Noddies were present when we crossed the Baltra channel (Canal de Itabaca) on the first day after our arrival. This was the first seabird we saw. Except for some frigatebirds circling around above the airport (while we passed through customs). On 9, 10 and 11 July we saw them all the time in Ayora harbour. They were mostly younger birds, coming in from sea, always alone. They were very quick and elegant in flight, never settling on the cliffs where Blue-footed Boobies were breeding. Hovering over the calm water, they swooped down and caught small prey. I could not see what it was they were catching. Some looked very dark, rather long-tailed, elegant and a bit long-necked

9 VII   Many fishing in the Baltra Channel, mostly adults. Singles in Ayora, mostly young.

10–11 July all the time one or two in the harbour, never fishing together as we saw in the Baltra Channel the day before

12 VII   Plaga and Seymour. Many were seen, once, at sea fishing together with shearwaters. On Seymour many had dark caps, one had a white cap and was sitting in a large cave on a ledge near water. (breeding?)

13 VII   We did not see one on Genovesa, or did not notice them there was so much to see

14 VII   breeding on Santiago, Puerto Egas, in caves, constantly flying in and out

15 VII   Isabela, some fishing below the track to Alcedo

16 VII   some present on Punta Vincente Roca flying into a cave Many seen during the crossing to Fernandina, mostly near Punta Espinosa. On Fernandina we saw only one

19 VII   Six near Villamil harbour

20 VII   Rábida, many, often sitting with juveniles on rocks on the way to Sombrero Chino. Many at sea, also some on Chino in a shearwater colony

21 VII   On Daphne, many were feeding near our boat.

22 VII   In the Baltra channel, many were present in late evening, mostly adults fishing in the calm waters of the channel

20 July Sombrero Chino
When they sit on black lava,
it's not easy to spot them,
only the white cap shows.

stretched neck

long tail

10 July 95 Ayora harbour

long neck

typical

notched

tail spread

pale

brown

paler brown

brown

very dark
(black)

They can fly with rather
'stretched' neck, but
normally they are
'short-necked'

18 July on sea to Seymour, searching
for food on water, swimming
well, unlike other terns

26 July
St Cruz.
(North)

23 VII   On Champion, near Floreana, there was a colony with
shearwaters. Many adults were still feeding fairly
small chicks, but some were close to fledging.

25 VII   few (12) on Lobos Island

26 VII   St Cruz (North) There were some along the sandy beach
together with pelicans, fishing in the shallow
water between them. Sometimes they settled on
the pelicans, especially on their heads but never
on the sand, like other terns do. On our last day
some were in the Baltra channel, where we saw
our first noddies.

We saw none on Genovesa, Floreana
or San Cristobal. They were only
on Lobos. Why? They were most
numerous on the crossing from
Isabela to Fernandina (ooo 200)
out at sea and even more from
Rábida to Sombrero Chino
mostly with shearwaters.

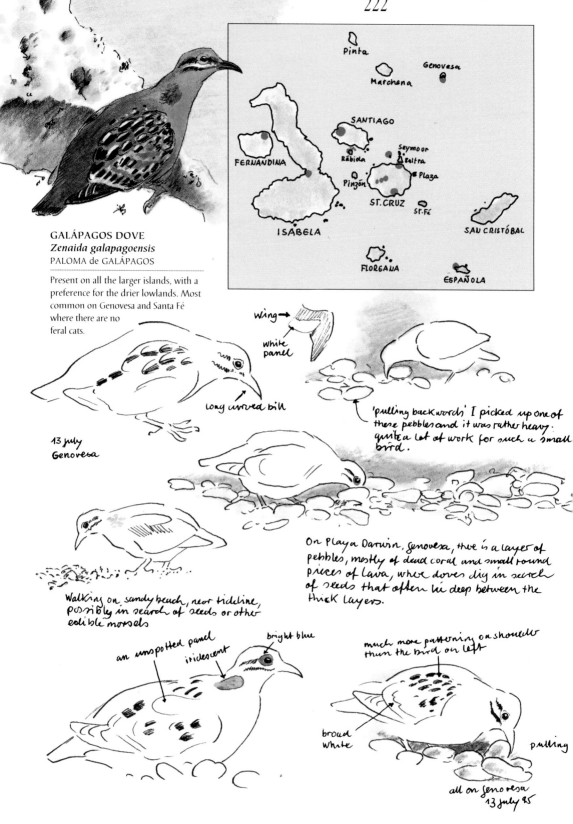

GALÁPAGOS DOVE
Zenaida galapagoensis
PALOMA de GALÁPAGOS

Present on all the larger islands, with a preference for the drier lowlands. Most common on Genovesa and Santa Fé where there are no feral cats.

Wing ➔

white panel

long curved bill

13 july
Genovesa

'pulling backwards' I picked up one of these pebbles and it was rather heavy. quite a lot of work for such a small bird.

On Playa Darwin, Genovesa, there is a layer of pebbles, mostly of dead coral and small round pieces of lava, where doves dig in search of seeds that often lie deep between the thick layers.

Walking on sandy beach, near tideline, possibly in search of seeds or other edible morsels

an unspotted panel

iridescent

bright blue

much more patterning on shoulder than the bird on left

broad white

pulling

all on Genovesa
13 July 95

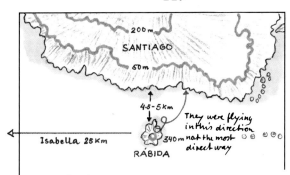

they wer flying in a compact flock, very fast with their short tail looking like European starlings, but heavier, more compact

pale panel

↑
short tail

Once on Rábida, I saw four doves circling higher and higher over the island, then flying out from the coast, coming back, joined by three more doves circling again higher and higher, then flying off towards Santiago, easily visible with my field glasses. I believe they have to gain altitude first befor crossing, in order to escape frigate bird attacks. They were at least 400 m in the air. Flying low over the sea, they could easily be pushed into the water. Eleonora Falcons in the Mediterranean prey on migrating birds in this manner. Buzzards (hawks) were also circling over Santiago so the inter-island trip can be a rather dangerous affair for this small dove.

22 July Rábida
One dove was taking seeds from a bush, a bit like African green pigeons do. I could not identify the bush, it was 3m. off the trail

not white more a brown colour

nearly no shiny patch

it appeared to be a rather young bird, calling not very loud

pale panel

very deep warm 'wine brown'

pale (white) edges on primaries

22 July St Cruz

two were digging in the ground, pulling out pebbles, stones etc. searching for seeds and possibly also insects
22 July St Cruz

22 July 90 St Cruz

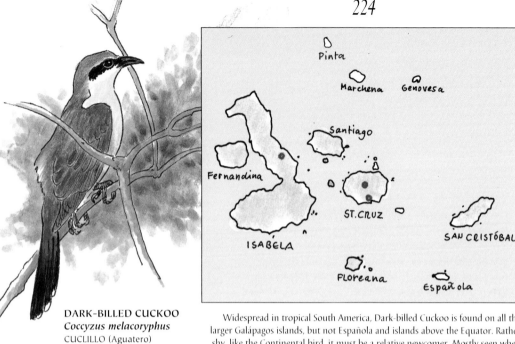

DARK-BILLED CUCKOO
Coccyzus melacoryphus
CUCLILLO (Aguatero)

Widespread in tropical South America, Dark-billed Cuckoo is found on all the larger Galápagos islands, but not Española and islands above the Equator. Rather shy, like the Continental bird, it must be a relative newcomer. Mostly seen when flying away with rather rapid wingbeats and identified by the characteristic white tip to its tail. It prefers to hop away in vegetation. Breeding starts with the first rains, 4–5 eggs are laid and the birds care for their broods themselves and are not parasitic like European Cuckoos. The chicks grow very rapidly and leave the nest before they can fly. They feed mainly on insects.

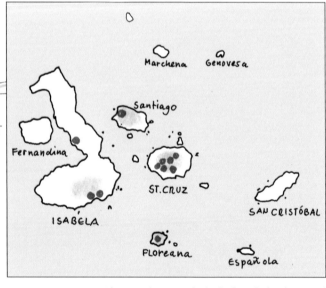

A recent newcomer (about 1960), it is not absolutely clear whether they arrived on their own or were introduced. Perhaps some farmers thought this would keep their cattle free from ticks and other insect parasites. However, the anis prefer to eat other insects, spiders and lizards, and to rob birds' nests, and even kill small birds. Now found on all farmland on St Cruz, Isabela and Floreana. We also saw them on Santiago, where there are far too many feral goats, which the anis warned of our presence with their alarm calls. Some were also in a lagoon in Elizabeth Bay, Isabela. There are now possibly over 5,000 anis on St Cruz alone.

SMOOTH-BILLED ANI
Crotophaga ani
GARRAPATERO COMÚN

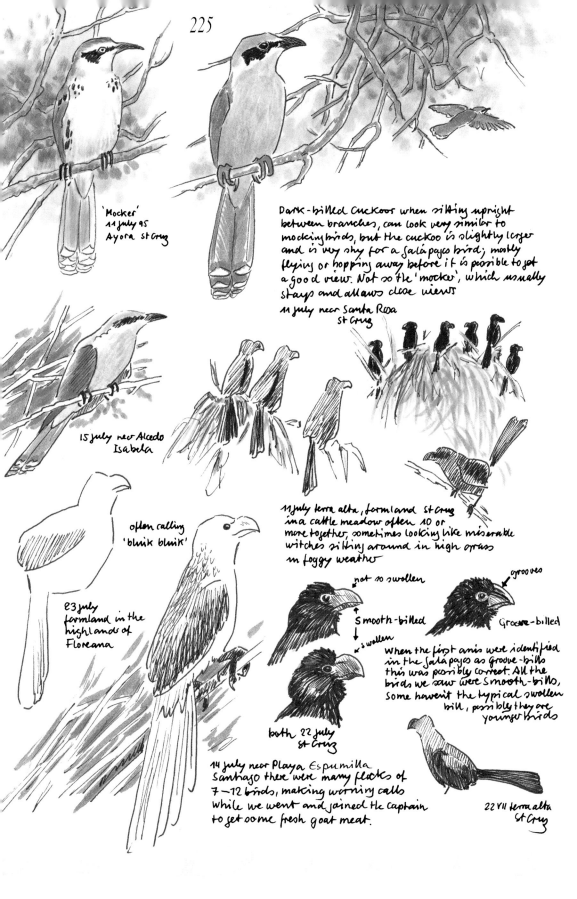

'Mocker'
11 July 95
Ayora St Cruz

Dark-billed Cuckoos when sitting upright between branches, can look very similar to mockingbirds, but the cuckoo is slightly larger and is very shy for a Galápagos bird; mostly flying or hopping away before it is possible to get a good view. Not so the 'mocker', which usually stays and allows close views.
11 July near Santa Rosa St Cruz

15 July near Alcedo Isabela

11 July terra alta, farmland St Cruz in a cattle meadow often 10 or more together, sometimes looking like miserable witches sitting around in high grass in foggy weather

often calling 'bluik bluik'

23 July farmland in the highlands of Floreana

not so swollen

grooves

Smooth-billed

Groove-billed

swollen

When the first anis were identified in the Galápagos as groove-bills this was possibly correct. All the birds we saw were smooth-bills, some haven't the typical swollen bill, possibly they are younger birds

both 22 July St Cruz

14 July near Playa Espumilla Santiago there were many flocks of 7-12 birds, making warning calls while we went and joined the captain to get some fresh goat meat.

22 VII terra alta St Cruz

BARN OWL
Tyto alba
LECHUZA de
CAMPANARIO

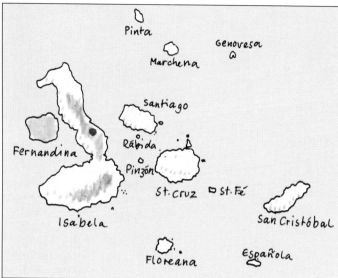

A cosmopolitan species. The small Galápagos Barn Owl *T. a. punctatissima* is not very common and only found on Fernandina, where the more successful Short-eared Owl is absent. Seen in drier, sparsely vegetated areas, mostly in lowlands but also at higher elevations. They roost during the day, hidden well away till dusk, in cavities in all kinds of rocks and trees, or in thick scrub. They nest on the floor of such cavities or even between roots of large trees. Usually three eggs are laid. Their food is small rats, mice, insects and small birds.

SHORT-EARED OWL
Asio flammeus
LECHUZA de CAMPO

In the Galápagos, this species is very successful and widespread, and found on all islands, except Wolf, Darwin and, oddly, Fernandina. This is an endemic subspecies, *A. f. galapagoensis*. Short-eared Owl is widespread in both Americas and Northern Eurasia, occurring in 10 subspecies. (Barn Owl is even more widespread, in 95 subspecies.) In the Galápagos, Short-ears prefer the moist highlands but are also found near the coast, often in seabird colonies, as on Genovesa where they prey on storm-petrels. Normally they take small birds and mice but will catch birds up to the size of shearwaters. They are strongly territorial, and more active in the mornings and evenings, but are also seen hunting in daylight, being less nocturnal than Barn Owl.

few spots

panting
in the sun

foot of
the rat

rat tail
Long = Black rat

eyes rather small

very dark
greyish/blue
violet

few spots

pale

reddish

small eyes

— rather large bill

small spots

orange

yellowish/reddish

grey

tinted pale orange

grey

all 15 July below Alcedo
Isabela

chick

About 1 Km from the coast, in a barranco, on the
track up to the Alcedo, we found this Barn Owl in a hole,
pressed against the wall and clutching a dead rat. It
moved a bit while I made sketches. On the way back,
about eight hours later, it was still there and this
time we saw a chick as well.

this in an old sketch
I made years ago on
Genovesa, at the same
spot where, this time,
we found only an
Owl's feather and
the remains of
a petrel eaten
by an owl,
and some
pellets

This photo, taken by Barnaby
in 1994 up in the terra alta on St Cruz,
shows very well the preferred habitat of
this species. It will also hunt in the open,
especially where there are no buzzards
(hawks), as on Genovesa.

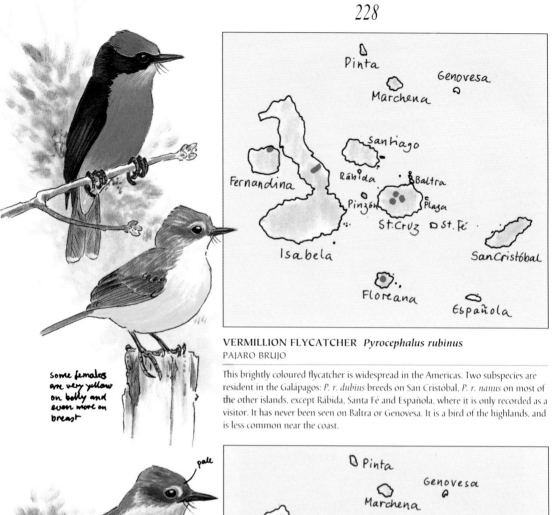

VERMILLION FLYCATCHER *Pyrocephalus rubinus*
PAJARO BRUJO

This brightly coloured flycatcher is widespread in the Americas. Two subspecies are resident in the Galápagos: *P. r. dubius* breeds on San Cristóbal, *P. r. nanus* on most of the other islands, except Rábida, Santa Fé and Española, where it is only recorded as a visitor. It has never been seen on Baltra or Genovesa. It is a bird of the highlands, and is less common near the coast.

some females
are very yellow
on belly and
even more on
breast

pale

GALÁPAGOS FLYCATCHER *Myiarchus magnirostris*
PAPAMOSCAS de GALÁPAGOS ou MARIA

Also called Large-billed Flycatcher, this bird is endemic to the Galápagos, originating from a widespread American genus. It is found on all the islands, mostly in the lowlands, but we saw them also in the terra alta on St Cruz. (Be careful, they look a bit like female Vermillion's.) There is only one record of this species from Genovesa, where no flycatchers breed.

Often seen in its spectacular courtship flight

drab white

greyish pink

courtship flight
11 july St Cruz

11 july highlands St Cruz
I think this was a young
male, looked rather drab
and dull

back very dark brown nearly black

throat paler pinkish

deep orangered looks paler on continent

black feet

pink

pale edges

10 july St Cruz highlands 650 m

a bright yellow female had also a yellow spot before/above eyes

Smaller than Large-billed flycatcher no grey on breast some females very bright yellow on belly

15 july Alcedo Isabela

23 july near 'Willmer's house in the hills on Floreana

watching me the yellow is never so bright as in female Vermillion. I saw them once side by side 5 m apart

yellowish

15 july Alcedo track Isabela

grey

yellow

11 july Ayora

not always visible but very typical

14 july Playa Espumilla Santiago

Large tail

'notch'

On St Cruz not shy, often sitting on the wires near the houses or even on the roofs in Ayora, but somehow a bit secretive. On the walk to the Alcedo on Isabela they sometimes followed us, singly or two at a time, and one took an insect from my finger

brown

pale

pale rump

bill from above this is how it came by its name

wing bars easily visible in field.

yellowish

has quite a melodious song, and a liquid 'tweet-tweet-twee' call

23 july Lagoon at Cormorant Point Floreana

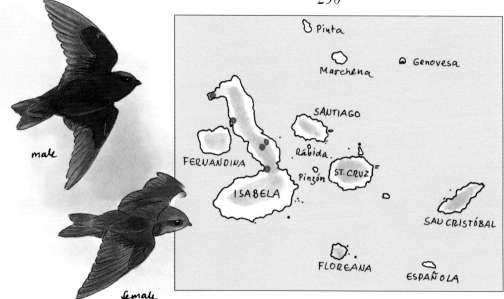

male

female

GALÁPAGOS MARTIN
Progne modesta
GOLONDRINA de GALÁPAGOS

Galápagos Martin is the most isolated form of a widespread South American species group. When Darwin brought this martin home from his voyage on the Beagle, John Gould, then curator at the British Museum, described it in 1837 as *Hirundo concolor*, and in 1838 gave it the scientific name of *Progne modesta*. In 1865, Baird described a similar bird from Argentina as *Progne elegans*, and in 1925 Chapman described another from Peru as *Progne murphyi*. Now they are mostly lumped together as one species, Southern Martin. Certainly they are closely related, although separated in their distribution and also in their behaviour. The southern *elegans* is a migratory bird, moving north after breeding. The coastal *murphyi* from Peru also moves in winter but only down to Chile, while most Galápagos Martins stay in their breeding haunts. So the different populations never meet in nature and could be seen as three separate species, or as one species with three subspecies or, and this is my preference, as one superspecies of three closely related, similar species.

Resident all year round in the central and southern islands but not on outlying islands such as Darwin-Wolf, Marchena-Pinta and Genovesa. Nor do they breed on Rábida and Española, but have been seen there, possibly only as visitors? Common nowhere, except on Isabela, where they are numerous. They prefer highlands, where they are more common, but they can be seen in all other habitats, even along the coast. They breed in small colonies and make their nests in crevices and holes inland or on sea cliffs. The nest is small, made of grass, and lined with feathers. Only 2-3 eggs are laid, mostly between August and March.

15 VII Isabela, on the track to Alcedo near the ridge our first martins, then one pair when we arrived on the ridge. Soon 10–12 birds around us, flying in to the crater Alcedo, possibly breeding down there; they flew in to the crater walls. Flight is fast, they look heavy and very dark, blue-black from above

16 VII Punta Vicente Roca, one pair circling over the Blue-footed Booby colony; the female looks much browner than any bird yesterday. Perhaps we only saw males on Alcedo

17 VII One pair in Pirate Bay over the sea. They were flying high in the air and dropped down, nearly touching the water. When we went ashore they flew over the crater ridge of Lago Beagle

18 VII Bahia Elizabeth, three birds, all males, above the lagoon, one caught a dragonfly, let it go again, caught it once more, and this three times and then let it drop where I could not retrieve it since it was off the visitor trail

22 VII St Cruz. On the long straight part of the road from Baltra to Puerto Ayora, we were beside the road looking for wild tomatoes. A bird flew out of the mist and over our heads, arced around and then disappeared. I saw it for about five minutes: a large pale-bellied martin with heavy wing beats. Possibly a Purple Martin

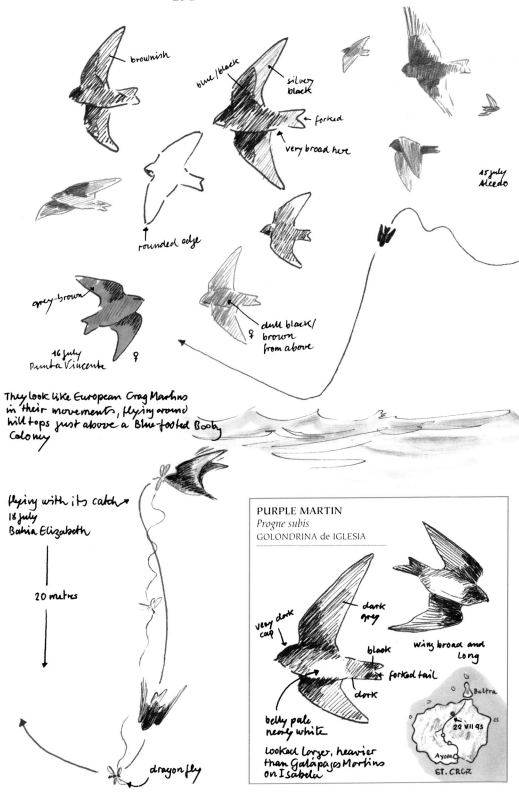

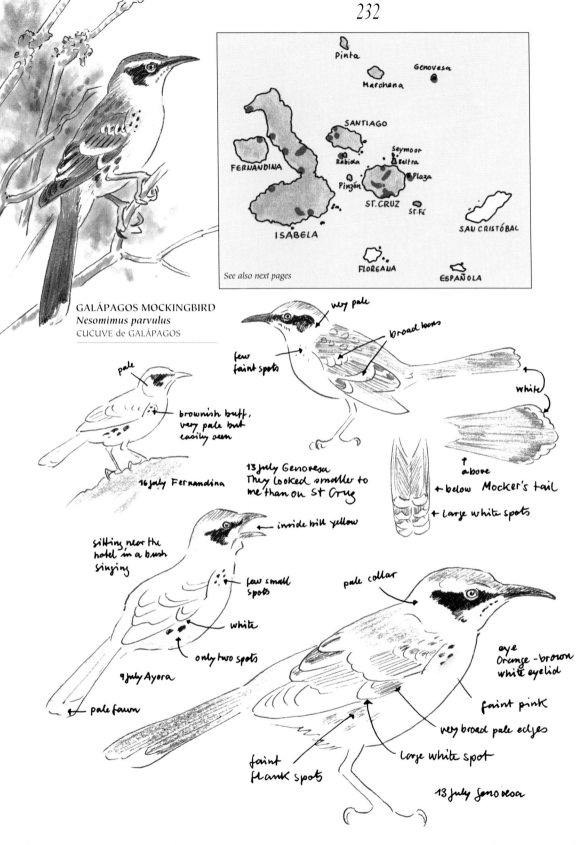

GALÁPAGOS MOCKINGBIRD
Nesomimus parvulus
CUCUVE de GALÁPAGOS

Pinta

Genovesa

Marchena

SANTIAGO

Seymour

Baltra

Rábida

Plaza

FERNANDINA

Pinzón

ST. CRUZ

St. Fé

ISABELA

SAN CRISTÓBAL

FLOREANA

ESPAÑOLA

See also next pages

very pale

broad bars

few faint spots

white

pale

brownish buff, very pale but easily seen

13 july Genovesa
They looked smaller to me than on St Cruz

16 July Fernandina

above

below   Mocker's tail

Large white spots

inside bill yellow

sitting near the hotel in a bush singing

few small spots

white

only two spots

9 July Ayora

pale fawn

pale collar

eye
Orange-brown
white eyelid

faint pink

very broad pale edges

Large white spot

faint flank spots

13 July Genovesa

the white spots are easily visible in flight

on wing as well

hair-like spines

20 July Rábida

reddish brown lava

fairly small spots

20 July Rábida

On Rábida we saw only three Mockers. Their heads and backs were darker than those seen on St Cruz. The light was good. One was pecking at a dead whale, perhaps feeding on flies, or tackling a rather large meal!

◁ GALÁPAGOS MOCKERS

26 July Beach near Caleta Tortuga Negra St Cruz. A Mocker was searching for food on a seal's placenta. When another arrived, it bent down and opened its bill like a young bird begging for food. The other stood with bill pointing upwards, wagging its tail, then froze motionless. Both then fed peacefully together on flies.

very pale look

no white spots

broad wing bars

Looked smaller than the St Cruz Mocker otherwise very similar to that widespread species

CHATHAM ▷
◁ MOCKER

few spots

stripes, no spots as in other Mockers

25 July near Punta Pitt San Cristóbal a single bird

25 July near Isla Lobos on San Cristóbal a single bird with a broken leg in a poison apple tree. – not shy but it was very difficult for Barnaby to take a good picture inside the dense bush

see also next pages ➤

GALÁPAGOS MOCKINGBIRD *See also previous pages*
Nesomimus parvulus
CUCUVE de GALÁPAGOS

Found on all the islands (including the two most northerly, Darwin and Wolf), but not recorded from Pinzón. On the three main southern islands, it is replaced by the similar species of each island (or are they subspecies?). The Floreana Mocker is extinct on the main island and now found only on the nearby satellite islets Champion and Gardner, in a stable but endangered population. Why they disappeared from Floreana is not known, possibly introduced cats and other predators, such as rats, killed them or robbed their nests.

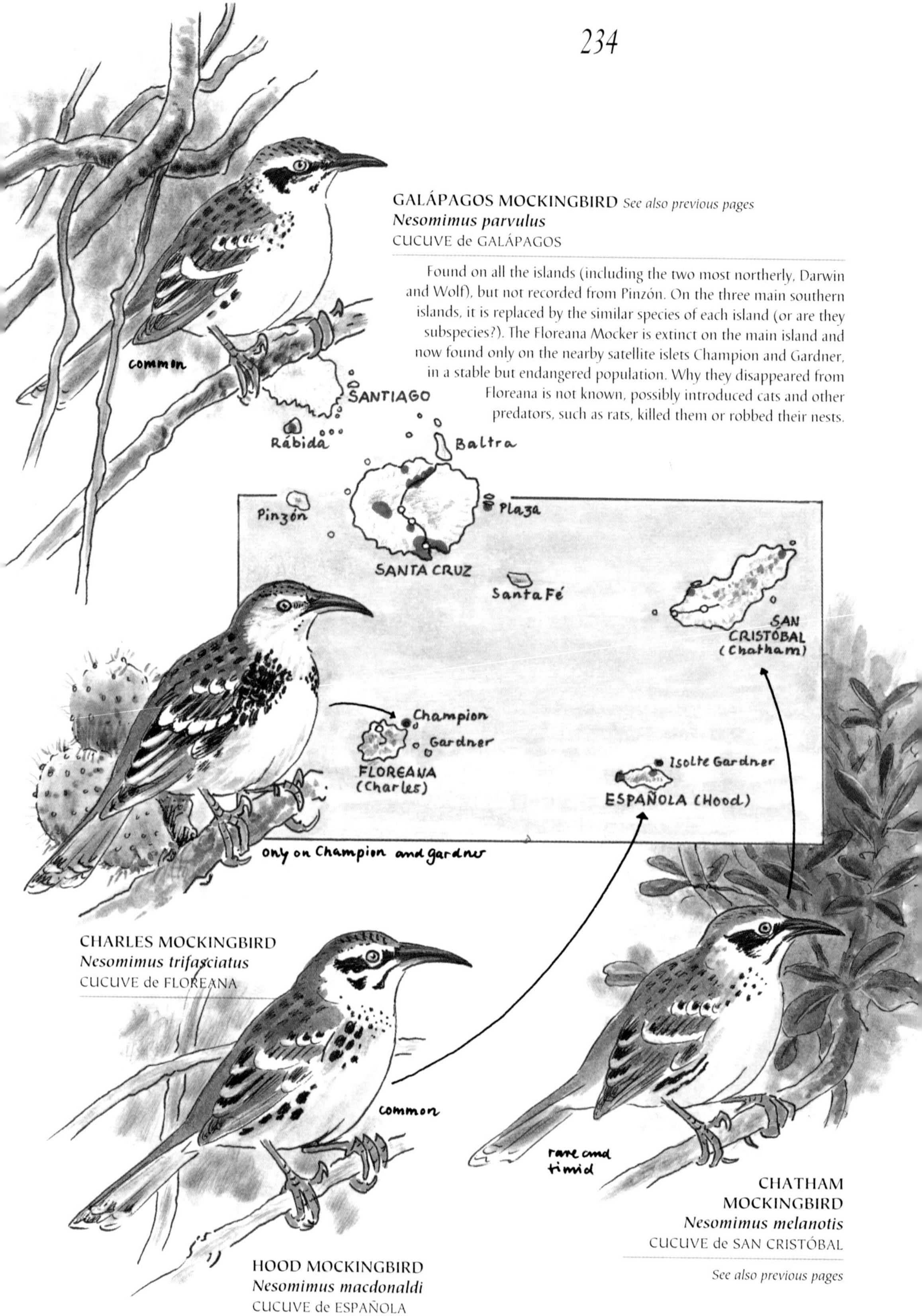

common

SANTIAGO
Rábida
Baltra
Pinzón
Plaza
SANTA CRUZ
Santa Fé
SAN CRISTÓBAL (Chatham)
Champion
Gardner
FLOREANA (Charles)
Isolte Gardner
ESPAÑOLA (Hood)

only on Champion and gardner

CHARLES MOCKINGBIRD
Nesomimus trifasciatus
CUCUVE de FLOREANA

common

rare and timid

HOOD MOCKINGBIRD
Nesomimus macdonaldi
CUCUVE de ESPAÑOLA

CHATHAM MOCKINGBIRD
Nesomimus melanotis
CUCUVE de SAN CRISTÓBAL

See also previous pages

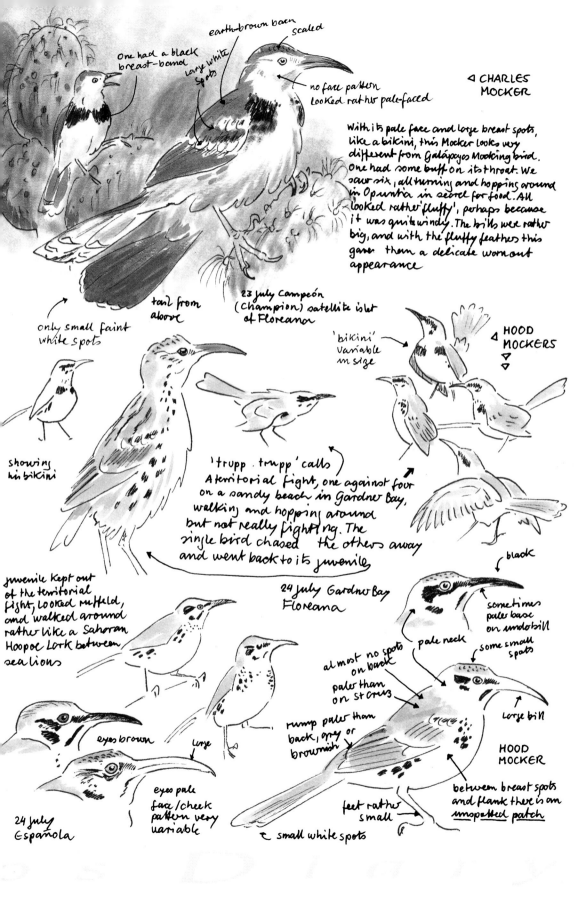

One had a black breast-band

earth-brown back

scaled

Large white spots

no face pattern
looked rather pale-faced

◁ CHARLES MOCKER

With its pale face and large breast spots, like a bikini, this Mocker looks very different from Galápagos Mockingbird. One had some buff on its throat. We saw six, all turning and hopping around in Opuntia in search for food. All looked rather 'fluffy', perhaps because it was quite windy. The bills were rather big, and with the fluffy feathers this gave them a delicate worn out appearance

only small faint white spots

tail from above

23 July Campeón (Champion) satellite islet of Floreana

'bikini' variable in size

◁ HOOD MOCKERS
◁
▽

showing his bikini

'trupp . trupp' calls
A territorial fight, one against four on a sandy beach in Gardner Bay, walking and hopping around but not really fighting. The single bird chased the others away and went back to its juvenile

juvenile kept out of the territorial fight, looked ruffled, and walked around rather like a Saharan Hoopoe Lark between sea lions

24 July Gardner Bay Floreana

black

sometimes paler base on underbill

pale neck

some small spots

almost no spots on back

paler than on St Cruz

rump paler than back, grey or brownish

Large bill

HOOD MOCKER

eyes brown

Large

24 July Española

eyes pale
face/cheek pattern very variable

feet rather small

between breast spots and flank there is an unspotted patch

↵ small white spots

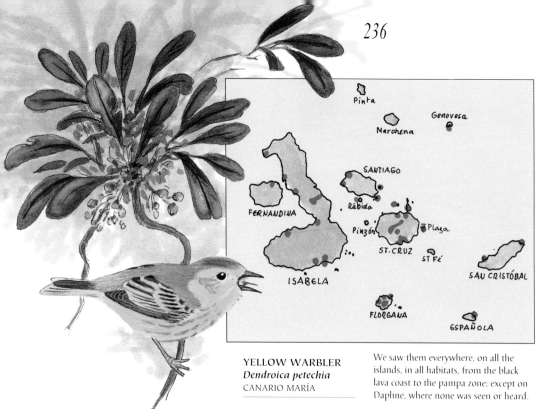

YELLOW WARBLER
Dendroica petechia
CANARIO MARÍA

We saw them everywhere, on all the islands, in all habitats, from the black lava coast to the pampa zone; except on Daphne, where none was seen or heard.

The Yellow Warbler which breeds in the Galápagos is of the same subspecies as Cocos Island Yellow Warbler *D. p. aureola*. Today, most scientists place Yellow Warblers in three allopatric groups. The northern Yellow Warblers, which breed from Alaska to Northern Mexico and Florida, have an all-yellow head in full breeding plumage; they spend their winter in Northern South America. This is the '*aestiva*' group. The West Indian warblers, with only a rufous cap (the so called 'Golden' Warblers) are in the '*petechia*' group, and Mangrove Warblers, with an all brown head (from Coastal Central and Northern South America) are in the '*erithachorides*' group. From its colour, the Galápagos bird is part of the Golden *petechia* group, but is mostly placed with the Mangrove Warblers. On Martinique, there is also a 'brown-headed' Golden Warbler *D. p. ruficapilla*, which is like a Mangrove Warbler. So the taxonomy of Yellow Warblers is rather complicated. I firmly believe that the Galápagos Yellow Warbler came from the West Indies, like other Galápagos birds. Yellow Warblers in the Galápagos vary in colour. You can see pale grey birds with no yellow at all, and bright yellow, rust-brown capped, breeding-plumaged males. Females are always duller, more greenish yellow, and only some have a little brown on the crown. There is no difference from one island to another, just individual variation, or possibly age-related differences. I heard dull-coloured birds singing, so these are not always females. Even with all the different shades of colour, Yellow Warblers are easy to identify. The only other warbler recorded in the islands is a rare vagrant, Blackpoll Warbler, *Dendroica striata*, which in its winter plumage (the plumage most likely to be seen in the Galápagos) is darkish grey-green, striped on breast and back, and with two pale wingbars. It is strange that none of the more numerous North American warbler species has yet been recorded in the Galápagos. Many are migratory, but most winter just down to Central America, the Caribbean and northern South America. They migrate mostly along the eastern seaboard, unlike the high-arctic waders which occur regularly in the archipelago.

Around our hotel in Ayora there were many Yellow Warblers in many shades of colour. They don't flock like ground-finches, but tolerate each other (at some distance). When one comes too close to another individual, they chase each other, but not fiercely. When I was sitting still beside a nearby lagoon, they even inspected my shoes for food. At breakfast, one was on our table, trying a bit of butter and some breadcrumbs as well as small pieces of dried banana. They have no fear of humans.

I sketched them on the first three days only, none afterwards, since they all looked the same to me. On a road in Ayora, I found a beautifully coloured old male lying dead on the street, possibly killed by a car. Others were close to ground-finches feeding on spilled rice, like European sparrows. The warblers seemed to like this as well and took little pieces of crushed rice grains. Normally they are insect eaters and will even enter houses in search of them. Often you can hear their bill snapping when they catch insects in the air, like flycatchers.

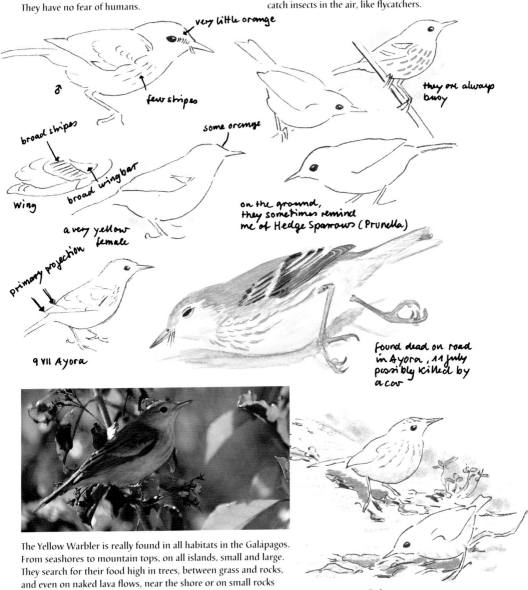

very little orange

♂

few stripes

broad stripes

some orange

wing

broad wing bar

they are always busy

on the ground, they sometimes remind me of Hedge Sparrows (Prunella)

a very yellow female

primary projection

9 VII Ayora

found dead on road in Ayora, 11 July possibly killed by a car

The Yellow Warbler is really found in all habitats in the Galápagos. From seashores to mountain tops, on all islands, small and large. They search for their food high in trees, between grass and rocks, and even on naked lava flows, near the shore or on small rocks jutting out of the water. But their preferred feeding and nesting is in lower vegetation in bushes and trees. They are more tied to this than the Warbler Finch. You will see them most commonly searching for insects, their main food, in shrubs and bushes, always busy, sometimes flying into the air to catch a small insect. They also nest in dense bushes or trees, make a cup-, not dome-shaped, nest with a side entrance hole like the Warbler Finch.

24 July on Española, one Yellow Warbler and a Warbler Finch were feeding on the sandy beach. Both very grey. The very busy Yellow Warbler has a much longer tail, is also more slender-billed and much larger than the short-tailed Warbler Finch

Darwin's finches hypothetical family tree

bill, as in all ground-finches, variable in size

often white

all adult males of the six Geospiza finches are black in full breeding plumage

in some populations rufous undertail coverts

♂ not yet in full breeding plumage

♀

♂ not in full black plumage

♀

Genovesa

Española

♀

Darwin's Finches are sparrow-sized, some smaller, some larger. They are found on all islands in different habitats: St Cruz, Isabela and Santiago, the large islands, have 10 species; the outlying Darwin, Wolf and Española have only three species, while distant Genovesa has four, but small St. Fé has seven. There are no other Galápagos birds that provide such identification 'headaches' as these finches. Some, such as Woodpecker or Warbler Finch, are not difficult, but to identify the ground-finches with certainty, even when next to each other in a mixed feeding flock, is often impossible. There are no colour differences and the bill size and form varies, often individually. To make it more complicated, there can be freaks and hybrids. Even with long experience, some individuals are just impossible, and only a fool would say that he could identify them all.

SMALL GROUND-FINCH *Geospiza fuliginosa*
The smallest of the ground-finches and, on most islands, the most common. Looks rather dumpy, toy-like with its short conical bill. Mostly smaller than Medium Ground-finch, and also smaller-billed. However, on Floreana, I had great difficulties in separating them from Medium Ground-finches. Many seemed to be rather small for Medium but too large for Small. Old males are all black, as in all ground-finches, often with white or rufous undertail-coverts. This rufous can also be reddish lava dust, sometimes also seen in females.

MEDIUM GROUND-FINCH *Geospiza fortis*
This is the finch that poses the most identification problems. In colour, male and female are like Large and Small Ground-finch, in size they are just between these two, but in bill size there is overlap. Some have small, others larger bills but their bill is rather longer than deeper. Not even those with the smallest bills among Medium Ground-finches have such pointed bills as those of Small Ground-finch. With some experience, most can be identified, except for the largest-billed individuals on St Cruz.

LARGE GROUND-FINCH *Geospiza magnirostris*
The largest ground-finch with the biggest head and an enormous bill. Colours and pattern like the next species. On St Cruz it is often impossible to separate them from large-billed individuals of Medium Ground-finch. The Mediums are often seen in large mixed flocks in company with small ground-finches, while Large Groundfinch is a more solitary bird. However, sometimes it's seen in small flocks of 5-6, feeding together, but it only mixes with others at open drinking water sites.

SHARP-BEAKED GROUND-FINCH *Geospiza difficilis*
Very much like Small Ground-finch, females and juveniles are darker. For most visitors this finch poses no identification problems since they will only see them on Genovesa, where they replace Small Ground-finch. There is a population on Darwin and Wolf, often called Vampire Finches as they suck blood out of fresh seabird feathers. They are possibly a separate species and are also found in the highlands of Fernandina, Santiago and Pinta where tourists are not permitted. It's possible they are still on St Cruz where we identified one near Ayora. Or was it a freak?

COMMON CACTUS-FINCH *Geospiza scandens*
Like the other Ground-finches but not so stockily built, more elegant with a longer, slightly curved bill. Females are quite dark and heavily streaked; some are like younger males, rather dark-faced. We saw them only at *Opuntia*, feeding on cactus or pecking out the seeds from fallen cactus figs. When visiting Plaza, which most tourists do, they can be seen on the first patch of cactuses after landing (on your right). On St Cruz, at the Darwin research station in Ayora, they come to the tortoise breeding pens to drink or bathe in the open water pans.

LARGE CACTUS-FINCH *Geospiza conirostris*
Like Cactus Finch, but females are darker still, some are really dull black. On Española they have large heavy bills, nearly the same size as some Large Ground-finches, but more elongated. On Genovesa, they more closely resemble cactus-finches from Marchena and are possibly related to them. On Darwin and Wolf they are also smaller-billed. Identification is more a question of which island one is on since the two species of cactus-finch don't occur on any island together.

all three tree-finches are alike in colour. Only bill shape and size separates them

all are arboreal but also search on the ground for food, sometimes in company with ground-finches

sex alike

both occasionally use tools

imm. ♂

sex alike

♀ -black

sexes alike some adult males have orange reddish throat patches

COSTA RICA

COCOS ISL.

GALÁPAGOS   ECUADOR

♀

VEGETARIAN FINCH *Platyspiza crassirostris*

When perched, mostly in an upright posture, with their short, deep curved bill, they look somehow like little parrots. The adult male plumage is very distinctive: dark on head, mantle, wing and tail with a pale, often creamy or even yellowish belly. Most males only have blackish heads and greyish upperparts. The females are similar but paler on head and mantle. They feed mainly in trees on buds, blossoms and fruits in a rather leisurely manner. They also search on the ground for fallen fruit or young shoots of plants. They remind me not only of a little parrot but also of a northern Pine Grosbeak or Bullfinch.

SMALL TREE-FINCH *Camarhynchus parvulus*

Size of Small Ground-finch but much greener or olive in colour. The adult males have black heads but the young are only black on the face, which gives them a masked look. Females are paler with a slightly paler eye-ring, like a pair of spectacles. The bill is small and short, giving them a baby face. They mostly feed in trees, even hanging upside-down on small branches, like northern tits or chickadees. When perched normally, they are rather upright. They also search on the ground, between fallen leaves, for insects, soft seeds and plant shoots.

MEDIUM TREE-FINCH *Camarhynchus pauper*

Found only on Floreana, the only island where all three tree-finches live. In colour, they are similar to Small Tree-finch below but darker on the upperparts, more like Large Tree-finch. Females have a less conspicuous pale pair of 'spectacles', but this is variable. The bill is longer and larger than in Small Tree-finch but not so parrot-like as is Large Tree-finch's. We only saw them up in the highlands near the old Wittners family settlement, coming to sip water, and in the nearby large orange and avocado trees; once feeding with Small Tree-finch on ripe papaya.

LARGE TREE-FINCH *Camarhynchus psittacula*

Larger and more strongly built than the other two tree-finches. The adult male is often very dark, black on head, extending down over breast to belly and flanks. The mantle and wings are also very dark. Most males we saw were only black on the face, producing a mask-like effect. Females have large 'spectacles' and are often yellowish on breast and belly. On Floreana, they seem to have bills that are less curved. Males were darker and females more yellowish from throat to belly.

WOODPECKER FINCH *Cactospiza pallida*

Looks rather pale, uniformly sandy or olive brown with a pale rump patch and a paler underside, sometimes with a yellow cast. The rather long bill is stout, and with its more elegant shape reminds me of some African weaverbird females (possibly to Americans, more like a pale tanager). Mainly an insect eater, it searches on trees or decaying wood. Normally it probes in dead wood, cracks in bark or under moss, but it also uses a tool. This is not often observed.

MANGROVE FINCH *Cactospiza heliobates*

A slightly smaller version of Woodpecker Finch with a more slender and smaller bill. Overall colouring is more brownish slate than the often yellowish-tinged Woodpecker Finch. Mangrove Finches also use tools. Their rarity and very restricted distribution (possibly now only in some mangroves on Isabela) avoids any confusion with the more upland and widespread Woodpecker Finch.

WARBLER FINCH *Certhidea olivacea*

The smallest of all the finches and the least finch-like. Variable in colour on the different islands. Very pale on St Fé, grey on Española, darker on upperparts on Genovesa. On Santiago, many have reddish faces, throat and breast but on Floreana and Isabela only a reddish cast. Short-tailed and short-billed, like a warbler, it is the most distinctive small insectivore. When searching for insects in a bush, when the bill is not easily seen, they can be confused with female Small Tree-finch or with a grey-coloured female Yellow Warbler.

COCOS ISLAND FINCH *Pinaroloxia inornata*

Not a Galápagos bird nor resident in the islands but generally included in the Darwin's finches. The adult males are shiny, silky steel blue-black. Young males moult into adult plumages differently from Darwin's finches. The females are also coloured quite differently from any finch in the Galápagos. They look so completely different that I wonder if they are really Geospizas or even related to them. DNA testing might answer this question.

SMALL GROUND-FINCH
Geospiza fuliginosa
PINZÓN PEQUENO de TIERRA

Before they acquire their full black plumage, males have a female-like plumage, gradually moulting into black, starting with their head. They often look masked and could at this stage be mistaken for a tree-finch.

The most common Galápagos landbird and found on all islands, except Genovesa, Wolf and Darwin, where they are replaced by Sharp-beaked Ground-finch. We saw them everywhere from the coastline to the highlands in nearly all habitats but most commonly in drier areas, often in large mixed-species flocks.

MEDIUM GROUND-FINCH
Geospiza fortis
PINZÓN MEDIANO de TIERRA

This is the most puzzling ground-finch. Their bills vary in size and shape, individually and from island to island. Some are small-billed, nearly as small as Small Ground-finch. Others have strong, curved bills.

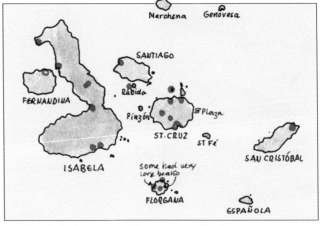

Found on all islands except Española, Genovesa, Wolf and Darwin. Most common in arid areas, preferring lowlands but will feed higher up and often seen on farmland. You will see them when landing on St Cruz, crossing from Baltra, and while waiting for your bus. Also common in Ayora or Puerto Velasco Ibarra in mixed flocks with Small Ground-finch.

LARGE GROUND-FINCH
Geospiza magnirostris
PINZÓN GRANDE de TIERRA

The shape of ground-finches is important in identification. Large really has an enormous bill and a big head.

Breeds on most islands, except Española, Seymour and Baltra, and possibly not on Plaza. Thought to be extinct on San Cristóbal, Floreana and St Fé, possibly not on Fernandina. Prefers the arid coastal zones and never common where there are many Medium Ground-finches. Most of those we saw were at the Darwin Station.

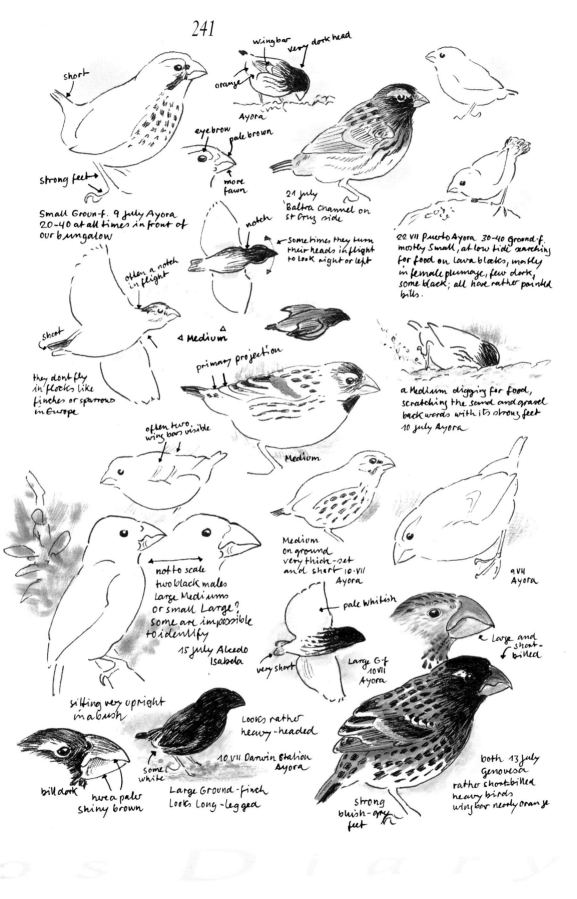

short

wingbar
very dark head

orange

Ayora

eyebrow
pale brown

more
fawn

21 July
'Baltra channel on
St Cruz side

strong feet →

Small Groun-f. 9 July Ayora
20-40 at all times in front of
our bungalow

notch

← Sometimes they turn
their heads in flight
to look right or left

often a notch
in flight

short

◁ Medium ▷

primary projection

22 VII Puerto Ayora 30-40 Ground-f.
mostly Small, at low tide searching
for food on lava blocks, mostly
in female plumage, few dark,
some black; all have rather pointed
bills.

they don't fly
in flocks like
finches or sparrows
in Europe

a Medium digging for food,
scratching the sand and gravel
backwards with its strong feet
10 July Ayora

often two
wing bars visible

Medium

Medium
on ground
very thick-set
and short 10·VII
Ayora

9 VII
Ayora

not to scale
two black males
Large Mediums
or small Large?
some are impossible
to identify

15 July Alcedo
Isabela

pale Whitish

Large G-f
10 VII
Ayora

very short

← Large and
short-
billed

sitting very upright
in a bush

Looks rather
heavy-headed

10 VII Darwin Station
Ayora

both 13 July
Genovesa
rather short-billed
heavy birds
wingbar nearly orange

bill dark

have a pale
shiny brown

some
white

Large Ground-finch
looks Long-legged

strong
bluish-grey
feet

SHARP-BEAKED GROUND-FINCH
Geospiza difficilis
PINZÓN VAMPIRO para la population de Darwin et Wolf

Very similar to Small Ground-finch, but in most populations the young males and females are very dark in colour and heavily streaked. Males in full black plumage have rufous undertail-coverts, some females also. The sharp bill is an identifying feature but often not easy to see well in the field.

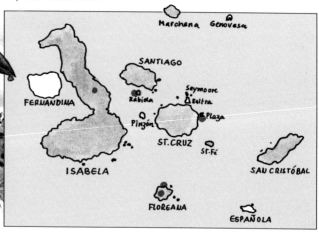

Has a very patchy distribution. Most easily seen on Genovesa where they are very common, and also found at sea level. In Fernandina, Santiago and Pinta, breeds only in the highlands in areas not open to visitors. Thought to be extinct on St Cruz, Floreana, Isabela and San Cristóbal. After the breeding season, disperses to lower lands.

COMMON CACTUS-FINCH
Geospiza scandens
PINZÓN del CACTUS

Adult males are all black, often with some white or reddish brown fringes to the undertail-coverts. The young males and females are rather dark and heavily streaked.

Found on all main islands, except Española, Genovesa and Fernandina, now possibly extinct on Pinzón. Common in the drier areas where prickly pears, *Opuntia*, grow, and never found far from them. They eat seeds, nectar and the pulp of cacti figs and always build their nests in *Opuntia*.

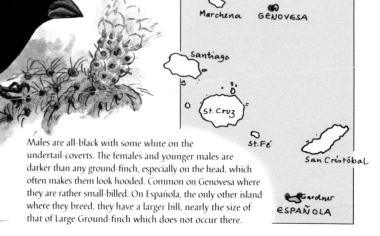

Males are all-black with some white on the undertail-coverts. The females and younger males are darker than any ground-finch, especially on the head, which often makes them look hooded. Common on Genovesa where they are rather small-billed. On Española, the only other island where they breed, they have a larger bill, nearly the size of that of Large Ground-finch which does not occur there.

LARGE CACTUS-FINCH
Geospiza conirostris
PINZÓN GRANDE de CACTUS

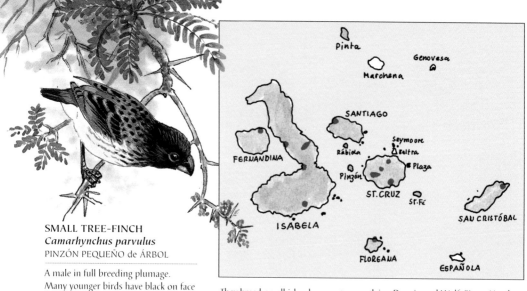

SMALL TREE-FINCH
Camarhynchus parvulus
PINZÓN PEQUEÑO de ÁRBOL

A male in full breeding plumage.
Many younger birds have black on face
only, and the females no black at all.
Underparts are variable – whitish or
yellowish.

They breed on all islands, except on outlying Darwin and Wolf, Pinta, Mordena
and Genovesa; also absent from Española. Most common in the humid highland
areas, but in small numbers, also at lower levels and even in the more arid
zones as long as there are bushes and trees where they feed on nectar, buds,
leaves, blossoms and also insects, sometimes on the ground under trees.

Endemic to Floreana, where
it is found in the highlands,
coming down to about 300
m. It's the only island where
all three tree-finches occur.

MEDIUM TREE-FINCH
Camarhynchus pauper
PINZÓN MEDIANO de ÁRBOL

Takes same food as Small Tree-finch. I watched them also searching and
probing in tree bark, also in moss and lichen on trees, possibly in search of
insects. Its slightly longer bill is probably better adapted to these food sources.
Woodpecker Finch now does this on other islands but is missing on Floreana?

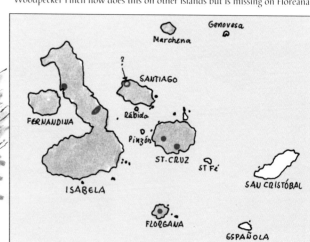

LARGE TREE-FINCH
Camarhynchus psittacula
PINZÓN GRANDE de ÁRBOL

Males are rather darker than other
tree-finches. Most diagnostic is the
sharply curved parrot-like bill.

Extinct on San Cristóbal and not found on Española, Genovesa or the two
far northern islands. A bird of the more humid highlands, but we also
saw them on Santiago near the coast, feeding like parrots in a tree
with fruit, and on Isabela in a dry area in thick bush.

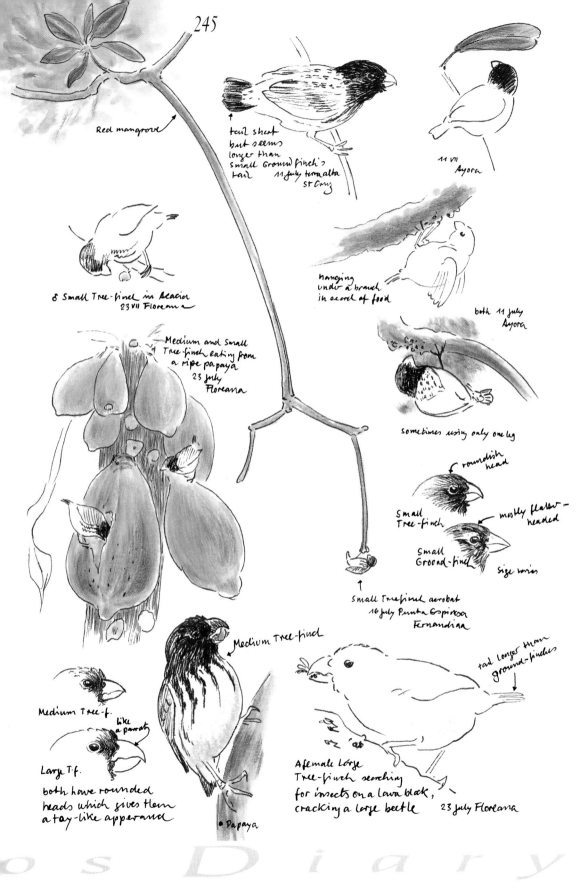

245

Red mangrove

tail short
but seems
longer than
small Ground finch's
tail   11 July terra alba
St Cruz

11 VII
Ayora

hanging
under a branch
in search of food

both 11 July
Ayora

♂ Small Tree-finch in Acacia
23 VII Floreana

sometimes using only one leg

Medium and Small
Tree-finch eating from
a ripe papaya
23 July
Floreana

roundish
head

Small
Tree-finch

mostly flatter-
headed

Small
Ground-finch

Size varies

Small Tree-finch acrobat
16 July Punta Espinosa
Fernandina

Medium Tree-finch

tail longer than
ground-finches

Medium Tree-f.

like
a parrot

Large T.f.

both have rounded
heads which gives them
a tay-like appearance

A female Large
Tree-finch searching
for insects on a lava black,
cracking a large beetle   23 July Floreana

• Papaya

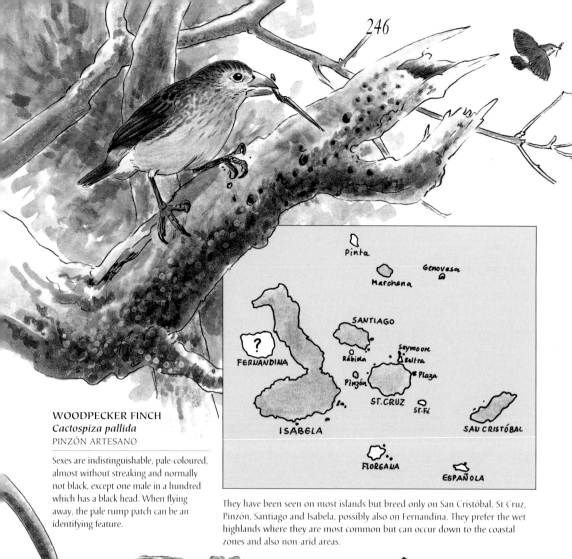

WOODPECKER FINCH
Cactospiza pallida
PINZÓN ARTESANO

Sexes are indistinguishable, pale-coloured, almost without streaking and normally not black, except one male in a hundred which has a black head. When flying away, the pale rump patch can be an identifying feature.

They have been seen on most islands but breed only on San Cristóbal, St Cruz, Pinzón, Santiago and Isabela, possibly also on Fernandina. They prefer the wet highlands where they are most common but can occur down to the coastal zones and also non-arid areas.

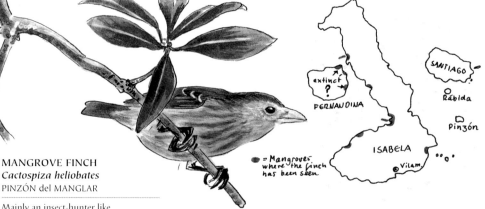

MANGROVE FINCH
Cactospiza heliobates
PINZÓN del MANGLAR

Mainly an insect-hunter like Woodpecker Finch, with a similar but less heavy bill. Possibly searches more in mangroves under leaves than probes in dead wood etc. (as Woodpecker Finches mostly do).

The rarest and least known Darwin's finch. Found only on Isabela, and is very restricted, being located in dense mangroves. Possibly still on Fernandina but we did not see or hear them at Punta Espinosa. I searched for them carefully and only heard one in the lagoon of Bahía Elizabeth, Isabela, where I had watched them 25 years ago.

Is this normal? Or was it unnatural. A black bill similar to breeding ground finches. Possibly only dirty from pulling grows finches but it was shiny black moss

after working for a while on the tree-trunk, the bird flew away with open tail and rather rounded wings

pale bill

one with a black bill

11/VII St Cruz

One bird had an entirely black bill, a second paler bird was pale-billed. They both were unstreaked, the plumage being yellowish washed with a greenish cast. They looked a bit like tanagers with their relatively long bills, but they also reminded me of small barbets.
11 July St Cruz farmland in the tierra alta

The bird was hanging upside-down on the tree-trunk, pulling and pushing a large clump of moss with its beak, helping with its feet. Bits of moss were falling under the tree where other finches waited for them (mostly small Ground-f.)

Wood pecker finch

lichen

22/VII St Cruz in a wet Scalesia forest one in search for food

one holding bits with its feet. They seem to use their feet quite often for holding or pulling
22 July St Cruz

On 18 July after a lengthy search and wait at the lagoon in Bahia Elizabeth out of a red mangrove I heard a loud, repeated 'tschedde tschedde tschedde' song. This must have been a Mangrove Finch. To some it could sound more like 'ts'hur s'hur ts'hur'. Then two birds flew out of the mangrove and could have been of this species. There were also some Small Ground-finches nearby

11 July terra alta, St Cruz

A Woodpecker Finch, very busy and active climbing around in an old tree like a nuthatch (*Sitta* sp.), with its head down in search of insects between the bark and under lichen. It was not easy to take a photograph.

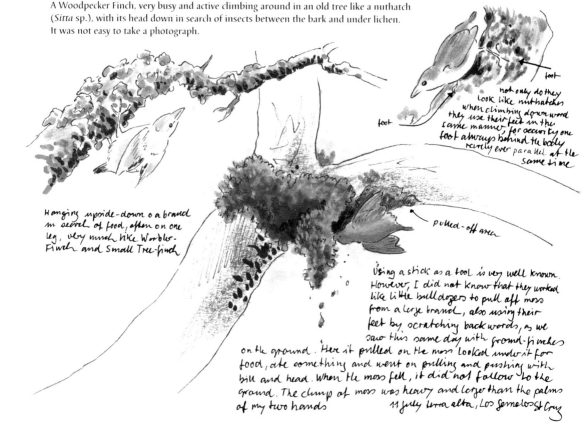

not only do they look like nuthatches when climbing downward they use their feet in the same manner, for securety one foot always behind the body rarely ever parallel at the same time

foot

foot

Hanging upside-down o a branch in seorch of food, often on one leg, very much like Warbler-Finch and Small Tree-finch

pulled-off area

Using a stick as a tool is very well known. However, I did not know that they worked like little bulldozers to pull off moss from a large branch, also using their feet by scratching backwords, as we saw this same day with ground-finches on the ground. Here it pulled on the moss looked under it for food, ate something and went on pulling and pushing with bill and head. When the moss fell, it did not follow to the ground. The clump of moss was heavy and larger than the palms of my two hands   11 July terra alta, Los Gemelos St Cruz

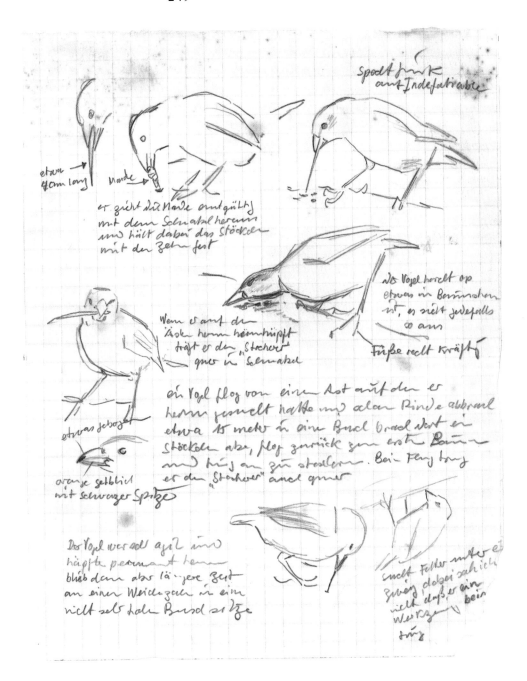

This is an original page from my sketch book, made over 25 years ago, whilst I stayed for a week up in the terra alta on St Cruz farmland. I wanted to watch Woodpecker Finches using tools. They were common up there, always seen singly or in pairs. Out of the dozen I saw daily, only one bird showed me the technique. I watched a 'Woodpecker' with rather pale spectacles searching very busily in a fallen dead tree, probing with its bill in the bark. Then it flew off, 15 m away to a bush, and came back with a stick in its bill. Hopping over the branch, probing here and there it demonstrated its expertise to me. Next day, I watched what I believed was the same bird. I wonder why I only saw one bird using a tool. Perhaps they don't all know the technique.

most we saw here in a rather dry habitat

VEGETARIAN FINCH
Platyspiza crassirostris
PINZÓN VEGETARIANO

In both sexes, the most distinctively coloured finch. Bill rather short, swollen and curved, rather parrot-like. Its song, which is several loud musical notes, is not unlike that of the American Red-winged Blackbird.

Found on all the main islands, except Española and Genovesa. Extinct on Pinzón and Santa Fé. Most common in the transitional zones where there are trees and bushes, but we saw them on the Alcedo walk, also in rather dry areas, and on St Cruz in the humid zone. Usually they feed quietly in trees but are also found on the ground.

very common

WARBLER FINCH
Certhidia olivacea
PINZÓN CANTOR

The smallest Galápagos bird, weighing only 8 g compared with the 34 g of Vegetarian Finch and 35 g of the heavy-billed Large Ground-finch. Small Ground-finch weighs 14 g, Small Tree-finch 13 g, and a Yellow Warbler 12 g.

Breeds on all the islands, except on the rather bare and windswept Daphne. Found in all habitats but said to be most common in the humid zones, though we saw most individuals on dry Genovesa, with plenty also on Española, but none in the highlands of Floreana. The different populations vary greatly in number, especially in the coastal areas.

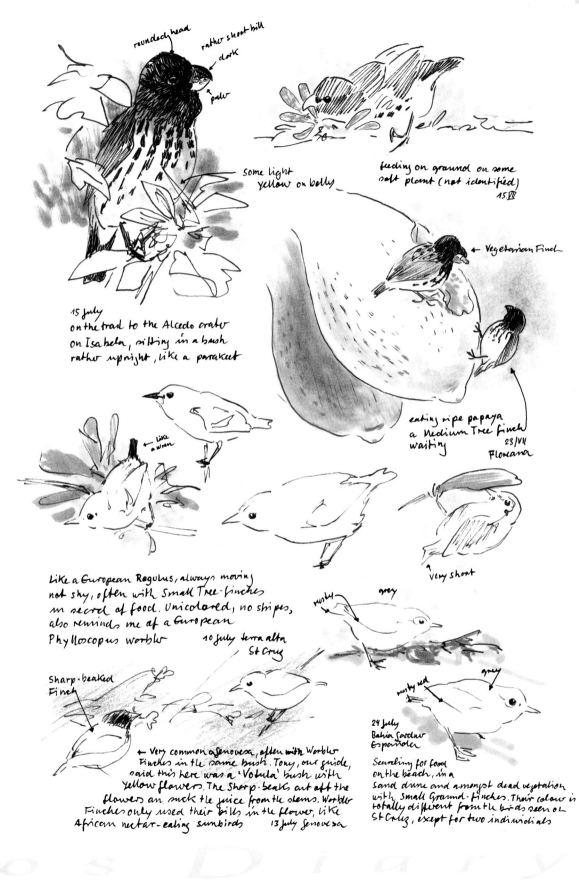

rounded head

rather short bill

dark

pale

some light
yellow on belly

feeding on ground on some
soft plant (not identified)
15.VII

15 July
on the trail to the Alcedo crater
on Isabela, sitting in a bush
rather upright, like a parakeet

← Vegetarian Finch

eating ripe papaya
a Medium Tree Finch
waiting
23/VII
Floreana

← like
a wren

Very short

Like a European Regulus, always moving
not shy, often with Small Tree-finches
in search of food. Unicolored, no stripes,
also reminds me of a European
Phylloscopus warbler

10 July terra alta
St Cruz

rusty   grey

Sharp-beaked
Finch

rusty red   grey

24 July
Bahia Gardner
Española

← Very common at Genovesa, often with Warbler
Finches in the same bush. Tony, our guide,
said this here was a 'Votula' bush with
yellow flowers. The Sharp-beaks cut off the
flowers an suck the juice from the stems. Warbler
Finches only used their bills in the flower, like
African nectar-eating sunbirds   13 July Genovesa

Searching for food
on the beach, in a
sand dune and amongst dead vegetation
with Small Ground-finches. Their colour is
totally different from the birds seen on
St Cruz, except for two individuals

1994 on St Cruz.

grub

The bird in the photo seems to have a rather stumpy bill, but only two-thirds is visible, the rest is covered by its prey – a grub.

Taking a good photo of Warbler Finch is very difficult. They are always on the move and mostly found in dense vegetation.

Darwin's finches form the Geospizinae, a very interesting subfamily of the worldwide Bunting family, Emberizidae. There are 13 species, all found in the Galápagos, a 14th lives on Cocos Island, but does not, I think, belong to the Geospizinae. Darwin's finches are, in many ways, all very similar, but at the same time vary greatly in detail. The most aberrant and peculiar member of this group is the small-sized Warbler Finch. When John Gould described this little bird in 1837 he included it rightly with the 'finches' but thereafter he was not sure if he was correct in doing so. Later on, other scientists placed Warbler Finch in a variety of bird families, mostly with New World warblers, the Parulidae. Superficially it looks like a member of that family.

Modern field studies have solved this problem and the little bird, which looks and lives like a warbler, is 'back home' with the Geospizinae.

All Darwin's finches build similar, and for such small birds, rather large nests which are cup-shaped, bulky, roofed and with a side entrance. All use the same material, and it is difficult to tell to which species a nest belongs. Often one species will take over a nest from another. Sometimes they will 'borrow' a nest for a quick courtship display when a female passes an unpaired male and he is too far from his own nest. Males start building the nest with dry grass and small twigs and conduct courtship from them. When a female accepts a nest (and the male goes on courting) she will finish the building job. The eggs of all species are very similar (only varying in size), white with only a few small pink spots. A normal clutch has four eggs.

All Darwin's finches look similar, especially in female plumage, which is drab greyish brown with dark streaks. Males have some black on their face, a black head or are all black in full breeding plumage. Woodpecker/Mangrove Finches of both sexes are like unstreaked female ground-finches, but sometimes males of Woodpecker Finch can have a blackish head. Warbler Finches are quite

different: unstreaked, even in the juvenile plumage (but juveniles from Floreana are heavily streaked). Adult males on some islands have orange-fawn faces and throats, but on St Cruz I saw a bird I thought was a female Sharp-beaked Finch which had a pinkish fawn throat as well. This pinkish, reddish or orange colour could sometimes also be seen in the wingbars of other species. The Sharp-beakeds from Genovesa have reddish brown undertail-coverts, this is also seen sometimes in all-black males of other species. So colour links all 13 species.

Warbler Finches, because they are small, short-winged and poor fliers, have developed quite varied colours and bill sizes on different islands. They are also the most widespread species, found on all islands and in all habitats; most common in the humid zones where vegetation is luxurious but also found in dry areas as long as there are bushes or trees. We also saw them on creeping vegetation in the dunes and even at low tide on the beach. Next to Small Ground-finches, they are the most common Galápagos landbird but are never seen in large flocks like ground-finches.

The Yellow Warbler, which has more or less the same lifestyle as Warbler Finch, must have arrived much later in the Galápagos, otherwise the finch would never have developed competing against its more powerful rival. The two species compete now, but the Warbler Finch manages to survive quite well. For another warbler or similar insect-eater there would be no ecological niche on the islands since other finches also take some insects in addition to seeds. On Santa Cruz I watched a Warbler Finch extracting nectar from a flower in the manner of an African sunbird. There are few large flowers in the Galápagos so there is no 'space' for a solely nectar-feeding bird, although finches, particularly cactus-finches, will take nectar when available. I wonder if any of the tree-finches will become fruit-eating birds, like tanagers, with the current abundance of introduced exotic fruiting trees.

253

Adult male Warbler Finches have no black in their plumage as in most other species. Instead they often have an orange-brown throat patch. This differs from island to island, as well as individually. The patch is most developed in birds on Santiago and found as only a trace in a few males on Santa Fé.

C. o. fusca from Pinta and Marchena is rather grey with little or no 'orange' on throat. The bill is about 8 mm long.

7·5mm

8-10mm

C. o. olivacea from Santiago has males with the most developed throat patch, but this is not so bright in all adult males.

Pinta

Marchena

Genovesa

C. o. mentalis from Genovesa is very dark, often with fine paler spots on the back and no red on throat. Very common and found in all habitats, even on the beach.

Fernandina

All islands west of St Cruz have the same subspecies, *olivacea*, with varied orange throat patches. On St Cruz there are often only a few mosaic-like spots. Bill sizes vary from 7.3 mm on Fernandina to 7.6 mm on St Cruz.

Rábida

Pinzón

Baltra

St Cruz

St Fé

Isabela

C. o. lutea from San Cristóbal is yellowish on the underside with broad wingbars.

San Cristóbal

8-10mm

8mm

Floreana

Española

C. o. bifasciata from Santa Fé is the palest subspecies with a really pale face and no trace of orange (nearly white on underside), sometimes with a yellowish wash.

8mm

11mm

C. o. becki from Floreana is greyish brown with some orange on face and has a rather strong bill. Some have buff-brown wingbars (many on Isabela).

C. o. cinerascens from Española is a very grey subspecies with no orange throat patch. However, I saw some with a rusty tail and strong bill.

♀ grey individ.

Some Yellow Warblers, *D. p. aureola*, are rather grey and could look like a Warbler Finch but they generally have some yellowish grey/green in the wings, on the rump or in the longer tail. They are not so acrobatic in their movements. Once I saw a grey bird singing, so they are not always females when this colour.

At St Cruz near Ayora I watched a Warbler Finch in a tree, sucking nectar out of a flower or possibly searching there for insects. Its face was bright yellow, stained by the pollen of the flowers. Otherwise it was very olive above like the birds on Santiago but had no orange throat patch.

When looking at the map above, with the different Warbler Finch subspecies, you see that on the western islands of St Cruz, Santiago, Isabela and Fernandina there is one subspecies, *C. o.olivacea*, with locally different populations. On the more distant islands there is a different subspecies on each island. A most peculiar fact is that on Santa Fé, which is near St Cruz, is found a quite different very pale form. On San Cristóbal is *C. o. lutea*, which resembles the western island subspecies group. There is a further subspecies, *C. o. becki*, on the most northern islands of Wolf and Darwin, which closely resembles the southern island form on Floreana. Again the *C. o. fusca* from Pinta and Marchena is most like birds from Española.

9 July, Ayora

The first landbird we saw in the Galápagos was a rather dull female Small Ground-finch. This occurred inside the airport hall at Baltra while we were waiting for our luggage. Coming out of the building the puzzle began. There were finches just outside the hall feeding under some bushes and also under the waiting bus. I was quite sure they were Small Ground-finches, except for one which had a larger bill. A few minutes later we were waiting for the ferry on the Canal de Itabaca. There were many finches both sides of the channel, Small and Medium Ground-finches, but some had rather large bills. They were all shades of grey with blackish stripes and all were rather drab. Arriving at our hotel in Ayora, just beyond the doorstep of our bungalow, there were many Small and Mediums feeding quietly together, hopping around and often concentrating on one spot; also an odd-coloured bird with an orange-brown throat and a more pointed bill. I thought it was a Sharp-beaked Finch. Barnaby took this photo when the light was not very good. Next day they were there again from very early in the morning. Identification was not easy, and we were only 2–3 m away. They came and went and did not fly off in a flock like American or European sparrows; each bird went its own way. Once a Common Cactus-finch appeared but only for a minute. Large-billed birds were flying overhead, sometimes two together. The colour of all these birds was of no help in identification. They had drab grey stripes, some had black heads and a few were all black. Their bill colour varied also, some that were black had pale bills, other female birds had black bills, and some had yellow fawn underbills and dark 'uppers' — an endless puzzle. A small-sized tree-finch joined the birds on the ground but then flew back into low vegetation, searched for food and caught an insect. Just behind our bungalow there was a 2-m high stone wall. Finches were sitting there around a dripping water pipe, drinking and also taking baths under the single falling drops. This went on all day long, and even very late in the day there were still Small Ground-finches scratching in the soil like little hens.

Depending upon what they are doing, the shape of the ground-finches varies and is of no great help in identification. This one here, a Small Ground-finch, which looks like a little stumpy African Quailfinch, is searching in the soil for seeds, its staple food. They often dig a little hole by scratching and pulling, so that just their backs are visible.

9 July, Ayora

The silhouette of the female Cactus finch in the photo (left) looks like a little crow, with her long pointed bill and dark plumage. This is one of the easiest black Darwin's finches to identify. They are mostly found near cacti but also feed on ground. The male above is searching for insects, an important part of their diet.

On Daphne, 20 July – A very dark Common Cactus-finch eating seeds out of a fallen over-ripe *Opuntia* fig, possibly a younger male, or was it an older female? In shape, these finches look more elongated than any other ground-finch, long-billed, flat-headed, long-necked, and longer-bodied.

A lighter (but still very dark) bird arrived, chased the 'dark' away and started eating. I first thought it was a very common Medium Ground-finch, but seeing its bill there was no doubt about identity, it was a female Common Cactus-finch. Mediums are also less striped.

10 July Ayora St Cruz – To the left is a Small Ground-Finch.

24 July Española – A typical Small Ground-finch but to me they seem to be larger than on St Cruz. The bill in this picture is also more pointed.

10 July Ayora – A group feeding together.
I call it a group and not a flock because each individual keeps to itself. There is no fighting and it appears that they aren't worried about the bird next to them nor do they attempt to call other birds to the group.

This bird puzzled me with its rather long bill. Same body size as nearby Mediums, same colour, a bit longer but too small for a Common Cactus-finch. Was it a Sharp-beaked or just a sharp-billed Medium?

The Darwin Station at Ayora is a good place for finches. Here they bathe in the shade of a tree in a basin of water provided for tortoises. It was difficult to photograph since a flash bulb is not allowed.

this bill is not very large but comparing the body size with the nearby Cactus-finches, it must be a Large-Ground-finch

The first black male and the brown wingbarred female on the left are Common Cactus-finches. They are too large for Sharp-beaks, and the male would have reddish undertail-coverts if the latter species; they are white here on the photo.

Small Ground-finch
both from St Cruz

breeding ♂♂
of all ground
finches have
black bills
bill size varies

24 July Punta Suarez on Española – The first bird is easy to identify, a younger male Small Ground-finch. The second bird is larger, much larger, but there are no Large Ground-finches on Española, or Medium Ground-finches either. There is, however, another large-billed species, Large Cactus-finch, and this could only be that bird. It is very dark in female plumage, the darkest of all ground-finches. (There were no cacti nearby.) The female is moving into breeding condition; the bill is changing colour to black.

bill size varies

Medium Ground-finches make identification so difficult. If there were only Small and Large it would be much easier.

Mediums have smaller bills than Large and bigger than Small. This one should be a Medium Ground-finch but I still have some doubt about its identification. Generally, Small Ground-finch has a more conical bill.

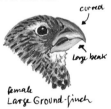

curved

Large beak

female
Large Ground-finch

A typical female Large Ground-finch, compact build with a strong head, formed by the muscles of the large bill. With such a bill they can crack hard seeds. This one's bill is not very large. There are much larger-billed individuals. On San Cristóbal, where there are no Large Ground-finches, I saw a Medium with a very large bill, but there are also other islands with large-billed Mediums.

A special permit is required to visit Daphne Mayor, a small island of only 34 hectares, west of Baltra and 8 km from St Cruz. Only small groups are allowed to visit. Landing is not easy and not always possible. Many seabirds breed inside the crater, but to us the most interesting birds were the finches. The vegetation is sparse, mostly of *Opuntia* and Palo Santo trees, which here are more of a shrub. There are also about 40 other plant species, like Tiquilias and Chamesyce.

The Darwin's finches living here have been studied by a group of American scientists for many years, day by day. Most, if not all individuals, had been marked with rings as you see here on the photo of a male Common Cactus-finch which has two rings. The Large Ground-finch female above (or is it a Medium?) also had a ring on her right foot, not visible on the photo. The story of this important study, which was made under relatively primitive conditions, is told in the book, *The Bill of the Finch*, by Jonathan Weiner, published in 1994. I wish I had read it before our visit to Daphne; I would have gone there with 'different' eyes!

20 July Rábida - A female Large Ground-finch, the only Large we saw on this island. There were a few Small Ground- finches, all with rather pointed bills, also some Medium and Common Cactus-finches. There was not one unopened prickly pear fig!

while sitting on a lava block, a female Large watched some Small Ground-finches searching for food between pebbles. She flew down and started digging, using her bill and large feet to scratch stones and gravel backwards. One stone was really large, 4—5 times her weight which is about 35g. Quite hard work for a small bird.

Ground-finches do not just feed on the ground, nor tree-finches only in trees, but cactus-finches feed mostly in cacti. Behind our bungalow in Ayora, I watched Small and Medium Ground-finches feeding in a flowering tree.

An all-black male Small Ground-finch picked off a flower and flew with it onto a nearby branch, kept it under its feet and 'nibbled' on the flower stem. A female came to have a look. Mediums were feeding in the same tree, also using their feet, as did a single Large and single Small Tree-finch
19 July Ayora St Cruz

A Warbler Finch holding a large grub with its feet, tearing off little bits to eat. All Darwin's finches often use their feet to hold things. A Sharp-beak on Genovesa was holding a pink piece of crab with its bill. A Woodpecker Finch holding a tool with its feet while pulling an insect out of a hole with its bill

24/VII/95
Española

ere, at the end of our diary, is a small collection of some Darwin's finches. They are quite easy to identify. It's just as you see them in the Galápagos, but there they move around and do not always show their bills for long in the 'perfect' position. Be careful, their colour can mislead. In one kind of light, a pale bill looks small, but in another light, larger. It is best to compare with birds close by; but I am sure it will always be a puzzle.

Back home in France, while preparing this book, I felt I should go to the British Museum of Natural History and examine their collection of bird skins from the Galápagos islands. This was not immediately possible since I was very short of time. Years before it would have been much easier when the collection was housed in London, but now it is in Tring outside London, and I would need a few days to complete my work. I only managed to get to the museum in 1997. Coincidentally, the first skin I examined was of a Large Ground-finch collected on Jervis, now officially called Rábida, in 1897, 100 years before. I started work in the museum on 29 September, the skin had been collected on the 24 September a century ago.

For most people, a museum with drawers stuffed full of dead birds sounds very unattractive. Not for me, however, apart from the strong smell of the preservatives used to protect the specimens. Here I have the opportunity to minutely examine a skin. If I am drawing and painting I prefer to go into the field to sketch live birds to get the right shape and pattern. To finish a painting I like to use a skin to get the right colours. Most museum collections are rather old, often from the nineteenth century, but even after 100 years the colours change little. So a well-kept museum collection is not only useful for scientists, but also for bird artists who want to get the details right, even when skins look more like feathered cigars than real birds.

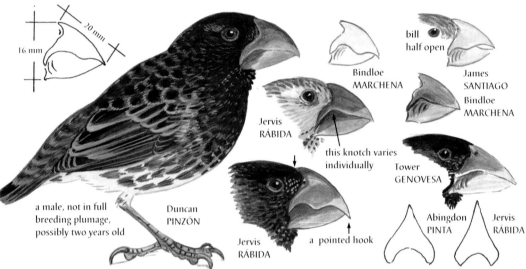

The bills of some Large Ground-finches (males and females) from different islands. They vary in shape and size from island to island and within an island population itself. Three individuals from Rábida (Jervis) are shown here. This difference is not sex-related.

The bills seen from below are also different in shape as these two examples illustrate

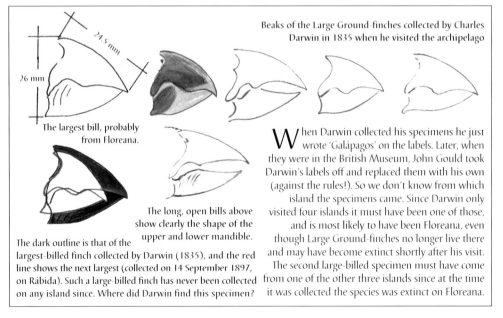

Beaks of the Large Ground-finches collected by Charles Darwin in 1835 when he visited the archipelago

The largest bill, probably from Floreana.

The long, open bills above show clearly the shape of the upper and lower mandible.

The dark outline is that of the largest-billed finch collected by Darwin (1835), and the red line shows the next largest (collected on 14 September 1897, on Rábida). Such a large-billed finch has never been collected on any island since. Where did Darwin find this specimen?

When Darwin collected his specimens he just wrote 'Galápagos' on the labels. Later, when they were in the British Museum, John Gould took Darwin's labels off and replaced them with his own (against the rules!). So we don't know from which island the specimens came. Since Darwin only visited four islands it must have been one of those, and is most likely to have been Floreana, even though Large Ground-finches no longer live there and may have become extinct shortly after his visit. The second large-billed specimen must have come from one of the other three islands since at the time it was collected the species was extinct on Floreana.

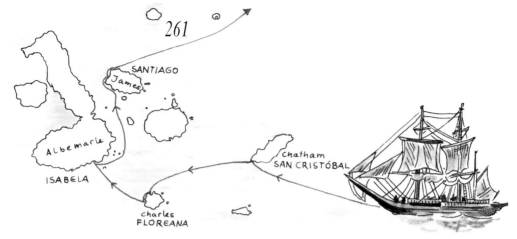

SANTIAGO
James
Albemarle
ISABELA
Chatham
SAN CRISTÓBAL
charles
FLOREANA

The Beagle, with Darwin aboard, arrived in the Galápagos on 15 September 1835, travelling from South America en route to other Pacific islands. Darwin only stayed a short time, leaving in October. At this time, Darwin had not formulated his theories on evolution, and it was only after he returned to London to be told by Gould that the finches and mockingbirds he had collected were not individually variable birds but separate species, did he begin to focus on evolutionary theory. Nevertheless, Darwin was deeply impressed by the complex world he found on these tiny islands, isolated in the wide Pacific.

Darwin was not the only collector from The Beagle, Rober Fitzroy, the ship's captain, made his own collection, but unlike Darwin he put the name of the relevant island on each label, so we know the origin of these skins. However, Darwin's lengthy diary entries from that time have helped to pinpoint the correct islands.

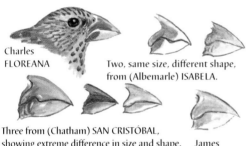

Charles
FLOREANA

Two, same size, different shape, from (Albemarle) ISABELA.

Three from (Chatham) SAN CRISTÓBAL, showing extreme difference in size and shape. There are no Large Ground-finches on this island (extinct).

James
SANTIAGO

Barrington
SANTA FÉ

Two from (Duncan) PINZÓN, from large to massive, and the same size as Large Ground-finches from Marchena. All three ground-finches are found on Pinzón and Rábida, there the 'Large' have massive bills.

As in the field, **Medium Ground-finches** are always difficult to identify. On some islands such as Pinzón or San Cristóbal they have a bill as large as that of Large Ground-finch. On Pinzón and San Cristóbal, Large Ground-finches are now extinct, and possibly Medium's have developed a larger bill. It's not only in the Galápagos where seed-eating birds have developed bill-size differences. The crossbill (Loxia species) from Scottish pine forests has a larger bill than English crossbills. Parrot Crossbill from Scandinavia has an enormous bill, while Two-barred Crossbill, which feeds mainly on larch, is slender-billed. The Philippine Crossbill has an even smaller, nearly goldfinch-sized bill. In the Americas this is even more pronounced with Red Crossbill, which may actually be 5-6 different species.

head from above

The **Bobolink**, Dolichonyx oryzivorous, not familiar to Darwin, and a bird he described as 'a finch, with a stiff tail and a long claw to its hinder toe', is the only specimen in the Darwin collection at the B.M. in Tring which has an original Darwin field label: Nr 3374, to which John Gould may have added 'James' (now Santiago). The skin is still in very good condition. It's possibly a moulting male since it has some black feathers on throat and breast. It is peculiar that Darwin collected a species not often found in the Galápagos, being a vagrant from North America which has possibly bred in the savannah-like highlands of San Cristóbal. Darwin may have collected this specimen in September 1835 in the highlands on St Cruz or Santiago.

COMPLETE CHECKLIST OF GALÁPAGOS BIRDS

This checklist contains all the species recorded in the archipelago. The most interesting birds are the **endemics**, species living and breeding only in the Galápagos. These are marked with an asterisk *. Two species, Waved Albatross and Swallow-tailed Gull, also breed in small numbers on an island off the South American coast; they are also marked with an asterisk. Birds with distinct subspecies occurring in the Galápagos, such as Masked Booby, *S. d. granti*, are marked with a circle ●.

Waders form the largest group of birds in the Galápagos, but only the oystercatcher breeds here. The others are winter visitors, and most are accidentals, having occurred once or twice. They are not an important part of the archipelago's birdlife. Some waders stay all year round on the islands, and one or two, such as Semipalmated Plover, could one day breed here.

It is always exciting to see a rare species, but of course the endemics are the birds everyone wants to see. You can personalize this list by 'ticking' each species you see during your visit.

Legend

* — endemic species
● — endemic subspecies

━━━ new family

R – resident, common breeder on this island
r – resident, but rare breeder
iv – inter-island visitor, Galápagos breeder
Wv – winter visitor, mostly from North America
wv – rarer winter visitor; some stay throughout the year
A – accidental; over 20 records on all islands
a – accidental; fewer than 5 records
→ – regularly seen passing near this island's coast

	Species	Galápagos waters	WESTERN		CENTRAL ISLANDS									SOUTHERN			OUTLYING			N.
			Fernandina (Narborough)	Isabela (Albemarle)	Santiago (James)	Rábida (Jervis)	Pinzón (Duncan)	Daphne	Seymour	Baltra	St Cruz (Indefatigable)	Plaza	St Fé (Barrington)	Floreana/St Mariá (Charles)	Española (Hood)	San Cristóbal (Chatham)	Genovesa (Tower)	Marchena (Brindloe)	Pinta (Abingdon)	Darwin & Wolf (Culpepper & Wenman)
*	Galápagos Penguin / *Spheniscus mendiculus*		R	R	iv						iv			iv						
	Pied-billed Grebe / *Podylymbus podiceps*			Wv							Wv			Wv r?	Wv					
	Wandering Albatross / *Diomedea exulans*	× ?																		
	Black-footed Albatross / *Diomedea nigripes*	×																		
	Black-browed Albatross / *Diomedea menlanophris*	×																		
*	Waved Albatross / *Diomedea irrorata*	×													R					
	Southern Giant Petrel / *Macronetes giganteus*	×																		
	Southern Fulmar / *Fulmarus glacialodes*	×																		
	Cape Petrel / *Daption capense*	×																		
	White-winged Petrel / *Pterodroma leucoptera*	×																		
●	Dark-rumped Petrel / *Pterodroma phaeopygia*	×	→	R							r			r		r			→	
	Dove Prion / *Pachyptila desolata*													a dead						

Legend

★ endemic species
● endemic subspecies

R – resident, common breeder on this island
r – resident, but rare breeder
iv – inter-island visitor, Galápagos breeder
Wv – winter visitor, mostly from North America
wv – rarer winter visitor; some stay throughout the year
A – accidental; over 20 records on all islands
a – accidental; fewer than 5 records
→ regularly seen passing near this island's coast

	Species (new family)	Galápagos waters	Fernandina (Narborough)	Isabela (Albemarle)	Santiago (James)	Rabida (Jervis)	Pinzón (Duncan)	Daphne	Seymour	Baltra	St Cruz (Indefatigable)	Plaza	St Fé (Barrington)	Floreana/St María (Charles)	Española (Hood)	San Cristóbal (Chatham)	Genovesa (Tower)	Marchena (Bindloe)	Pinta (Abingdon)	Darwin & Wolf (Culpepper & Wenman)
	Parkinson's Black Petrel — *Procellaria parkinsoni*	×																		
	Wedge-tailed Shearwater — *Puffinus pacificus*	×																		
	Flesh-footed Shearwater — *Puffinus carneipes*	×	→				→													
	Sooty Shearwater — *Puffinus griseus*	×	→				→										→			
●	Audubon's Shearwater — *Puffinus lherminieri*	×	breeds on all islands in rock cavities in cliffs																	
●	Elliot's Storm-petrel — *Oceanites gracilis*	×	often follows ships; breeding haunts in Galápagos unknown																	
	White-faced Storm-petrel — *Pelagodroma marina*	×			→						→					→				
	White-bellied Storm-petrel — *Fregatta grallaria*	×	→																	
●	Wedge-rumped Storm-petrel — *Oceanodroma tethys*	×														R– Pitt islet	R			
	Galápagos Storm-petrel — *Oceanodroma castro* (breeds on islets near the coast of ×)	×	×	×	R				R	×	R			×		×	R			
	Leach's Storm-petrel — *Oceanodroma leucorhoa*	×												→	→		→			→
	Markham's Storm-petrel — *Oceanodroma markhami*	×	a																	
	Black Storm-petrel — *Oceanodroma melania*	×		a																
	Red-billed Tropicbird — *Phaethon aethereus*	×		a	R		R	R		R	R			→	→	→	R			
●	Brown Pelican — *Pelecanus occidentalis*	×	→	R	R	R	R		→	→	R	→	→	→	R	→		R		
●	Blue-footed Booby — *Sula nebouxii*	×	breeds on all islands with suitable habitats; rare on Genovesa																	
●	Masked Booby — *Sula dactyla*	×	breeds on all islands (at different times during year), mostly in small colonies																	
●	Red-footed Booby — *Sula sula*	×	→				→									→	R	R	R	R

Legend

■■■■■ new family

R – resident, common breeder on this island
r – resident, but rare breeder
iv – inter-island visitor, Galápagos breeder
Wv – winter visitor, mostly from North America
wv – rarer winter visitor; some stay throughout the year
A – accidental; over 20 records on all islands
a – accidental; fewer than 5 records
→ regularly seen passing near this island's coast

★ endemic species
● endemic subspecies

	Species	Galápagos waters	WESTERN		CENTRAL ISLANDS									SOUTHERN			OUTLYING			N.
			Fernandina (Narborough)	Isabela (Albemarle)	Santiago (James)	Rábida (Jervis)	Pinzón (Duncan)	Daphne	Seymour	Baltra	St Cruz (Indefatigable)	Plaza	St Fé (Barrington)	Floreana/St María (Charles)	Española (Hood)	San Cristóbal (Chatham)	Genovesa (Tower)	Marchena (Brindloe)	Pinta (Abingdon)	Darwin & Wolf (Culpepper & Wenman)
★	Flightless Cormorant *Nannopterum harrisi*		R	R																
●	Great Frigatebird *Fregata minor*	×	R	×				R						R	×	R				R
●	Magnificent Frigatebird *Fregata magnificens*	×	→	×	→	→	→	×	R	→	→	→	→	×	→	×	R	→	→	R
			breeds on islets near the coast of islands marked with an ×																		
	Snowy Egret *Leucophoyx thula*			wv							wv			wv						
	Great Blue Heron *Ardea herodias*		R	R	R	iv	?	iv	iv	iv	R	iv	iv	R	r	R	r			
	Great Egret *Casmerodius alba*		r	r	iv						r			r		r				
	Cattle Egret *Bulbulcus ibis*			R	iv					iv	R	iv		R		R				
★	Lava Heron *Butorides sundevalli*		*breeds in mangroves along the coast of all islands, also in lagoons*																		
	Striated Heron *Butorides striatus*		r	r			r				r								r	
●	Yellow-crowned Night Heron *Nycticorax violacea*		*found on all islands except Darwin and Wolf*																		
	Greater Flamingo *Phoenicopterus ruber*	→		R	R	R					R			R						
	Black-bellied Whistling-duck *Dendrocygna autumnalis*			a																
●	White-cheeked Pintail *Anas bahamensis*		R	R	R	iv	iv			iv	R		iv	R	iv	R	iv			
	Blue-winged Teal *Anas discors*			Wv							Wv						Wv			
★	Galápagos Hawk *Buteo galapagoensis*		R	R	R	r	r				r		R	R	+	R				
	Osprey *Pandion haliaetus*		a →	a →							a →					a →				
	Peregrine Falcon *Falco peregrinus*			wv						wv	wv	wv		wv						
	Sora Rail *Porzana carolina*				a													a	a	

Legend

★ endemic species
● endemic subspecies

new family

R – resident, common breeder on this island
r – resident, but rare breeder
iv – inter-island visitor, Galápagos breeder
Wv – winter visitor, mostly from North America
wv – rarer winter visitor; some stay throughout the year
A – accidental; over 20 records on all islands
a – accidental; fewer than 5 records
→ regularly seen passing near this island's coast

	Species	Galápagos waters	Fernandina (Narborough)	Isabela (Albemarle)	Santiago (James)	Rábida (Jervis)	Pinzón (Duncan)	Daphne	Seymour	Baltra	St Cruz (Indefatigable)	Plaza	St Fé (Barrington)	Floreana/St María (Charles)	Española (Hood)	San Cristóbal (Chatham)	Genovesa (Tower)	Marchena (Bindloe)	Pinta (Abingdon)	Darwin & Wolf (Culpepper & Wenman)
★	Galápagos Crake *Laterallus spilonotus*		R	R	r						R			?		r			r	
	Paint-billed Crake *Neocrex erythrops*			R		iv					R			r		R	iv			
	Common Moorhen *Gallinula chloropus*	?		R							R			R		R				
	Purple Gallinule *Porphyrula martinica*										a						wv	wv		
●	American Oystercatcher *Haematopus palliatus*	found on most islands along rocky shores or on sandy beaches																		
	American Golden Plover *Pluvialis dominica*										a									
	Black-bellied Plover *Pluvialis squatarola*		Wv		Wv									Wv				Wv		
	Semipalmated Plover *Charadrius semipalmatus*	sandy shores or lagoons, also in highlands on most islands; some stay all year																		
	Wilson's Plover *Charadrius wilsonia*															a				
	Killdeer *Charadrius vociferus*			a																
	Marbled Godwit *Limosa fedoa*			a							a					a				
	Whimbrel *Numenius phaeopus*	in lagoons on all islands throughout the year																		
	Greater Yellowlegs *Tringa melanoleuca*				a						a			a						
	Lesser Yellowlegs *Tringa flavipes*			A							A			A			a	a		
	Solitary Sandpiper *Tringa solitaria*										A					A				
	Spotted Sandpiper *Actitis macularia*			A							A			A					A	
	Wandering Tattler *Heteroscelus incanum*	on coasts of all islands throughout the year																		
	Willet *Catoptrophorus semipalmatus*		a	a	a						a			a						

Legend:

★ endemic species
● endemic subspecies

- **R** – resident, common breeder on this island
- **r** – resident, but rare breeder
- **iv** – inter-island visitor, Galápagos breeder
- **Wv** – winter visitor, mostly from North America
- **wv** – rarer winter visitor; some stay throughout the year
- **A** – accidental; over 20 records on all islands
- **a** – accidental; fewer than 5 records
- **→** regularly seen passing near this island's coast

Species	Galápagos waters	Fernandina (Narborough)	Isabela (Albemarle)	Santiago (James)	Rabida (Jervis)	Pinzón (Duncan)	Daphne	Seymour	Baltra	St Cruz (Indefatigable)	Plaza	St Fé (Barrington)	Floreana/St Mariá (Charles)	Española (Hood)	San Cristóbal (Chatham)	Genovesa (Tower)	Marchena (Bríndloe)	Pinta (Abingdon)	Darwin & Wolf (Culpepper & Wenman)
		WESTERN		CENTRAL ISLANDS									SOUTHERN			OUTLYING			N.
Ruddy Turnstone *Arenaria interpres*		wv	Wv	possible on all islands						Wv	Wv				wv	Wv			
Black Turnstone *Arenaria melanocephala*															a				
Short-billed Dowitcher *Limnodromus griseus*			wv	wv									wv		wv				
Surfbird *Aphriza virgata*			wv	wv						wv	wv								
Red Knot *Calidris canutus*													a						
Sanderling *Calidris alba*		a	a	a	a			a	a	a		a	a	a	a		a	a	
Semipalmated Sandpiper *Calidris pusilla*			a							a			a						
Western Sandpiper *Calidris mauri*				a								a	a						
Least Sandpiper *Calidris minutilla*				Wv						Wv			Wv		Wv				
White-rumped Sandpiper *Calidris fuscicollis*		a											a						
Baird's Sandpiper *Calidris bairdii*				a									wv	wv					
Pectoral Sandpiper *Calidris melanotos*										a									
Stilt Sandpiper *Micropalma himantopus*			wv							wv									
Wilson's Phalarope *Phalaropus tricolor*			Wv	Wv						Wv			Wv				wv		
Red-necked Phalarope *Phalaropus lobatus*	×	often in large numbers from August–April, around all islands, rarely on land																	
Grey (Red) Phalarope *Phalaropus fulicarius*	×	×	rarely on land, most common in water near islands marked with an ×										×		×				
Black-necked Stilt *Himantopus himantopus*		from December to June on salt and freshwater lagoons on all islands																	
Kelp Gull *Larus dominicanus*		a																	

new family

★ endemic species
● endemic subspecies

R – resident, common breeder on this island
r – resident, but rare breeder
iv – inter-island visitor, Galápagos breeder
Wv – winter visitor, mostly from North America
wv – rarer winter visitor; some stay throughout the year
A – accidental; over 20 records on all islands
a – accidental; fewer than 5 records
→ regularly seen passing near this island's coast

	Species	Galápagos waters	WESTERN		CENTRAL ISLANDS									SOUTHERN			OUTLYING			N.
			Fernandina (Narborough)	Isabela (Albemarle)	Santiago (James)	Rábida (Jervis)	Pinzón (Duncan)	Daphne	Seymour	Baltra	St Cruz (Indefatigable)	Plaza	St Fé (Barrington)	Floreana/St María (Charles)	Española (Hood)	San Cristóbal (Chatham)	Genovesa (Tower)	Marchena (Bindloe')	Pinta (Abingdon)	Darwin & Wolf (Culpepper & Wenman)
★	Lava Gull *Larus fuliginosus*			R	R						R	iv				R	r			
	Laughing Gull *Larus atricilla*			wv							wv					wv				
	Franklin's Gull *Larus pipixcan*		wv	wv	wv					wv	wv			wv		wv				
★	Swallow-tailed Gull *Larus furcatus*			R	R	r	r	r	R	R	R	R	R	R	R	R	R	R	R	?
	Royal Tern *Sterna maxima*			wv							wv									
	Common Tern *Sterna hirundo*			wv							wv					wv	wv			
	Sooty Tern *Sterna fuscata*			a																R
	Black Tern *Chlidonias niger*	a																		
	White Tern *Gygis alba*	a															a			
●	Common Noddy *Anous stolidus*			R	R	R	R	R	R	r	R	r	R	R	R	R	R	R	R	R
	South Polar Skua *Catharacta maccormicki*			a																
	Pomarine Skua *Stercorarius pomarinus*			→									→	→						
	Eared Dove *Zenaida auriculata*										a									
★	Galápagos Dove *Zenaida galapogoensis*		R	r	R	R	R			r	R		R	r	R	R	R	R	R	R
	Black-billed Cuckoo *Coccyzus erythropthalmus*														a					
	Dark-billed Cuckoo *Coccyzus melacoryphus*		R	R	R		R				R			R		R				
	Smooth-billed Ani *Crotophaga ani*			R	R		erad				R		erad	R						
●	Barn Owl *Tyto alba*		R	R	R						r					R				

Legend (new family):

- R – resident, common breeder on this island
- r – resident, but rare breeder
- iv – inter-island visitor, Galápagos breeder
- Wv – winter visitor, mostly from North America
- wv – rarer winter visitor; some stay throughout the year
- A – accidental; over 20 records on all islands
- a – accidental; fewer than 5 records
- → regularly seen passing near this island's coast
- ★ endemic species
- ● endemic subspecies

	Species	Galápagos waters	Fernandina (Narborough)	Isabela (Albemarle)	Santiago (James)	Rábida (Jervis)	Pinzón (Duncan)	Daphne	Seymour	Baltra	St Cruz (Indefatigable)	Plaza	St Fé (Barrington)	Floreana/St María (Charles)	Española (Hood)	San Cristóbal (Chatham)	Genovesa (Tower)	Marchena (Brindloe)	Pinta (Abingdon)	Darwin & Wolf (Culpepper & Wenman)
●	Short-eared Owl *Asio flammeus*		r	r	r	r					R			r	r	r	R	r	r	
	Common Nighthawk *Chordeiles minor*		a	a							a				a					
	Chimney Swift *Chaetura pelagica*										a									
	Belted Kingfisher *Ceryle alcyon*			wv			a				wv			wv	wv		wv			

The following families all belong to the order Passeriformes and are mostly small to medium-sized birds. For these landbirds it was and is difficult to reach the outlying islands in the archipelago. Two, the mockingbird and a finch must have reached the Galápagos a long time ago, both spreading over all islands, with the finch evolving into 12 different species. Alongside one warbler they are now the most successful Galápagos landbirds. The Bobolink, a winter visitor, is probably on its way to becoming a regular breeding bird in the highlands of the larger islands. Most Galápagos endemics are from this order of birds.

	Species	Galápagos waters	Fernandina (Narborough)	Isabela (Albemarle)	Santiago (James)	Rábida (Jervis)	Pinzón (Duncan)	Daphne	Seymour	Baltra	St Cruz (Indefatigable)	Plaza	St Fé (Barrington)	Floreana/St María (Charles)	Española (Hood)	San Cristóbal (Chatham)	Genovesa (Tower)	Marchena (Brindloe)	Pinta (Abingdon)	Darwin & Wolf (Culpepper & Wenman)
●	Vermillion Flycatcher *Pyrocephalus rubinus*		R	R	R	iv	R				R		iv	R	iv	r		R	R	iv
★	Galápagos Flycatcher *Myiarchus magnirostris*		R	R	R	r	R		r	r	R			R	R			r	r	
	Eastern Kingbird *Tyrannus tyrannus*															a				
	Purple Martin *Progne subis*										a				a					
● ?★	Galápagos Martin *Progne modesta*		R	R	r		r				r			r	iv	r				
	Sand Martin *Riparia riparia*													wv	wv	wv				
	Barn Swallow *Hirundo rustica*										wv			wv	wv	wv				
	Cliff Swallow *Petrochelidon pyrrhonota*																			a
	Cedar Waxwing *Bombycilla cedrorum*															a				
★	Galápagos Mockingbird *Nesomimus parvulus*		R	R	R	r			r		R			R			R	R	R	R
★	Charles Mockingbird *Nesomimus trifasciatus*													only on Champion and Gardner/Floreana						

Legend

* endemic species
• endemic subspecies

▬ new family

- R – resident, common breeder on this island
- r – resident, but rare breeder
- iv – inter-island visitor, Galápagos breeder
- Wv – winter visitor, mostly from North America
- wv – rarer winter visitor; some stay throughout the year
- A – accidental; over 20 records on all islands
- a – accidental; fewer than 5 records
- → regularly seen passing near this island's coast

	Species		WESTERN		CENTRAL ISLANDS									SOUTHERN			OUTLYING			N.
		Galápagos waters	Fernandina (Narborough)	Isabela (Albemarle)	Santiago (James)	Rábida (Jervis)	Pinzón (Duncan)	Daphne	Seymour	Baltra	St Cruz (Indefatigable)	Plaza	St Fé (Barrington)	Floreana/St María (Charles)	Española (Hood)	San Cristóbal (Chatham)	Genovesa (Tower)	Marchena (Brindloe)	Pinta (Abingdon)	Darwin & Wolf (Culpepper & Wenman)
*	Hood Mockingbird — *Nesomimus macdonaldi*														R					
*	Chatham Mockingbird — *Nesomimus melanotis*															R				
	Red-eyed Vireo — *Vireo olivaceus*																			a
•	Yellow Warbler — *Dendroica petechia*	→ breeds on all islands, found from sea level to the highest points. (Also on Cocos Isl.)																		
	Blackpoll Warbler — *Dendroica striata*										a									
	Summer Tanager — *Piranga rubra*										?					a				a
	Rose-breasted Grosbeak — *Pheucticus ludovicianus*		a														a			
	Indigo Bunting — *Passerina cyanea*										a									
	Bobolink — *Dolichonyx oryzivorus*			×							×			×		r?	×			
	(Bobolink note)	→ common from Oct.–Dec., also found July–Aug.; possibly breeds in highlands of San Cristóbal																		
*	Large Ground-finch — *Geospiza magnirostris*		R	R	R	R	R	R			R	iv	+	+		+	R	R	R	R
*	Medium Ground-finch — *Geospiza fortis*		R	R	R	R	R	R	R	R	R	r	R	R		R		R	R	
*	Small Ground-finch — *Geospiza fuliginosa*		R	R	R	R	R	r	R	R	R	R	R	R	R	R		R	R	
*	Sharp-beaked Ground-finch — *Geospiza difficilis*		R	?	R						+					+	?	R		R	R
*	Common Cactus-finch — *Geospiza scandens*			R	R	R	r	R	R	r	R	R	R	R		R		R	R	
*	Large Cactus-finch — *Geospiza conirostris*														R		R			
*	Vegetarian Finch — *Platyspiza crassirostris*		R	R	R	R	+				R		+	R				R	R	
*	Large Tree-finch — *Camarhynchus psittacula*		R	R	R	R	+				R			R		iv?		R	R	
*	Medium Tree-finch — *Camarhynchus pauper*													R						

★ endemic species ● endemic subspecies	new family		WESTERN		CENTRAL ISLANDS									SOUTHERN			OUTLYING			N.
	R – resident, common breeder on this island r – resident, but rare breeder iv – inter-island visitor, Galápagos breeder Wv – winter visitor, mostly from North America wv – rarer winter visitor; some stay throughout the year A – accidental; over 20 records on all islands a – accidental; fewer than 5 records → regularly seen passing near this island's coast	Galápagos waters	Fernandina (Narborough)	Isabela (Albemarle)	Santiago (James)	Rábida (Jervis)	Pinzón (Duncan)	Daphne	Seymour	Baltra	St Cruz (Indefatigable)	Plaza	St Fé (Barrington)	Floreana/St María (Charles)	Española (Hood)	San Cristóbal (Chatham)	Genovesa (Tower)	Marchena (Bindloe)	Pinta (Abingdon)	Darwin & Wolf (Culpepper & Wennman)
★	Small Tree-finch *Camarhynchus parvulus*		R	R	R	R	R			R	R		R	R		R			iv	
★	Woodpecker Finch *Cactospiza pallida*			R	R	iv	R			iv	R			iv		R			iv	
★	Mangrove Finch *Cactospiza heliobates*		+?	r																
★	Warbler Finch *Certhidia olivacea*		R	R	R	R	R		R	R	R		R	R	R	R	R	R	R	R

Species new to the Galapagos, recorded since the publication of this book

INDEX

Actitis macularia 208, 209

Albatross, Waved 69, 84, 89, 126–9, 140, 144, 162–5

Anas bahamensis 74, 87, 88, 113, 198, 199

Ani, Groove-billed 21, 225
  Smooth-billed 8, 21, 51, 110, 224, 225

Anous stolidus 30, 31, 55, 60, 64, 69, 70, 96, 101, 107, 148, 157, 220, 221

Ardea herodias 17, 31, 46, 55, 73, 75, 92, 96, 101, 107, 149, 152, 153, 157, 188, 189

Arenaria interpres 25, 30, 88, 114, 132, 144, 212, 213

Asio flammeus 41, 49, 111, 226, 227

Bobolink 136, 261

Booby, Blue-footed 10, 19, 30–2, 37, 38, 41, 42, 44, 49, 55, 60, 63–70, 80, 89, 101, 102, 104, 105, 107, 114, 123–5, 132, 136, 137, 139–44, 148, 164, 165, 176, 177, 180, 181
  Masked 30, 32, 38, 41–4, 49, 68, 96, 101, 104, 105, 107, 131, 132, 136, 138–41, 178–81
  Red-footed 38, 40, 41, 42, 44–6, 49, 104, 138–41, 176, 178, 181

Bubulcus ibis 6–8, 12, 15, 21, 28, 77, 110, 155, 156, 190, 191

Buteo galapagoensis 51, 52, 57, 63, 64, 69, 73, 96–8, 132, 200–3

Butorides striatus 77, 81, 84, 192, 193

Butorides sundevalli 12, 13, 15, 19, 26, 29, 41, 68, 72, 75, 77, 81, 84, 96, 148, 192, 193

Butorides virescens 77

Cactospiza heliobates 62, 73, 81, 82, 84, 86, 166, 239, 246, 247, 252

Cactospiza pallida 22, 62, 63, 110, 239, 246–9, 252

Cactus-finch, Common 62, 92, 106, 118, 147, 238, 242, 243, 254–6, 258
  Large 39, 122, 133, 147, 165, 238, 242, 243, 257

Calidris alba 53, 208

Calidris mauri 208, 209

Camarhynchus parvulus 10, 12, 20, 22, 24, 50, 62, 73–5, 82, 86, 110, 118, 136, 239, 244, 245

Camarhynchus pauper 239, 244, 245

Camarhynchus psittacula 24, 62, 74, 239, 244, 245

Casmerodius albus 6, 7, 17, 77, 155, 190

Catoptrophorus semipalmatus 210, 211

Certhidia olivacea 20, 22, 39, 62, 96, 122, 133, 159, 237, 239, 250–3, 259

Charadrius semipalmatus 17, 53, 88, 208

Coccyzus erythropthalmus 20

Coccyzus melacoryphus 20, 62, 224, 225

Cormorant, Flightless 68, 70–2, 75, 76, 80, 83–5, 96, 182, 183

Crake, Galápagos 108, 112, 204, 205
  Paint-billed 113, 205

Crotophaga ani 8, 21, 51, 110, 224, 225

Crotophaga sulcirirostris 21, 225

Cuckoo, Black-billed 20
  Dark-billed 20, 62, 224, 225

Dendroica petechia 10, 12, 14, 17, 18, 20, 24, 26, 37, 41, 50, 62, 64, 70, 72, 74, 75, 86, 96, 97, 118, 142, 148, 207, 236, 237, 252–4

Dendroica striata 236

Diomedea irrorata 69, 84, 89, 126–9, 140, 144, 162–5

Dolichonyx oryzivorus 136, 261

Dove, Eared 8, 9
  Galápagos 38, 41, 48, 49, 51, 52, 72, 92, 107, 110, 122, 128, 222, 223
  Zenaida 8

Egret, Cattle 6–8, 12, 15, 21, 28, 77, 110, 155, 156, 190, 191
  Great 6, 7, 17, 77, 155, 190

Falcon, Peregrine 203

Falco peregrinus 203

Finch, Cocos Island 239
  Mangrove 62, 73, 81, 82, 84, 86, 166, 239, 246, 247, 253
  Vegetarian 62, 108, 120, 239, 250, 251
  Warbler 20, 22, 39, 62, 96, 122, 133, 159, 237, 239, 250–3, 259
  Woodpecker 22, 62, 63, 110, 239, 246–9, 252

Flamingo, Greater 50, 52, 114–17, 150, 151, 196–8

Flycatcher, Galápagos *see* Large-billed
  Large-billed 13, 14, 51, 62, 74, 92, 121, 159, 228, 229
  Vermillion 23, 24, 60–2, 73, 108, 110, 228, 229

Fregata magnificens 15, 19, 31–8, 41, 64, 68, 96, 101, 102, 104, 107, 114, 139, 140, 142, 184, 185, 187

Fregata minor 32–8, 41, 43, 49, 58, 59, 132, 139, 164, 184–6

Fregetta grallaria 107

Frigatebird, Great 32–8, 41, 43, 49, 58, 59, 132, 139, 164, 184–6
  Magnificent 15, 19, 31–8, 41, 64, 68, 96, 101, 102, 104, 107, 114, 139, 140, 142, 184, 185, 187

Gallinula chloropus 12, 19, 86, 113, 204, 205

Gallinule, Common 12, 19, 86, 113, 204, 205

Geospiza conirostris 39, 122, 133, 147, 165, 242, 243, 257

Geospiza difficilis 13, 39, 107, 136, 238, 242, 243, 252, 259

Geospiza fortis 10, 12–14, 22, 24, 50, 62, 64, 68, 74, 82, 86, 92, 106, 118, 136, 142, 238, 240, 241, 254, 256–9, 261

Geospiza fuliginosa 10, 12–15, 17, 18, 22, 24, 50, 56, 62, 72, 74, 75, 82, 84, 86, 92, 106, 118, 122, 133, 136, 142, 238, 240, 241, 254, 256–9, 261

Geospiza magnirostris 12, 24, 39, 50, 62, 74, 86, 92, 106, 238, 240, 241, 256, 258, 260, 261

Geospiza scandens 62, 92, 106, 118, 147, 238, 242, 243, 254–6, 258

Ground-finch, Large 12, 24, 39, 50, 62, 74, 86, 92, 106, 238, 240, 241, 256, 258, 260, 261
  Medium 10, 12–14, 22, 24, 50, 62, 64, 68, 74, 82, 86, 92, 106, 118, 136, 142, 238, 240, 241, 254, 256–9, 261
  Sharp-beaked 13, 39, 107, 136, 238, 242, 243, 252, 259
  Sharp-billed *see* Sharp-beaked
  Small 10, 12–15, 17, 18, 22, 24, 50, 56, 62, 72, 74, 75, 82, 84, 86, 92, 106, 118, 122, 133, 136, 142, 238, 240, 241, 254, 256–9, 261

Gull, Franklin's 50, 218
  Kelp 148, 218
  Lava 15–19, 38, 41, 46, 69, 70, 72, 84, 86, 89, 96, 142, 146, 156, 216, 217
  Swallow-tailed 25, 27, 28, 30–2, 37, 38, 40, 41, 50, 64, 69, 101, 107, 114, 129, 132, 136, 144–6, 214, 215

Haematopus palliatus 53, 55, 85, 114, 131, 206

Hawk, Galápagos 51, 52, 57, 63, 64, 69, 73, 96–8, 132, 200–3

Heron, Great Blue 17, 31, 46, 55, 73, 75, 92, 96, 101, 107, 149, 152, 153, 157, 188, 189
  Green 77
  Lava 12, 13, 15, 19, 26, 29, 41, 68, 72, 75, 77, 81, 84, 96, 148, 192, 193
  Striated 77, 81, 84, 192, 193
  Yellow-crowned Night 41, 47, 52, 59, 129, 194, 195

Heteroscelus incanum 30, 53, 72, 133, 207, 209–11, 213

Himantopus mexicanus 212, 213

Larus dominicanus 148, 218
Larus fuliginosus 15–19, 38, 41, 46, 69, 70, 72, 84, 86, 89, 96, 142, 146, 156, 216, 217
Larus furcatus 25, 27, 28, 30–2, 37, 38, 40, 41, 50, 64, 69, 101, 107, 114, 129, 132, 136, 144–6, 214, 215
Larus pipixcan 50, 218
Laterallus spilonotus 108, 112, 204, 205

Martin, Galápagos 62, 63, 74, 230
  Purple 231
Mockingbird, Charles 120, 234, 235
  Chatham 143, 233, 234
  Galápagos 11, 13, 14, 17, 20, 39, 41, 62, 72, 74, 92, 148, 232–4
  Hood 120, 122, 125, 129, 132–5, 159, 234, 235
Moorhen *see* Common Gallinule
Myiarchus magnirostris 13, 14, 51, 62, 74, 92, 121, 159, 228, 229

Nannopterum harrisi 68, 70–2, 75, 76, 80, 83–5, 96, 182, 183
Neocrex erythrops 113, 205
Nesomimus macdonaldi 120, 122, 125, 129, 132–5, 159, 234, 235
Nesomimus melanotis 143, 233, 234
Nesomimus parvulus 11, 13, 14, 17, 20, 39, 41, 62, 72, 74, 92, 148, 232–4
Nesomimus trifasciatus 120, 234, 235
Noddy, Common 30, 31, 55, 60, 64, 69, 70, 96, 101, 107, 148, 157, 220, 221
Numenius phaeopus 16, 17, 53, 72, 89, 133, 140, 210, 211
Nyctanassa violacea 41, 47, 52, 59, 129, 194, 195

Oceanites gracilis 80, 84, 89, 96, 140, 148, 168, 169
Oceanodroma castro 41, 49, 69, 107, 140, 168
Oceanodroma melania 89, 169
Oceanodroma tethys 41, 49, 136, 140, 168
Osprey 203
Owl, Barn 20, 60, 63, 226, 227
  Short-eared 41, 49, 111, 226, 227
Oystercatcher, American *see* Galápagos
  Galápagos 53, 55, 85, 114, 131, 206, 207

Pandion haliaetus 203
Pelecanus occidentalis 10, 13, 15, 19, 30, 31, 55, 57, 58, 63, 68, 70, 73–5, 78–80, 82, 84, 90, 91, 96, 114, 140, 148, 149, 154, 156, 171–4
Pelican, Brown 10, 13, 15, 19, 30, 31, 55, 57, 58, 63, 68, 70, 73–5, 78–80, 82, 84, 90, 91, 96, 114, 140, 148, 149, 154, 156, 171–4
Penguin, Galápagos 70, 72, 80, 85, 96, 100, 114, 160, 161, 207
Petrel, Dark-rumped 69, 80, 166, 167
Phaethon aethereus 29, 38, 41, 48, 101, 103, 107, 145, 148, 170, 171
Phoenicopterus ruber 50, 52, 114–7, 150, 151, 196–8
Pinaroloxia inornata 239
Pintail, White-cheeked 74, 87, 88, 113, 198, 199
Platyspiza crassirostris 62, 108, 120
Plover, Black-bellied 53, 208, 209
  Grey *see* Black-bellied
  Semipalmated 17, 53, 88
Pluvialis squatarola 53, 208, 209
Progne modesta 62, 63, 74, 230, 231
Progne subis 231

Pterodroma leucoptera 69, 80
Pterodroma phaeopygia 166, 167
Puffinus lherminieri 10, 30, 41, 60, 63, 69, 80, 86, 96, 107, 132, 148, 166, 167
Pyrocephalus rubinus 23, 24, 60–2, 73, 108, 110, 228, 229

Rail, Galápagos *see* Crake, Galápagos

Sanderling 53, 208
Sandpiper, 208, 209
  Western 208, 209
Shearwater, Audubon's 10, 30, 41, 60, 63, 69, 80, 86, 96, 107, 132, 148, 166, 167
Sparrow, Rufous-collared 8, 9
Spheniscus mendiculus 70, 72, 80, 85, 96, 100, 114, 160, 161, 207
Sterna fuscata 218, 219
Sterna maxima 219
Stilt, Black-necked 212, 213
  Black-winged *see* Black-necked
Storm-petrel, Black 89, 169
  Elliot's 80, 84, 89, 96, 140, 148, 168, 169
  Galápagos 41, 49, 69, 107, 136, 140, 168
  Madeiran *see* Galápagos
  Wedge-rumped 41, 168
  White-bellied 107
Sula dactylatra 30, 32, 38, 41–4, 49, 68, 96, 101, 104, 105, 107, 131, 132, 136, 138–41, 178–81
Sula nebouxii 10, 19, 30–2, 37, 38, 41, 42, 44, 49, 55, 60, 63–70, 80, 89, 101, 102, 104, 105, 107, 114, 123–5, 132, 136, 137, 139–44, 148, 164, 165, 176, 177, 180, 181
Sula sula 38, 40, 41, 42, 44–6, 49, 104, 138–41, 176, 178, 181

Tanager, Blue and yellow 8, 9
Tattler, Wandering 30, 53, 72, 133, 207, 209–11, 213
Tern, Royal 219
  Sooty 86, 218, 219
Thraupis bonariensis 8, 9
Thrush, Great 9
Tree-finch, Large 24, 62, 74, 239, 244, 245
  Medium 239, 244, 245
  Small 10, 12, 20, 22, 24, 50, 62, 73–5, 82, 86, 110, 118, 136, 239, 244, 245
Tropicbird, Red-billed 29, 38, 41, 48, 101, 103, 107, 145, 148, 170–1
Turdus fuscata 9
Turnstone, Ruddy 25, 30, 88, 114, 132, 144, 212, 213
Tyto alba 20, 60, 63, 226, 227

Warbler, Blackpoll 236
  Yellow 10, 12, 14, 17, 18, 20, 24, 26, 37, 41, 50, 62, 64, 70, 72, 74, 75, 86, 96, 97, 118, 142, 148, 207, 236, 237, 252–4
Whimbrel 16, 17, 53, 72, 89, 133, 140, 210, 211
Willet 210, 211

Xema sabini 214

Zenaida auriculata 8, 9
Zenaida aurita 8
Zenaida galapagoensis 38, 41, 48, 49, 51, 52, 72, 92, 107, 110, 122, 128, 222, 223
Zonotrichia capensis 8, 9